THE PRICE of GOLD

McGill-Queen's Rural, Wildland, and Resource Studies Series

SERIES EDITORS: Jennifer Bonnell, James Murton, and R.W. Sandwell

The Rural, Wildland, and Resource Studies Series includes monographs, thematically unified edited collections, and rare out-of-print classics. It is inspired by Canadian Papers in Rural History, Donald H. Akenson's influential occasional papers series, and seeks to catalyze reconsideration of communities and places lying beyond city limits, outside centres of urban political and cultural power, and located at past and present sites of resource procurement and environmental change. Scholarly and popular interest in the environment, climate change, food, and a seemingly deepening divide between city and country is drawing non-urban places back into the mainstream. The series seeks to present the best environmentally contextualized research on topics such as agriculture, cottage living, fishing, the gathering of wild foods, mining, power generation, and rural commerce, within and beyond Canada's borders.

JOHN SANDLOS and ARN KEELING

THE PRICE OF GOLD

MINING, POLLUTION, and RESISTANCE in YELLOWKNIFE

McGill-Queen's University Press
Montreal & Kingston | London | Chicago

ISBN 978-0-2280-2617-4 (paper)
ISBN 978-0-2280-2618-1 (ePDF)
ISBN 978-0-2280-2619-8 (ePUB)

Legal deposit third quarter 2025

Bibliothèque et Archives nationales du Québec

Printed in Canada on acid-free paper that is 100% ancient-forest-free, containing 100% sustainable, recycled fibre, and processed chlorine-free.

This book has been published with the help of a grant from the Federation for the Humanities and Social Sciences, through the Awards to Scholarly Publications Program, using funds provided by the Social Sciences and Humanities Research Council of Canada.

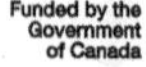

We acknowledge the support of the Canada Council for the Arts.
Nous remercions le Conseil des arts du Canada de son soutien.

McGill-Queen's University Press in Montreal is on land which long served as a site of meeting and exchange amongst Indigenous Peoples, including the Haudenosaunee and Anishinabeg nations. In Kingston it is situated on the territory of the Haudenosaunee and Anishinaabek. We acknowledge and thank the diverse Indigenous Peoples whose footsteps have marked these territories on which peoples of the world now gather.

LIBRARY AND ARCHIVES CANADA CATALOGUING IN PUBLICATION

Title: The price of gold : mining, pollution, and resistance in Yellowknife / John Sandlos and Arn Keeling.
Names: Sandlos, John, 1970– author | Keeling, Arn, author
Series: McGill-Queen's rural, wildland, and resource studies series ; 19.
Description: Series statement: McGill-Queen's rural, wildland, and resource studies series ; 19 | Includes bibliographical references and index.
Identifiers: Canadiana (print) 20250170493 | Canadiana (ebook) 2025017054X | ISBN 9780228026174 (paper) | ISBN 9780228026181 (PDF) | ISBN 9780228026198 (EPUB)
Subjects: LCSH: Giant Mine (Yellowknife, N.W.T.) | LCSH: Gold mines and mining—Environmental aspects—Northwest Territories—Yellowknife. | LCSH: Gold mines and mining—Health aspects—Northwest Territories—Yellowknife. | LCSH: Gold mines and mining—Government policy—Northwest Territories—Yellowknife. | LCSH: Arsenic trioxide—Health aspects—Northwest Territories—Yellowknife. | LCSH: Environmental protection—Northwest Territories—Yellowknife. | LCSH: Yellowknife (N.W.T.)—Environmental conditions. | CSH: Dene—Social conditions—Northwest Territories—Yellowknife.
Classification: LCC TD195.G64 S26 2025 | DDC 363.73909719/3—dc23

This book was designed and typeset by Lara Minja in EB Garamond 11 pt/14.5 pt.
Copyediting by Correy Baldwin.

McGill-Queen's University Press
Suite 1720, 1010 Sherbrooke St West, Montreal, QC, H3A 2R7

Authorized safety representative in the EU: Mare Nostrum Group BV, Mauritskade 21D, 1091 GC Amsterdam, the Netherlands, gpsr@mare-nostrum.co.uk

To the Tatsǫ́t’ıné and Yellowknifers

who so generously shared their knowledge.

Contents

Table, Map, and Figures

Table

Map

Figures

Acknowledgments

In one form or another, our work on Giant Mine stretches back nearly fifteen years and we have developed many relationships and incurred many debts along the way. The foremost among these have involved discussions and collaborations with members of the Yellowknives Dene First Nation, who provided direction, help, support, and inspiration in many ways over the years. Special thanks to Mary Rose Sundberg, Johanne Black, William Lines, and Fred Sangris. Interpretation support for oral history interviews was provided by Lena Drygeese and Jeannie Martin. We also acknowledge the Elders and community members who contributed their knowledge and feedback, especially during workshops held as part of the Toxic Legacies project.

Other Yellowknifers also played important roles in supporting and guiding this research. In addition to his passion for environmental justice, community activist Kevin O'Reilly contributed his deep knowledge of the Giant Mine case, access to files and information he had collected over the years, and his delicious pad Thai. France Benoit's film *Guardians of Eternity*, on which she collaborated with the Yellowknives Dene First Nation and the Toxic Legacies project (including collaborators Ron Harpelle and Kelly Saxberg), featured northern voices and experiences. Robin Weber at the Northwest Territories Archives assisted with navigating the many archival and photographic holdings related to Giant at the Prince of Wales Northern Heritage Centre. Various staff members at the Mackenzie Valley Land and Water Board provided invaluable assistance as we waded through the very large paper public registry on Giant Mine. Ben Nind at the Giant Mine Oversight Board generously shared his knowledge and resources while supporting student projects in Yellowknife. We also greatly benefitted from the conversations we had with Ryan Silke, whose passion for local mining heritage preservation helped us better understand the community pride associated with Yellowknife's gold mining legacy. Our Yellowknife research assistants, Rosanna Nicol and Nimisha Bastedo, provided invaluable help keeping our research going when teaching and other responsibilities prevented us from heading north.

Graduate students working with us at Memorial University of Newfoundland contributed amazing energy and insight through their research projects on Giant, including Caitlynn Beckett, Amanda Degray, Heather Leard, and Sally Western.

We also wish to thank Kevin O'Reilly and two anonymous reviewers who provided extremely valuable feedback on an earlier draft of this book. Thanks also to Kyla Madden, Catherine Bienvenu, and the rest of the editorial team at McGill-Queen's University Press, who believed in this project from the very beginning (even as we took a very long time to finish it) and provided crucial editorial work on the finished manuscript. We also owe a debt of gratitude to Correy Baldwin for helping push the manuscript over the finish line with his thorough and attentive copyediting work.

Over the years, we have published community reports, book chapters, and journal articles related to Giant Mine's history and the challenges of remediation. Much of this work is collected on the Toxic Legacies project website (www.toxiclegacies.com), along with project descriptions, student publications, and the film *Guardians of Eternity*. The Toxic Legacies project was supported through a Social Sciences and Humanities Research Council Partnership Development Grant. The Toxic Legacies team also contributed research support for community reports by the Yellowknives Dene First Nation and Trailmark Systems, and we thank Trailmark's Peter Evans for his engagement around Giant.

A Note on the Terminology

The Indigenous people who live near the present-day settlement of Yellowknife, and who are at the centre of this history, are called the Tatsǫ́t’ıné in their own language of Wılıìdeh. In English they are called the Yellowknives Dene, or sometimes just the Yellowknives. Their nation is now called the Yellowknives Dene First Nation. We have used all of these terms in this book, most often using Tatsǫ́t’ıné as a general reference to individual people or the cultural group, and Yellowknives Dene, or Yellowknives Dene First Nation, to refer to the communities, the nation, or their government.

A NOTE ON THE TRANSLATION

Abbreviations

AANDC	Aboriginal Affairs and Northern Development Canada
ANFO	ammonium nitrate and fuel oil (explosive)
BEAR	Bear Exploration and Radium
CASAW	Canadian Association of Smelter and Allied Workers
CBC	Canadian Broadcasting Corporation
CEPA	Canadian Environmental Protection Act
CLRB	Canadian Labour Relations Board
CM&S	Consolidated Mining and Smelting Company of Canada (Cominco after 1966)
CPHA	Canadian Public Health Association
DIAND	Department of Indian Affairs and Northern Development
GSC	Geological Survey of Canada
MVEIRB	Mackenzie Valley Environmental Impact Review Board
MVLWB	Mackenzie Valley Land and Water Board
NIB	National Indian Brotherhood
NIOSH	National Institute for Occupational Safety and Health (United States)
OSHA	Occupational Safety and Health Administration (United States)
RCMP	Royal Canadian Mounted Police
USWA	United Steelworkers of America
YES	Yellowknife Environmental Survey
YKDFN	Yellowknives Dene First Nation

THE PRICE of GOLD

Introduction

> Had I a right, for my own benefit, to inflict this curse upon everlasting generations?
>
> DR VICTOR FRANKENSTEIN,
> in Mary Shelley's novel *Frankenstein*

> Shit happens but you move on.
>
> One of the maxims of PEGGY WITTE, former CEO of Royal Oak Mines (attributed in *Chatelaine* magazine, January 1995)

One of the most famous characters of Greek mythology is Prometheus, a trickster figure who stole fire from Zeus and brought it back to Earth after the god had hidden it to punish humans. Over time, the story evolved as a symbolic exaltation of technology and civilization; to be Promethean today is to be creative and bold, a person who will take risks or defy the rules in the name of progress. There is a darker side to being Promethean. In some versions of the story, Prometheus pays dearly for his rebellion against Zeus, chained to a rock for all eternity and tortured by an eagle who eats his liver each day, only to have it grow back again. Earlier versions of the story are even more ominous: Zeus imposes a form of collective punishment on humanity. He orders his son Hephaestus, a craftsman, and other gods to create the first woman, Pandora. Zeus gives Pandora to a man named Epimetheus, but the woman carries with her a jar (in later centuries mistranslated to be a box), which she opens and thereby "scattered the evils" and "contrived pernicious woes for the people," including disease and hard toil.[1] As a bringer of evil and as the first woman, Pandora has long been associated with Eve, both characters who are important symbolic markers of misogyny in Western society. But Pandora's story can also be interpreted as a warning about the terrible consequences that accompany powerful and potentially destructive technologies when they are placed in the hands of humans.

Mining, especially in its modern form, is often understood as a Promethean activity. Whether it is the image of the lone prospector striking it rich in a remote region, a junior company hoping for pay dirt from a new mine, or giant companies pushing the mineral frontier into new territory, the mining business has certainly evoked Promethean boldness as it has unlocked mineral wealth from below the Earth's surface. Modern mineral extraction relies on gargantuan earth-moving technologies to disassemble ore-bearing landscapes or plumb the earth to extreme depths. Mining has also been strongly associated with progress, providing vast amounts of materials critical to nearly all forms of industry and the development of new technologies.

And yet, there is also something distinctly Pandora-like about the mining industry. When mining companies have opened the earth and extracted thousands of tons of ore, then crushed, pounded, and chemically altered it so as to get at the tiny percentage of valuable material contained within, they have often released all manner of "pernicious woe" into the surrounding environment, toxic material that has worked its way through the watersheds surrounding the mine, or polluted the air, eventually to settle on the ground and contaminate the soil. Exactly what form this pollution has taken has depended entirely on the geological composition of the ore body, but the waste products of mining have very often included heavy metals that are toxic to living things, whether it be cadmium, selenium, lead, uranium, or arsenic. Mines have also released toxic material as a by-product of processing ore, including mercury and cyanide used to separate gold from crushed rock, sulfuric acid used to leach copper from ore, or sulphur dioxide, a gaseous emission produced by many smelting operations. Mining companies have employed an array of technologies to combat pollution: scrubbers, precipitators, baghouses, tailings dams, settling ponds, and water treatment plants. But Promethean optimism has never been able to fully overcome Pandora and her jar. Some pollution almost always escapes efforts to contain it, pollution control technologies may break down, and very often long-term problems arise as toxic material collected with the control equipment begins to pile up at the mine site.[2]

Giant Mine, a gold extraction site located next to the northern city of Yellowknife, in Canada's Northwest Territories, was one of the worst polluting mines in Canadian history. Pollution began in 1949, when Giant Yellowknife Gold Mines began to roast refractory ore (also called arsenopyrite) to burn off sulphur, a prerequisite to treating this type of ore in a cyanide circuit to produce pure gold.[3] One by-product of the roasting process was the emission of poisonous arsenic trioxide in the form of fine dust. On a daily basis, thousands of pounds of arsenic dust spread from Giant Mine's relatively short roaster stack and settled on land and water in the area surrounding the mine, accumulating in snow during the winter months, running off into waterways during the spring, and landing on food plants such as blueberries or garden produce in the summer months. Another nearby gold mining operation, Con Mine, contributed a smaller amount of arsenic trioxide to the overall load. Neither mine initially made any efforts to reduce pollution at their roaster facilities, even though technology to do so had been used at other mines and the dangers of arsenic trioxide (sometimes referred to as the world's oldest poison) were well known.[4]

Yellowknife at this time was a relatively small mining town perched on the North Arm of Great Slave Lake. It was built on rugged, Canadian Shield rock amid countless small lakes and the endless scrubby spruce and pine trees of the northern boreal forest. To a casual observer, the bustle of mining activity, the frequent roar of float planes taking prospectors on new exploratory missions, and the development of new housing and infrastructure to support Yellowknife's burgeoning workforce promised a bright future for this northern outpost of settler Canada. Amid this idealized scene, however, arsenic trioxide spread through the local environment in an insidious, almost secretive way: an invisible, tasteless, and odourless substance that eluded any sensory defences that might have helped humans and non-humans avoid it. By 1951, the health impacts of arsenic trioxide were abundantly clear, especially among the Yellowknives Dene (Tatsǫ̨t'ıné, in their own Wıìlıìdeh language), who lived adjacent to Yellowknife. At least one Tatsǫ̨t'ıné child died from acute arsenic poisoning that year, possibly more, and many people became sick from highly contaminated snow used for drinking water. Months later, Giant Yellowknife Gold Mines installed pollution controls on its roaster stack, as did Con Mine, but large amounts of arsenic trioxide still escaped from the roaster facilities. In addition, mine workers assigned to operate Giant's pollution control facilities (an

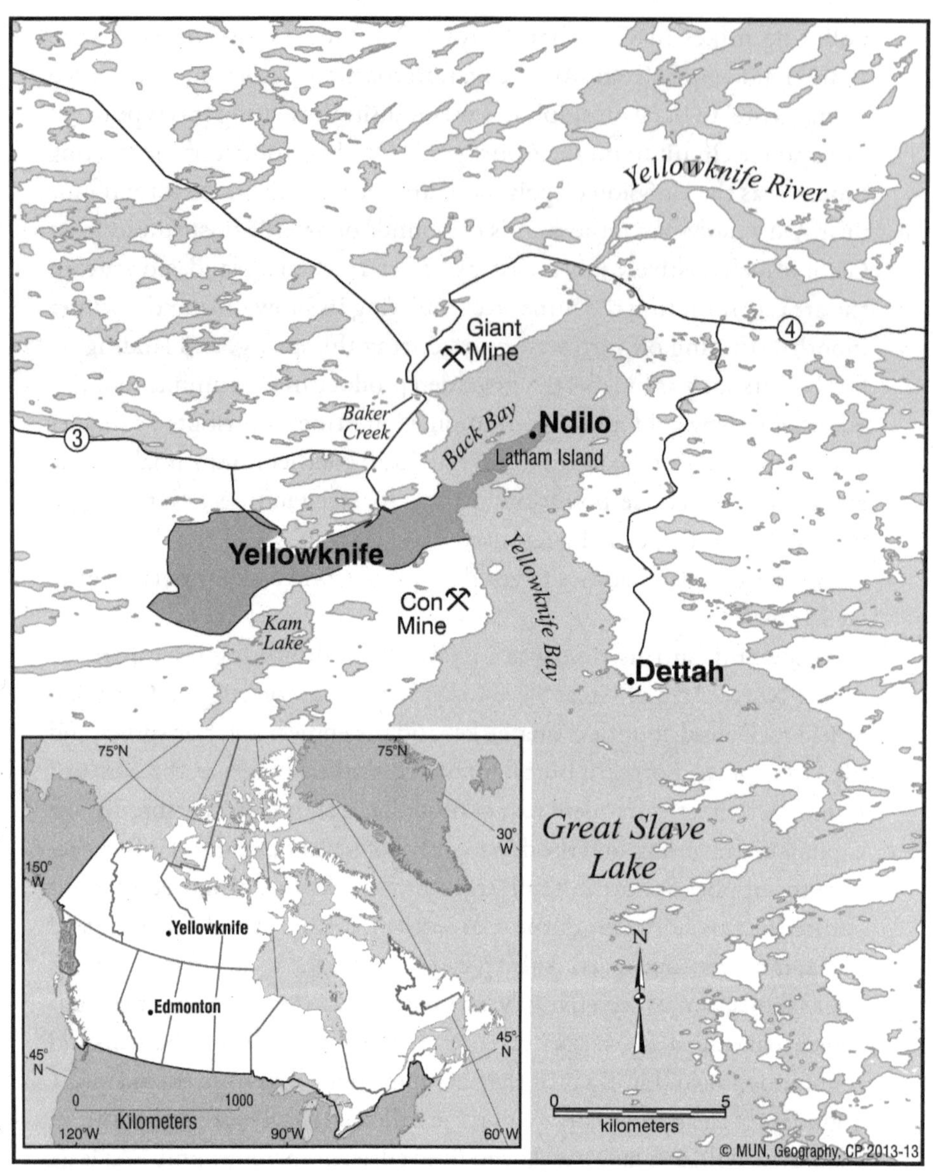

Map 0.1

Giant Mine and surrounding area, with the City of Yellowknife shaded.

electrostatic precipitator, and by 1959 a baghouse) faced high levels of occupational exposure to arsenic trioxide.

Giant Mine's pollution control technologies improved gradually over time, to the point where the company dramatically reduced (but certainly did not eliminate) airborne arsenic emissions by the early 1980s. However, merely capturing the arsenic trioxide dust did not make it disappear. Over five decades of production, the companies that operated Giant Mine collected massive amounts of arsenic trioxide in their Cottrell electrostatic precipitator and baghouse, and then deposited it under the mine surface, at first in abandoned stopes and eventually in purpose-built chambers. While the amounts of arsenic trioxide varied depending on production levels and the composition of the ore being processed at the mine, the company placed an average of thirteen tonnes per day of the toxic material in the underground chambers. Today, around 237,000 tonnes of arsenic trioxide lie buried under Giant Mine (approximately seven ten-storey buildings full of arsenic): a staggering amount of poison that the Canadian government plans to freeze in place until a more permanent solution can be found, possibly involving removal and treatment of the arsenic trioxide to a less toxic form.

At least four other gold mines roasted arsenopyrite ore in Canada, but none produced arsenic trioxide waste on this scale. Of these mines, only the Campbell Red Lake Mines operated an arsenic capture and underground storage program similar to Giant Mine's, but it produced only 20,000 tons of arsenic trioxide, most of which has been recovered and treated.[5] Such a removal and treatment plan is not currently feasible at Giant Mine because of the risks to workers and the nearby communities of mobilizing so much arsenic. Since the companies responsible for producing all of this arsenic trioxide no longer exist, the Canadian public will bear the multi-billion-dollar cost of the current surface cleanup and underground freezing programs, along with an unknown price tag attached to any future permanent solution. The burden of finding a method to remove the arsenic safely, and figuring out what to do with such a large amount of toxic material when it is brought to the surface, could very well fall to future generations – perhaps those who are children now or possibly those who will exist across the gulf of deep time.[6]

Figure 0.1
Aerial view of Giant Mine, 1948, with Back Bay (part of Yellowknife Bay) in the foreground.

When we have presented this troubling story to public audiences and students, many react with palpable shock, asking how and why such a thing could have occurred. Why were the companies that operated Giant Mine allowed to emit large amounts of arsenic trioxide into the Yellowknife environment without regard for the health risks to the local population, or bury such large amounts of toxic material without any regard for future costs and consequences? In part the answer reflects the standard historical practices of mining companies that acted with little restraint or regulation in a free-wheeling, capitalist economy. In remote areas throughout the globe, the goal of extraction was to generate corporate profits and shareholder value, which took precedence over all other concerns. Giant Mine's various owners were not the first mining companies to put profits before people, to emphasize short-term gain ahead of long-term planning, and to disregard the environmental and health consequences of pollution.[7] Our previous work, and the work of many other environmental historians, has documented innumerable cases of mines that have produced complex and difficult environmental problems, many of which continued to exert a malevolent influence after closure.[8] The "cyclonic" boom-and-bust nature of mining – the sudden rush of development pressure combined with the almost instant collapse of some mines and mining communities – has historically contributed to a lack of forethought and careful planning in the industry.[9] Indeed, historian Tim LeCain has gone so far as to describe the advent of low-grade, capital-intensive mining in the early twentieth century as a process of "mass destruction" that entailed the disassembly of landscapes and the production of massive quantities of waste (rock piles, fine tailings, toxic heavy metals, etc.).[10] While it is true that Giant Mine's relatively long operational life of more than five decades offered more economic stability to Yellowknife than many other mines in Canada, the sudden rush of mining development to the region, heedless of potential problems with mining arsenopyrite ore, and the abrupt abandonment of the mine without completing any meaningful remediation work suggest that the industry's boom-and-bust mentality was at least partly to blame for the intractable environmental problems at the mine.

Industry was not the only player in this drama. Many of the environmental problems at Giant Mine occurred and persisted because they were allowed to. As many historians have pointed out, Canadian governments (provincial and federal) of all political stripes have long resisted imposing strict environmental regulations on resource companies, lest they compromise production rates (and the resulting royalties and taxes), local employment, or even the very survival of a development project.[11] In the case of Giant Mine, the federal government's northern administration failed to impose limits on arsenic emissions, ignored warnings about the long-term consequences of storing arsenic underground, neglected to regulate workplace exposure to arsenic for decades (and then did so only weakly and reluctantly), and dismissed internal warnings about the dangers of arsenic from the government's own Department of National Health and Welfare. Almost invariably, federal and territorial governments relied instead on voluntary company pollution control initiatives that were not directly correlated with ongoing risks to human health and the environment. As long as the company made an effort to reduce pollution, that was enough for the federal government, regardless of whether arsenic trioxide levels in air, in water, and on vegetation presented risks to people and animals in the Yellowknife region. To be fair, the mining companies that operated Giant Mine were very adept at using threats of job reductions or an outright closure of the mine as a means to swat aside regulatory initiatives from the government. But the relationship between the companies and government was rarely adversarial: they often shared an attitude of indifference – at times outright negligence – toward the health and environmental impacts of arsenic trioxide pollution in Yellowknife.

The federal government's support for gold mining at Yellowknife was also a core element of Canada's colonial ambitions in the Yukon and Northwest Territories. By the end of the nineteenth century, the Canadian government had achieved one of the central goals of Confederation by settling the western prairies and pushing Indigenous people onto small reserves. The rush toward gold in the Klondike in 1898 inspired federal bureaucrats and politicians of all political stripes to imagine the North as the next frontier for national expansion. Although the harsh climate and terrain might limit agrarian settlement, the development of extractive industries could unlock the wealth of the region and eventually replace the Indigenous hunting and trapping with a modern industrial economy.[12] With gold fever in the Yukon, Ottawa quickly (1899–1900) sent a treaty commission northward to garner what it regarded as a land surrender from Cree and Dene groups living in the Athabasca region, Great Slave Lake, and northeastern British Columbia – the eventual Treaty 8 group of First Nations (which includes the Tatsǫ̨t'ınę́) – in their minds clearing the way for extractive development across 841,487 square kilometres of mostly boreal forest.[13]

After the First World War, the federal government began to take an even more active role in northern affairs, convinced by promoters such as the explorer Vilhjalmur Stefansson that the region could become a "polar Mediterranean," replete with mines and other industries supported with a food supply from ranches devoted to the production of reindeer and muskoxen (an idea the government took so seriously it convened a royal commission to investigate in 1919).[14] In 1920, Imperial Oil started pumping sweet crude oil at Norman Wells. Once again envisioning a resource rush, Ottawa sent a treaty delegation in 1921 to garner land surrenders from the Dene nations of the Deh Cho (Mackenzie River and delta drainage area) and Sahtu (Great Bear Lake) regions – the Treaty 11 group.[15] That same year, the federal government created the first administrative body for the northern territories (the Northwest Territories and Yukon Branch, which opened an office in Fort Smith) and established the Northwest Territories Council (six unelected bureaucrats who ruled the territory from Ottawa). While the Fort Smith office was initially set up to administer a huge land mass south of Great Slave Lake that had been designated as Wood Buffalo National Park in 1922, the new northern administration also set about cataloguing and promoting northern resources. One publication noted that the District of Mackenzie (i.e., the western Northwest Territories) boasted "extensive and varied" mineral resources, and "from similar geological formations elsewhere in Canada great mineral wealth is being recovered."[16]

General knowledge of the favourable geology for gold-bearing rock in the Yellowknife area dated back to the stories of prospectors who had surveyed the area while travelling the Mackenzie River route to the Klondike in 1898, but it was not until 1938 that a Canadian corporate giant – Trail, BC–based Consolidated Mining and Smelting (CM&S) – opened Con Mine as the first major gold mine in the region.[17] The smaller Negus Mine opened adjacent to Con a year later, and small mining camps emerged alongside the shore of Yellowknife Bay. Nobody was under any illusion that the Yellowknife gold developments could proceed without large-scale, heavily capitalized mining operations. Because the gold rested in the hard rock of the Canadian Shield, it was inaccessible to the archetypal heroic and hardscrabble individual gold panners who worked the alluvial deposits of the famous nineteenth-century gold rushes.[18] Setting up a hard-rock mine in such a remote environment was no small undertaking, requiring the import of heavy equipment, the generation of electrical power, the development of mine workings and ore processing facilities, an influx of workers and their families, and the construction of housing and other community infrastructure. It is no surprise then, that Con was only the third large-scale mining operation in Canada's northern territories after the Keno Hill silver mines in the Yukon, which entered production in 1914, and the Eldorado radium mine, which commenced full operations in 1933 on Great Bear Lake, Northwest Territories. The Great Depression slowed the government's plans for northern expansion: the Northwest Territories and Yukon Branch was dissolved, owing to budgetary challenges, in 1931 and the general economic downturn prevented the flow of much private capital to the region.

Nonetheless, the price of radium was extremely high by the late 1920s because of its utility for new cancer treatments, and the gold price also spiked during the Great Depression as people sought a safe haven for their money. Radium mining at Great Bear Lake and gold mining at Yellowknife thus kept the northern expansionist dream alive and demonstrated that industry could operate practically and profitably north of the sixtieth parallel.[19]

Yellowknife's mines were almost wholly dependent on linkages between northern mine sites and southern supply centres that government and industry developed after the First World War. A vastly increased capacity for air transportation (including bigger and better planes for cargo, passengers, and mineral exploration), the development of heavy barging infrastructure along major river routes, and the first use of caterpillar tractors to haul supplies to mining camps across the frozen expanse of the region's large lakes (the famous northern "cat train" network that began operation in the late 1930s) all promised access to a whole new northern frontier for settlement and resource development. The historian Liza Piper has argued persuasively that the mines and transportation infrastructure of the interwar period signal a much earlier origin point for northern industrialization than most historians have recognized (many of whom have pointed instead to the Diefenbaker-era "northern vision" and his government's "Roads to Resources" program).[20] The Second World War severely curtailed the growth of northern industry, especially in Yellowknife as wartime restrictions on gold production eventually brought mining activity in the region to a complete halt. But after the war, the re-opening of Con and Negus, along with the opening of a bright new prospect at Giant Mine in 1948, marked government's and industry's renewed commitments to opening the North through extractive development.[21]

The Tatsǫt'ıné have argued for decades that the advent of mining in Yellowknife was central to their historical experience of colonialism. The development of the mine sites, the growth of the town, and the spread of arsenic trioxide pollution all contributed to the dispossession of the Tatsǫt'ıné from land and resources. Giant Mine occupied an area that was important for fish and blueberry harvesting, while the land base that makes up the city of Yellowknife was once an important hunting area for moose. Arsenic trioxide pollution from the mines also behaved (albeit unwittingly) as an agent of colonialism by sickening the Tatsǫt'ıné communities, robbing them of their main water sources, contaminating local berries and vegetable gardens, and forcing them to confront the possibility that the fish and animals they relied on for food might not be safe to eat. Nobody asked the Tatsǫ̨t'ıné for permission to mine the region, and the economic benefits that flowed to the community were minimal, despite the immense amount of wealth extracted from Treaty 8 lands (over $8.6 billion in total gold revenue from the Yellowknife area in 2023 dollars).[22] From the beginning, the mining companies were largely indifferent toward Tatsǫ̨t'ıné concerns about contamination, health, and the degradation of local resources. As in other places where extractive industries have displaced Indigenous communities, mining at Yellowknife became the highest form of use for what the industry regarded as a remote and rocky wasteland, the taking of land justified in the minds of private capital and the state regardless of the environmental and environmental injustices that might result for the Tatsǫ̨t'ıné.[23] Or, as Johanne Black, director of lands management for the Yellowknives Dene First Nation, said on a CBC *Ideas* episode, "they got the gold and we got the shaft" – a fair summary of her community's historical encounter with gold mining.[24]

In 2009, close to the time we began our research on Giant Mine, Unangax̂ scholar Eve Tuck released an open letter calling for the suspension of damage-centred research in Indigenous communities. The risk, she argued, is that declensionist narratives may actually work against positive social change because they reinforce stereotypes that portray Indigenous communities as being in a state of decay, inhabited by people without hope.[25] We would be the first to admit that much of the Giant Mine story is bleak, focused as it is on contamination, environmental injustice, and the seemingly intractable problem of the underground arsenic. But there is also much that is hopeful and inspiring in the Giant Mine story. For at least the last half century, the Indigenous and settler communities in Yellowknife have contested the pollution from the mines and, since closure, have demanded more community control over the current remediation project at Giant Mine. Their creative activism reflects broader patterns in the history of local environmentalism: an emphasis on everyday, non-elite activism; mobilizing independent expertise to counter corporate and government control over environmental narratives; prying open every crack of light offered by local democratic processes (environmental assessments, public consultations, etc.); and coalition building across diverse communities.[26]

Remarkably, the labour union at Giant Mine (the United Steelworkers of America) forged an unprecedented alliance with the Indian Brotherhood of the Northwest Territories and the Tatsǫ̨t'ıné communities in the late 1970s, working across differences to question the prevailing discourse around "safe" levels of arsenic trioxide in the local environment. The reaction of both groups was part of a broader fluorescence of two political movements in the early 1970s: the surge of occupational health and anti-pollution activism across the North American labour movement,[27] and the continent-wide anti-colonial struggles of Indigenous people, inspired by the Red Power movement in the United States, but manifest among the Dene as a struggle for land rights and resistance to extractive developments such as the high-profile Mackenzie Valley Pipeline proposal.[28] Accordingly, their activism garnered intense local and national media attention, elicited much public sympathy, and pushed the federal government to adopt a defensive, and often panicky response to the arsenic issue. Decades later, a similar coalition of environmental activists and the Tatsǫ̨t'ıné worked toward the common cause of more public oversight and control over the controversial Giant Mine Remediation Project. As one might expect, the public discussion on the arsenic issue was not merely technical in nature (though there has been a great deal of that); it has also embraced activist discourses on decolonization, reconciliation, occupational health, and environmental justice. For the activists in Yellowknife, the problems at Giant Mine could not simply be engineered away; instead, they reflected broken social relationships, and unfulfilled obligations to each other, to the land, and to future generations.

As researchers, we became connected to these community conversations about the toxic legacies of Giant Mine. While our work in Yellowknife began in 2009 as a fairly conventional archival study of abandoned mines in Northern Canada, from 2013 to 2018 we worked closely with Yellowknives Dene First Nation members and non-Indigenous Yellowknifers on a community-based project to document the history of arsenic contamination and exposure in Yellowknife, and foster a community dialogue around the thorny issue of communicating with future generations about the underground arsenic hazard.[29] We took direction on project priorities from community members such as Mary Rose Sundberg, director of the Goyatiko Language Society (a cultural and language centre of the Tatsǫ̨t'ıné);

Johanne Black, director of lands management with the Yellowknives Dene First Nation; Kevin O'Reilly at Alternatives North (an environmental and social justice group); and France Benoit, a Yellowknife-based independent filmmaker. Together, we organized a multi-stakeholder "communicating with future generations committee" to generate ideas on what kind of physical monuments, text, and stories might promote intergenerational communication about the arsenic hazard at Giant Mine (assuming there was a reasonable chance that a permanent solution might not be found within the 100-year timeline of the remediation project). We travelled to schools in Yellowknife, Ndilǫ, and Dettah, and worked with students to build concept models representing landscapes of the future at Giant Mine. Drawing from scholarly literature and the voluminous research done on the nuclear waste repository at the Waste Isolation Pilot Project (WIPP) in Carlsbad, New Mexico, we produced public reports and lay summaries, including an overview of approaches to communicating with future generations at contaminated sites, a summary of the work of the communicating with future generations committee, and the results of a public workshop in which participants created drawings of signs and symbols that could warn the distant future of the dangers at Giant Mine.[30] We wrote a historical report as a background submission for the environmental assessment and articles on Giant's history for a local magazine, *EdgeYK*.[31] Perhaps most importantly, Benoit directed a film, *Guardians of Eternity*, that summarized the history of the mine and its impacts, as well as the challenges of communicating with future generations about toxic hazards, with a particular focus on the Yellowknives Dene experience. At the film's Yellowknife premiere in November 2015, many of the audience members reacted emotionally, an outpouring that reflected not only the community's long and arduous engagement with Giant Mine, but also apprehension over the fact that no permanent solution to the underground arsenic problem was on the horizon.[32]

During our many research trips to Yellowknife, Tatsǫ́t'ınė Elders would often ask, "Why's a couple of guys from Newfoundland interested in Giant Mine?" It is a fair question, highlighting our status as outsiders to both the Tatsǫ́t'ınė and Yellowknife's settler community, and forcing us to ask ourselves whether we should be writing this book. We certainly did not want to create a narrative that would rob the Tatsǫ́t'ınė of their own stories of Giant Mine, a history they have already documented from their perspective in several oral history studies, and one we do not presume to tell for them.[33] Instead, our primary purpose is to document the actions and inactions of the Canadian government and the mining companies that produced acute and long-term problems with arsenic contamination at Giant Mine. As our use of the Pandora analogy suggests, our key focus is to critically examine this history in the context of Western narratives of progress – more specifically Canada's colonial history of northward expansion, extractivism, and environmental degradation. At the same time, any history of Giant Mine that excludes the voices of the Tatsǫ̀t'ıné would be unforgivably incomplete. Not only were we fortunate to interview several Yellowknives Dene First Nations members about their memories of Giant Mine; we also uncovered many transcripts of public hearings, newspaper articles, and radio segments that allowed us to amplify the historical Tatsǫ̀t'ıné experience. Our hope is that the reclamation of these voices will be useful to the Yellowknives Dene First Nation members as they continue to document their historical encounter with gold mining on their territory and to call for compensation and an apology in response to the damage associated with pollution at Giant Mine.

Despite the intensely local nature of our research for this book, the book does not address important aspects of the settler community's historical experience in Yellowknife. When we were working in the city, we met with Yellowknifers who were active in the Northwest Territories Mining Heritage Society (now re-named the Yellowknife Historical Society), and who maintained a great deal of pride in the region's gold mining heritage. How to incorporate such perspectives into our work was a challenging issue to navigate. While we were wary of triumphal mining narratives that mask the history of colonialism and environmental issues associated with gold mining, Yellowknife's mining heritage enthusiasts were understandably skeptical of anything that might seem to demean the work that they and (in many cases) their parents and grandparents did to build the mines and the city. The work of these volunteer historians to document the operational history of the gold mines, to record the oral history reminiscences of Yellowknife's settler community, and to build a proposed mining museum is incredibly valuable, reflective of a deep sense of identity and connection to landscape that is typical of many mining communities.[34] Very often this community pride is founded on an *esprit de corps* among workers who face dangerous occupations and who build their workplace and community from scratch: not only the physical infrastructure of the mine and mining town, but also the sports teams, the service clubs, the churches, and the schools.[35] Our goal in this book is not to undermine that history, but to add another dimension to it, showing how workers and environmentalists from the settler community challenged the supposedly safe levels of arsenic trioxide exposure in the workplace and the community, and eventually asked tough questions about the long-term implications of storing massive amounts of arsenic trioxide beneath the mine.

The chapters in this book follow a fairly linear history of the mining cycle at Giant Mine, from the earliest exploration forays early in the twentieth century to the closure of the mine and the controversy over a proposed remediation plan in the early decades of the new millennium. Chapter 1 is in some ways a prequel to the Giant Mine story, as it covers the mineral exploration period in the Yellowknife area from roughly 1900 to the opening of Con Mine in 1930 and the early discovery of the Giant orebody. It describes the first encounters of the first prospectors and early settlers to the Yellowknife Bay area (or Wıı̨̀lıı̨̀cheh, in the Yellowknives' language) and the reactions of Tatsǫ́t'ıné to these newcomers on their land. Also highlighted are the competing stories about whether prospectors discovered the gold on their own initiative or by exploiting the traditional knowledge of the Tatsǫ́t'ıné. The chapter also summarizes what we know of the history and material culture of the Tatsǫ́t'ıné, and how their culture and economy had come under multiple stressors in the early twentieth century, owing to competition from outside hunters and trappers who migrated to the area in the 1920s and a devastating influenza epidemic in 1928. Finally, the chapter traces the rise of gold mining in Yellowknife, including the development of the Burwash, Con, and Negus mines, until the Canadian government–ordered shuttering of non-essential gold mines during the Second World War.

The second chapter begins with the post-war revival of gold mining in Yellowknife, including the reopening of the Con and Negus mines and the development and subsequent opening of Giant Mine in 1948. Much of the chapter is devoted to the beginning of gold roasting in the region and documents the devastating health and environmental impacts of arsenic trioxide dust emitted into the air and water, initially without any abatement technology. What is abundantly clear from this chapter is that the federal government's northern administration was well aware of the public health and environmental risks associated with arsenic trioxide but chose to ignore the advice of its own Department of National Health and Welfare to shut down Giant Mine, at least temporarily. As a result, people and animals were sickened, including at least one fatality due to arsenic poisoning. One final theme of the chapter is the fact that, although the mines were eventually required to install pollution controls, pollution abatement technology often caused new problems in the name of solving old ones. At Con, the wet scrubber used to capture arsenic trioxide dust led to water pollution as effluent seeped out into local lakes and streams. At Giant, the mining company used the so-called dry method of storing captured arsenic dust, a technique that mitigated the water pollution problem but which started the long buildup of arsenic trioxide in the underground.

Chapter 3 traces the slow realization that pollution abatement technologies installed in the 1950s may not have resolved the public health threats from arsenic trioxide. Survey work in the 1960s revealed high levels of arsenic trioxide in drinking water and on food plants in the Yellowknife area. The persistence of arsenic trioxide in the environment came with growing scientific evidence that arsenic might have hitherto unknown health effects, including various types of cancer, even at low levels of exposure. Public health advocates within the federal Department of National Health and Welfare in the 1950s had largely moved on a decade later, and those who did speak up were silenced by a government determined to keep Yellowknife's gold mines in production for the foreseeable future. The federal government's tendency to bury health and environmental surveys came to haunt it in the 1970s, as local activists in Yellowknife and from the outside accused the government of a cover-up when nobody could locate a major report that had been issued in the late 1960s. At the same time, the Tatsǫ̀t'ıné began to agitate publicly on the arsenic issue, both in terms of the health impacts on the community and the fact they had to pay for trucked-in water delivery because the mines had polluted their main source of drinking water in Yellowknife Bay. In the midst of a burgeoning anti-pollution movement in Canada and a strident assertion of Indigenous rights among Dene activists, the federal government had a full-blown crisis on its hands.

How the government dealt with this crisis, and how a loose coalition of Indigenous activists, labour unions, and environmentalists pressed the issue of arsenic contamination, is the focus of chapter 4. In 1974, the Canadian Broadcasting Corporation (CBC) picked up the story of Yellowknife's arsenic problem on its very popular radio news program *As It Happens*, bringing the story to the Canadian public for the first time. In response to the national media attention, the federal government organized new health and environmental studies, but activists and Indigenous leaders were critical of the results. The National Indian Brotherhood and the United Steelworkers of America went so far as to collaborate on their own arsenic studies, a remarkable effort, the results of which pointed to high levels of arsenic exposure among Tatsǫ̨t'ıné on Latham Island, across the bay from Giant Mine's smokestack. The federal government responded with a commissioned study by the independent Canadian Public Health Association (CPHA). The final report of the CPHA suggested that the general public in Yellowknife was not at risk from arsenic, but some mine workers and possibly Tatsǫ̨t'ıné on Latham Island faced high exposure risks. The report effectively ended the arsenic controversy at the end of the 1970s. With further improvements to pollution controls, many people thought that the government and industry had brought the arsenic issue under control.

But pollution problems at Giant Mine never did fade away. Chapter 5 traces ongoing public concern over arsenic pollution in the air and water in the 1980s and 1990s. It also highlights two new pollutants of concern at Giant Mine: ammonia, which is toxic to aquatic life, and sulphur dioxide, which destroys vegetation and exacerbates respiratory conditions in humans. Meanwhile, in 1990, Giant Mine's new owner, Royal Oak Mines, pursued an aggressive agenda with respect to labour relations and environmental deregulation. A devastating strike/lockout that began in 1992 featured picket line violence and murder in Yellowknife, events that dominated public discourse about Giant Mine for many years. Nonetheless, environmental activists did manage to build a campaign in the early 1990s pushing for zero emissions of arsenic, once again featuring an alliance of interests among environmentalists and Yellowknives Dene communities. Royal Oak countered the activists, and any potential regulatory initiatives from the government, through job blackmail and threats of closure. By the late 1990s, as ore grades declined and gold prices plummeted, the death of Giant Mine seemed imminent. Yellowknifers were forced to weigh the environmental and health impacts of pollution against a few more years of mining employment.

The final chapter begins with the financial collapse of Royal Oak in 1999 and the closure of Giant Mine in 2004. It documents the last days of the mine's life, including the reactions of workers, the company, and the general public to the closure. The core of the chapter, however, is the growing realization within government and among the general public that there was no simple way to remove the thousands of tonnes of arsenic beneath the mine. As mentioned previously, the Canadian government's proposed plan to freeze the underground arsenic for all time sparked a new wave of activism among Yellowknife residents and Tatsǫ́t'ıné, who asked hard questions about the plan to clean up Giant, including the perpetual care requirements for the site and whether the plan was simply foisting the problem off on future generations. Through a multi-year environmental assessment process, the activists managed to secure some tangible environmental standards and community oversight over the Giant Mine Remediation Project. Most importantly, they secured a commitment from the federal government to find a more permanent solution to the underground arsenic problem within the next 100 years. If such a solution is not found, the toxic legacies of Giant Mine will continue to haunt Yellowknife for decades, and perhaps for centuries to come.

At this point, with a basic outline of Giant Mine's history in hand, a reader might ask whether the wealth generated from fifty years of gold production outweighed the environmental and health problems in Yellowknife. Many mining executives are fond of pointing out that their industry is a creature of necessity, providing materials essential to so much of modern life: the cars we drive, the planes we fly, the buildings we inhabit, and the computers we use to write books. The environmental cost of extracting all this material must, they argue, be weighed against the impracticality of doing without it. This argument does not really apply to gold, a metal that is precious partly because it is malleable enough to use for craftwork and does not easily lose its lustre, but mostly because humans have made a cultural choice to assign to it a high value. As far as metals go, it is not really that useful; only in dreams do people live in houses or walk on streets made of gold. A significant amount of the world's gold – about half – has been fashioned into jewellery, a luxury that we could live without. About 10 per cent has some industrial application, but the remaining 40 per cent is essentially a financial instrument, used as a standard of value for currency or as a tradable commodity, sitting in bank vaults, doing nothing of direct utility for anyone.[36] Today you can even buy gold online in so-called e-gold exchanges, the abstract value of the commodity underlined by the fact that traders will never see or touch any of what they are buying and selling.

In Yellowknife, many argue that the city would not exist without gold, its identity so bound to the metal that a musical play about the town's early days referred to it as the place where "the gold was paved with streets." No doubt, wealth from the mine in the form of salaries, taxes, and royalties provided a great deal of financing for the houses, schools, and hospitals that make up the city, but it is also true that the projected $4.38 billion cost of remediating Giant Mine's environmental mess exceeds the $4.3 billion (in 2023 dollars) from the sale of the mine's total gold output (just over seven million ounces).[37] So, if the mine was worth it in financial terms, it was only for individual people who made a lot of money (investors, managers, executives, etc.) but who were not required to shoulder any of the long-term environmental costs. All of this individual wealth must be measured against the health and environmental costs of arsenic pollution that Giant Mine released from the highly mineralized hard rock that lay beneath the Yellowknife River area.

For this reason, *The Price of Gold* puts arsenic pollution, rather than wealth and progress, at the centre of the Giant Mine story. By doing so, it raises deeper moral questions about the environmental injustices that extractive development has inflicted on Indigenous people and their land in the sacrifice zones inherent to capitalist, extractive economies. More specifically, the book argues that the spread of arsenic pollution from Giant Mine was a colonial act: first, because the federal government and the mining companies assumed the air, land, and water around Yellowknife was a *terra nullius* that could be appropriated as a vast dump for industrial waste and pollution; and second, because arsenic pollution disrupted (but did not completely sever) Tatsǫ̨t'ıné connections to a land base that now seemed ominously dangerous to human health. Although Tatsǫ̨t'ıné and settler activists scored some significant victories over the course of many decades of stubborn activism, the mind-boggling amount of toxic material left behind at Giant Mine, and its potential to persist across a vast gulf of time, raises broader questions about whether industrial-scale resource extraction can ever be reconciled with the idea of sustainable human and natural communities. The journalist and graphic artist Joe Sacco invoked this idea while reflecting on an underground tour of Giant Mine, asking, "What is the worldview of a people who mumble no thanks or prayers, who take what they want from the land, and pay it back with arsenic?"[38] As the world hurtles headlong into a new era of massive mineral rushes to fuel the transition to non-fossil energy sources, struggling with such a question is more important than ever.

1

Claiming Wı̨ìlı̨ìcheh

Prospecting around the Yellowknife River area one evening in spring 1929, Ted Nagle heard the sound of dog teams streaming towards his camp on Walsh Lake. When the teams came into view, he saw the sleds bearing Tatsǫ̨t'ıné families travelling along their historical route from the Barrenlands southwards towards Wı̨ìlı̨ìcheh (Yellowknife Bay). Nagle recalled sharing tea and fish that his crew had cached with the Dene families before they moved on; at some point, Nagle must have discussed his need for travel assistance before the group continued south, because, as he noted, "[t]he next morning two Indian drivers from the Yellowknife Settlement magically appeared for us," to help the prospectors move their camp back to Fort Rae in search of rumoured gold prospects on the North Arm of Great Slave Lake.[1]

Led by Chief Baptiste Drygeese, the Tatsǫ̨t'ıné travellers might well have regarded Nagle and his partner with trepidation. Just the year previous, many Yellowknives had fled to the Barrenlands to escape the devastating influenza epidemic that swept through Mackenzie Valley communities in 1928, brought by White travellers from the south.[2] Baptiste's brother, Chief Joseph "Suzie" Drygeese, perished during the epidemic, and oral testimony describes its harrowing effects on Tatsǫ̨t'ıné settlements. But the Yellowknives were also concerned with the increasing presence of White trappers and traders in their territory; several oral histories recount that, when the strangers told them they were looking for rocks, Chief Drygeese (probably

Joseph) asked them to leave the territory and not return.[3] The chief was right to be wary. As it turned out, Nagle's team were merely the advance guard of a series of fly-in prospecting teams that summer, as geologists and explorers descended on the area in search of copper and gold.[4]

Nagle and Drygeese's encounter on Walsh Lake presaged many of the key circumstances surrounding gold exploration in the Northwest Territories and the establishment of the mines around Yellowknife Bay in the 1930s. As a prospector, Nagle was no mere "cheechako";[5] he worked for the exploration arm of Consolidated Mining and Smelting (CM&S), one of Canada's largest mining companies. In 1929, he was part of a coordinated corporate effort to explore the Yellowknife River and the North Arm of Great Slave Lake, informed by previous government geological surveys as well as older claims and rumours of gold. Though travelling around the area by dog team and canoe, prospectors increasingly arrived in the region by bush plane – Nagle claimed that his crew's flight into Yellowknife Bay in legendary bush pilot Punch Dickins's Fokker aircraft in April 1929 was the first of its kind into the area. While frontier mining still featured its prospector "characters" and influential individuals, the full origin story of the Yellowknife gold mines reflected the modern, increasingly corporate character of industrial mineral development rather than the individualistic, chaotic flavour of the earlier Klondike Gold Rush.

For the Tatsǫ́t'ıné, the arrival of prospecting parties by canoe, dog team, and aircraft in their territory in the late 1920s coincided with a period of difficult challenges and often wrenching change.[6] Generations of Yellowknives Dene oral histories trace their extensive land use and occupancy since time immemorial of the territory ranging from the North and East arms of Tinde'e (Great Slave Lake) to the southern shore of Sahtu (Great Bear Lake), and eastward to the Barrenland lakes of Nondìkatı̀ (MacKay Lake), Ewadinti (Courageous Lake), and Ek'ati (Lac de Gras).[7] The heart of Tatsǫ́t'ıné territory, however, was the mouth of Wıìllıìdeh, the Yellowknife River. As a recent community report noted, "[i]t's the place that, in many ways, defines who [the Tatsǫ́t'ıné] are. It's the beginning of the trail that plays a significant role in their Annual Cycle, a trail that connects their Yellowknife Bay villages, and nearby north shore villages, with their winter caribou hunting lands around the edge of the tree line to the north."[8] Five Tatsǫ́t'ıné villages stretched along the east shore Yellowknife Bay, providing access to rich fishing grounds and inland resources such as wood, berries, and medicinal plants. They avoided settling on the west side of the bay – around Giant Mine and the modern city of Yellowknife – because it featured both prime berry-picking areas and hunting grounds for moose and caribou.[9]

Tatsǫ́t'ıné territory spanned the central and eastern portions of Denendeh, "the land of the people," the vast Dene homelands stretching from the Mackenzie Mountains in the west to the Hudson Bay lowlands in the east, and from the Mackenzie Delta region in the north southwards to the lower Peace River and Athabasca River watersheds. The spine of Denendeh is Deh Cho (Mackenzie River), some 1,800 kilometres long, fed by several major tributaries and three very large lakes: Sahtu (Great Bear), Tindee (Great Slave), and Athabasca (a Cree name). Much of Denendeh is characterized by a subarctic climate, notable for long, cold winters, discontinuous permafrost, and low precipitation (mainly snow), although it also extends into the western Arctic barrens, a treeless landscape of continuous permafrost.

The Tatsǫ́t'ıné are one of several related Athabaskan-language speaking Dene groups whose cultures and economies developed in intimate relation with the land and resources of Denendeh.[10] Fishing, hunting (especially caribou), small game trapping, and plant harvesting provided the material and, in many ways, spiritual basis for Dene lifeways. "From generation to generation, Dene are taught to respect the land because it is the source of their survival," as the oral history *Weledeh Yellowknives Dene* notes.[11] Their deep knowledge of the land, travel routes, and harvesting techniques made Dene valued partners in the fur trade with Europeans, beginning in the early eighteenth century. Two fur trade outposts are noted as operating on the Yellowknife River in the mid-1920s.[12] While a full account of the fur trade's influence on Dene economy and society is beyond the scope of this book, in general, early non-Indigenous presence and influence in Denendeh was limited to trading posts and missionary activities, until the reverberations of the 1898 Klondike Gold Rush reached the territory. Spurred by rumoured gold deposits around Great Slave Lake and keen to promote northern development, Canada's federal government rushed to conclude treaties with South Mackenzie region Dene nations (Treaty 8 in 1899, Treaty 11 in 1920). But both government and private non-Dene presence remained relatively sparse until the 1920s, when White trappers, and later prospectors like Nagle, began arriving in the Wı̨ìlı̨ìcheh area. Ultimately, the signing of Treaty 8 and the establishment of the Yellowknife Game Preserve in 1923 offered little protection for Tatsǫ̀t'ıné against these incursions, and, in the wake of the devastating influenza epidemic, they struggled to resist the tide of gold seekers that followed the discoveries of gold around Yellowknife Bay in the early 1930s. By the end of that decade, hard-rock gold mining was firmly established, birthing the new settlement of Yellowknife and launching the ever-deepening industrial colonization of Wı̨ìlı̨ìcheh.

Nagle was not the first to prospect for gold and other minerals in the Wı̨ìlı̨ìcheh area. In fact, his (and others') growing interest in the mineral potential of Great Slave Lake built on three decades of intermittent geological exploration and prospecting activity in the region. In 1898 and 1899, prospecting parties passed through the Mackenzie region, attempting to reach the Klondike gold fields in the Yukon via an "all-Canadian" overland route. Exploring en route, some prospectors staked likely areas of mineralization on the southern shore of Great Slave Lake near Fort Resolution (the lead-zinc deposits of the future Pine Point Mine), as well as on the East and North arms.[13] A small prospecting and staking rush ensued, but unlike in the Yukon's Klondike or British Columbia's Cariboo, where miners sought "free" gold in alluvial deposits, the more complex deposits of the Yellowknife region mostly eluded easy detection – although some ore samples were sent to Ottawa for analysis by the Geological Survey of Canada (GSC).[14] In 1899, Robert Bell, director of the GSC, along with his nephew J. Mackintosh Bell, undertook a geological exploration and mapping expedition to Great Bear and Great Slave lakes, including Yellowknife Bay, and reported, "at Fort Resolution we met considerable numbers of men returning from prospecting around Great Slave Lake after having failed to find any indications of the precious metals or of any kind of ores or other minerals of economic value."[15]

Nevertheless, the arrival of prospectors stimulated government interest in the area, especially geological exploration. The younger Bell continued to explore the region the following year, hiring northerner Charles Camsell (himself a future federal deputy minister of mines) as a field assistant.[16]

Both Bell and Camsell returned several times to undertake topographical and geological surveys of the region for the GSC, publishing technical reports and travelogues to stimulate interest in the area. Though they did not identify confirmed gold deposits, scientific knowledge and mapping activities like those of the GSC made knowledge of northern geography and resources increasingly available to southern Canadian prospectors and companies.[17]

However haltingly, this interest in northern mineral resources increased both non-Indigenous activity and government interest in the region, especially after the First World War. Rapid developments in transportation, including steamer service running from Fort Smith to the Mackenzie Delta and the increasing use of aircraft to access remote territories, brought growing numbers of southern prospectors and White trappers northward.[18] By the end of the 1920s, the advent of aerial reconnaissance, mapping, and photography also permitted the circulation of information about northern geology and geography to centres of administration and mining capital, such as Edmonton, Ottawa, and Toronto.[19] When a subsidiary of Imperial Oil struck oil near Fort Norman on the Mackenzie River in 1920, another brief flurry of mineral exploration ensued. Among the prospectors, J.M. Bell also returned to the region in 1921 and 1922, staking a few claims himself around the Yellowknife River area – though he later reflected that he found the area "disappointing as one usually does a much-heralded distant bonanza."[20] If the prospects for both mineral and petroleum development remained uncertain (the well at Fort Norman was capped by 1925), burgeoning interest in the Northwest Territories' resources set the stage for a transformative period in the region's history.

In particular, resource potential motivated federal treaty making with the region's Indigenous Peoples. Reports of disputes between Klondike-bound prospectors and local Dene groups, as well as the desire to promote mineral exploration, resulted in the signing of Treaty 8 in 1899 at Fort Smith and in 1900 at Fort Resolution. The latter adhesions included Tłı̨chǫ and Tatsǫ́t'ıné on the north side of Great Slave Lake, and contained Crown promises to protect Indigenous land use and harvesting rights while permitting mineral exploration and other settler activities. Similarly, the signing of Treaty 11 with Dene in the northern reaches of the District of Mackenzie followed the Norman Wells oil strike in 1921.[21]

Treaty making, however, failed to forestall the upheaval faced by the Dene in this period. The advent of the fur trade beginning in the late eighteenth century had already brought significant cultural and political change for the Tatsǫ̨t'ıné (including affecting relations with their Tłı̨chǫ and Dënesųłı̨né relatives).[22] As treaty historian Rene Fumoleau describes, the early decades of the century saw increasing numbers of White trappers and free traders (unaffiliated with the Hudson's Bay Company) enter the Northwest Territories, which "broke the monopoly of the Hudson's Bay Company and altered the nature of the fur trade."[23] Competition for furs and the imposition of game laws on Dene (in spite of treaty promises to protect Dene land use) resulted in disputes with the government: in 1920, Tatsǫ̨t'ıné Chief Suzie Drygeese refused treaty payments over limits imposed on Dene harvesting. Drygeese's protest resulted in the creation of the Yellowknife Game Preserve in 1923, which was meant to protect Yellowknives harvesting within their traditional territories north of Great Slave Lake.[24] The game preserve, however, provided scant defence against non-Indigenous hunting and trapping, including by the growing presence of prospectors in the region by the early 1930s.

Dene resistance to the incursions of free traders, trappers, and prospectors was further undermined by the "world-changing" influenza epidemic of 1928 in the Deh Cho region.[25] That summer, passengers on the Hudson's Bay Company steamer *Distributor* brought the disease north, with devastating effects on Dene communities throughout the region. Hundreds of Dene perished, including many important leaders such as Suzie Drygeese; many survivors fled their settlements for the refuge of bush camps, only to carry the disease inland. The geologist J.M. Bell, who had returned to the North Slave area that summer to resume prospecting, encountered Yellowknives Dene who related a "harrowing story of the decimation of the population of Yellowknife Village by the pneumonic flu."[26] Yellowknives oral histories recount how survivors avoided their seasonal fishing grounds near Wı̨ìlı̨ìcheh for years thereafter, fearing the return of disease. As a recent report for the Yellowknives Dene community observes, the epidemic "weakened the Yellowknives at a time when they needed to be strong" – particularly as exploration for gold intensified around Yellowknife Bay.[27]

Locating a Giant

Mineral exploration and claim staking on Yellowknives territory was facilitated by the settler legal principle of "free entry." Canada's Dominion Quartz Mining Regulations (1898), based on previous Western Canadian and, ultimately, American gold rush models, permitted any registered "free miner" to enter "vacant" public lands to search for minerals and, where found, to "stake" a portion of land surrounding their location as a mining claim.[28] This entailed affixing posts into the ground at either end of a claim, indicating its length, which stretched to a specified breadth (1,500 feet square). A limited number of such claims could be staked by a single person, which meant prospectors working in teams or for companies often banded together to stake claim groups covering a promising mineralized area. Recording claims with a government-designated mining recorder enabled the prospector to turn them into a peculiar form of property: offering an exclusive right to explore for minerals located at the surface or below it on the claim area, and a lease right to mine them, but not fee-simple title to the land itself. In order to promote the timely exploitation of minerals, these regulations required claimants to undertake development work on their claims every year and ultimately to obtain a mining lease, or the claims would revert to the Crown and the lands become available for re-staking. Certain lands, including federal Indian reserves, were exempted from the free-entry system, but treaty lands in the Northwest Territories, where reserves had never been established, were not.[29]

Mineral exploration further north actually spurred the eventual staking and development in the 1930s of the long-suspected gold deposits around Wı̨ìlı̨ìcheh. Famed "mine maker" Gilbert LaBine's discovery of valuable radium deposits on the eastern shore of Great Bear Lake in 1930 led to a radium and uranium exploration boom (and, ultimately, the Eldorado Port Radium mine).[30] Lured to the region, prospectors – employed by hastily assembled exploration syndicates – fanned out around the eastern Great Bear Lake area. Among them was an English-born, geologically trained prospector working for Bear Exploration and Radium (BEAR), C.J. Baker. Along with his partner, Herb Dixon, Baker explored southward from the Coppermine River towards the Yellowknife River in 1933, staking likely locations, including at Quyta Lake north of Great Slave Lake. Encouraged

Figure 1.1

Prospector C.J. Baker ("Yellowknife Johnney") travelling from his base camp at the Giant claims in 1936. Baker claimed the deposits at Giant Mine.

by these prospects, BEAR created a subsidiary company (Yellowknife Gold Mines), and the following year dispatched Baker and a new partner to continue searching to the south. In late fall 1934, Baker identified gold-bearing quartz veins on the east side of Yellowknife Bay near the river's mouth. These promising claims he dubbed the "RICH" group, around which another BEAR subsidiary was created, Burwash Yellowknife Gold Mines (named for the mine's first manager, Major L.T. Burwash).[31]

Like many mineral discovery narratives, disputed stories surround the subsequent identification of the nearby Giant gold deposits. In interviews and articles, "Yellowknife Johnney" Baker was at pains to establish his pre-eminent role in the Giant discovery, which most mainstream accounts echo.[32] Certainly, as the Burwash company's field manager, Baker continued to prospect around Yellowknife Bay, and in July 1935 he staked additional claims along small, high-grade quartz veins on the west side of

Figure 1.2
Cabins at the Giant Mine exploration camp in 1936, built near the mouth of what would later be named Baker Creek. Before the arrival of mining, this was a popular berry-harvesting area for Tatsǫt'ıné. The sawhorse and large wood piles are a testament to the amount of burning required to keep the occupants of the cabins warm, and they hint at the mining companies' reliance on woodcutting for construction material at the early stages of exploration and development.

the bay near a small creek drainage. He was so impressed with their potential he named them the "GIANT" group.[33] But at Yellowknife, as in many other "discovery" narratives, Indigenous knowledge "was crucial to geological, prospecting, and mining development work."[34] Absent from Baker's accounts is the role of Tatsǫt'ıné Elder Liza Crookedhand. Oral histories recount that the elderly Crookedhand, whose family lived near the mouth of Wıìllıìdeh, discovered a "shiny, heavy rock" while picking berries around the creek (which came to be known as Baker Creek). At some point, she showed the rock to a prospector, who offered the woman one or more stove pipes in exchange for the rock and information about its location.[35] Based on this unequal exchange, many Tatsǫt'ıné maintain, Baker and his associates became wealthy and the Yellowknives' territory was subsequently overrun with prospectors and mining developments.

"Proving up" these initial indications of gold in the quartz veins required considerable investment and effort in drilling, sampling, and assessment of the deposits before mining could begin. Through 1935 and 1936, Baker and Burwash undertook development work at both the Rich and Giant claims, sharing work crews, equipment, and supplies, and reporting progress to financial backers in Toronto. A shaft was sunk at the Burwash property in 1935, yielding about fifteen tons of ore that was shipped to Trail, British Columbia, for refining. By fall 1936, after a summer of diamond drilling and trenching work, Baker declared the Giant claims "the most promising property in this area" and urged his Toronto backers to support consolidating the company's activities on these deposits, with an eye to potential underground mining.[36]

As news of the discoveries spread in 1935 to 1936, an influx of mining crews arrived from the Great Bear Lake camps as well as Edmonton, joined by a staking rush of prospectors and "eastern mining men." The GSC supported gold exploration in the region by providing mapping, aerial photographs, and field surveys, led annually by Dr A.W. Jolliffe.[37] Established companies quickly entered the field: a prospecting crew working on behalf of CM&S (Ted Nagle's employer) staked gold occurrences south of the Giant claims, near Kam Lake, that would become the Con Mine in 1936. CM&S subsequently optioned the Giant claims from BEAR, conducting drilling and exploration work in 1937 before a brief dispute over the claims led to the formation of a new company, Giant Yellowknife Gold Mines.[38] To service and accommodate prospectors, a tent camp quickly sprang up near the float plane moorage in Yellowknife Bay, while mine workers also lived in hastily constructed bunkhouses near the Giant, Burwash, and Con sites. By early 1939, there were reportedly over four thousand mining claims in good standing in the Yellowknife area.[39] This seizure of Yellowknives territory represented not just private fortune seeking, but the vanguard of national territorial and economic expansion. As heralded in the *Northern Miner*'s annual review issue for 1938, "[t]he government is anxious to have the vast areas, which produce practically no revenue at the present time apart from the fur trade, developed. Mining is the answer."[40]

Early prospecting and development activities around Yellowknife Bay brought major disruptions to Tatsǫ̨t'ıné settlements and resources. Prospectors travelling on the land hunted freely, in spite of nominal restrictions on non-Indigenous hunting in the Yellowknife Game Preserve. Indeed, prospectors and mining advocates repeatedly lobbied for exemptions to harvesting restrictions so that they could hunt and fish for provisions while exploring the territory; by 1932, they had requested that mineralized areas be removed from the Yellowknife Game Preserve altogether.[41] The Yellowknives repeatedly protested these incursions, including a second treaty boycott in 1937, triggered in part by the depredations of prospectors. "The mining itself did not seem to bother the [Dene]," according to Fumoleau, "but it was the abuse of their game preserve they protested."[42] Nevertheless, some Dene actively objected to staking in the game preserve and even demanded royalties. Federal officials, inclined to promote mineral development, tended to side with the industry, though stopping short of expelling Dene people from mining areas altogether, as some companies wished.[43]

Extensive oral testimony and historical land-use mapping demonstrates how early prospectors and miners overran areas around Wįìlįìcheh that were important to the Tatsǫ́t'ıné. Development at the Burwash claims near the mouth of the Yellowknife River displaced one of the main Tatsǫ́t'ıné settlements along the bay, Ts'i Naìkwi Dah Kò, as well as disturbing nearby grave sites.[44] The mouth of Baker Creek, on the west side of the bay, was an important fishing site, and the creek valley a cornucopia of berries and small game. As one Elder reported,

> It was the most important area of the whole bay. If you look at the whole Yellowknife Bay and you look at the eastern shore, the eastern shore, it's not as good as the one in Giant Mine because Giant Mine creek [Baker Creek] is the only place where blueberries grow, and a lot of raspberries, and many other berries. It's [an] abundance of berries, and to the Yellowknives, that berries are very, very important. ... Everything you need was right there – fish, muskrat, berries, your birch, everything you need, your medicine plants was all there.[45]

Still today, the Baker Creek valley is commonly remembered by Yellowknives Dene for the "blue blanket" of berries that covered the area; others recall berry picking and other harvesting activities near the Con Mine site to the south.[46] Further inland on the west side of the bay, sandy soils and vegetation around the current Yellowknife airport also attracted moose and caribou. "Right where the big town is right now, that's where the people used to go hunting for moose," recalled Helen Tobie in an interview published in 2000.[47] As described in a community oral history,

> Elders discouraged families from living where animals, especially moose, would come because the animals would stop coming there. Otter and mink, for instance, leave a river where people camp or settle on the banks; moose eventually leave an area where people stay. Thus, Weledeh Yellowknives families did not stay or build log homes in such places as the present-day Giant mine site, the townsite of Yellowknife, or recreation areas along the Ingraham Trail [today's highway].[48]

While the Dene avoided settling in these rich harvesting areas, prospecting and development activities in the 1930s, including the establishment of camps, deforestation, blasting, and drilling, directly targeted what one Elder described as "the lifeline of the Yellowknives," places that the community protected because of their value for food production:

> [T]hat's why the Dene people didn't really establish themselves or, you know, there's a lot of nice places around Yellowknife that we could have easily just start building cabins and setting up camp and stuff, but we never did because our ancestors always told us never to establish there because want to leave it for the animals to migrate, and it's a good hunting area. So we never did. So when the prospectors, they came, you know, they just plopped themselves everywhere and anywhere without any consultation of our people, or even ask anyone. So it kind of destroyed the whole Yellowknife area for us, not only Giant Mine but the whole Yellowknife area because it used to be a really good place for animals.[49]

Mining claims and prospecting activities also disrupted travel routes westward from Yellowknife Bay towards harvesting areas and traplines on inland lakes, though people continued to use and access the areas whenever they could.[50] Through the 1930s, as trenching, drilling, and development work continued at the Con and Giant claims on the west side of the bay, access to the key animal and plant resources of this area was increasingly affected, and some Dene avoided the noisy newcomers.[51]

Mineral development was also responsible for the growing number of forest fires in the region. As Liza Piper notes, "increased fire frequency heralded the establishment of new mining communities" across the north during this period.[52] In some cases, prospectors set fires to burn off dense forest for ease of travel and prospecting, though the exposed bedrock around much of the Yellowknife area made this less necessary. Forest fires were also sparked by travellers' campfires. Early Yellowknife settler, prospector, and newspaperman Jock McMeekan remarked on "disastrous bush fires" in 1936 and 1938.[53] Fires drove away game and furbearers, as well as contributing to forest depletion, already a problem in the vicinity of mining camps due to woodcutting for fuel and construction. Writing in the *Northern Miner*, Deputy Minister of Mines Charles Camsell warned the mining fraternity that "fires not only destroy future mine timbers and fuel, but they deprive the Indians of their means of livelihood through the destruction of trapping areas."[54] But lacking any capacity for fire suppression, federal officials remained largely powerless to stop the annual blazes that torched the Yellowknife District in the late 1930s, undoubtedly affecting wildlife and Dene harvesting activities.

Initially, the mining boom offered opportunities for some Tatsǫt'ıné, who engaged in work and trade with the newcomers. Dene men cut wood and helped with camp construction; others hunted to supply moose and caribou meat or traded berries with the camps. "A lot of men from Dettah got firewood for both mines," recalled Elder Isadore Tsetta, "but we still trapped and hunted during the different seasons."[55] Con Mine, for instance, contracted dozens of Dene and Métis men to cut cordwood for fuel, running into the hundreds of cords per month, from the 1930s through the war years.[56] Oral histories also link woodcutting to local deforestation. Elder Michel Paper discussed working at Burwash and Giant in the early days: "This mine and several later gold mines paid people to cut spruce trees for use in their mills before other power sources were available. As a result, spruce is now a rare tree species in Weledeh-Cheh."[57] While mineral development provided some new sources of cash and trade, the Yellowknives were also increasingly constrained in their access to traditional resources and territory – a situation that would only worsen as the mines moved towards full production.

In 1938 to 1939, gold development in the Yellowknife region gathered considerable momentum. CM&S led the way: miners at Con sunk development shafts and entered full production, pouring the camp's first gold brick on 5 September 1938. The company also began mining at its adjacent Rycon and Negus properties.[58] Promising deposits were located and then drilled at Thompson Lake, forty-eight kilometres northwest of Yellowknife Bay, which would become the Thompson-Lundmark Mine. While development at Burwash sputtered, BEAR, through the newly formed Giant Yellowknife Gold Mines, shifted crews and equipment across the bay to the more promising Giant claims, where a development shaft yielded high-grade ores that were shipped to Trail for smelting in 1939.[59] Progress at Yellowknife was widely reported to southern Canadian readers in both the mainstream press and the *Northern Miner*, the industry weekly. In martial rhetoric suited to the unsettled world of the late 1930s, observers declared that "Canada's last frontier" was yielding to an "invading army" of prospecting "troops."[60] Nor was the colonial context of mining deeply hidden: Toronto lawyer A. Kelso Roberts, reporting on a flying tour of the region, declared that the mining companies opening the Canadian north would rival "past epochs" of imperial expansion. "Out of such work," Roberts wrote, "will undoubtedly come a further instalment in the almost fairy tale of Empire building."[61]

While not quite a new Jerusalem (or Johannesburg), with these developments the settlement of Yellowknife quickly took on an air of permanence. For workers at Con Mine, CM&S constructed a bunkhouse camp, manager's houses, a cookhouse, and even a small "cottage" hospital, where the region's first doctor, Oliver Stanton, was based. North of Con, most other drilling crews, prospectors, and businesses congregated along a narrow, rocky peninsula that stretched into Yellowknife Bay just south of the river mouth. By 1939, there were nearly a thousand non-Dene in Yellowknife, many recruited from mining camps across the Canadian Shield, from Chibougamau to Lake Athabasca.[62] Most new arrivals were employees of local mining companies or other businesses, rather than independent prospectors, and government authorities tended to discourage the unemployed from coming to the camp.[63] Nevertheless, pre-war Yellowknife had the feel of a mining boomtown, likened by some to the Cobalt, Ontario, mining camp of three decades previous: "There was no land holding, land tenure

Figure 1.3

Old Town Yellowknife, ca. 1939–1940. Prominent buildings shown include the Ingraham Hotel, Hudson's Bay Company store, and Wildcat Cafe, along with a Mackenzie Air Service float plane on Back Bay.

or anything of that kind," noted lawyer Charles Perkins. "People stuck up a tent or built a log cabin wherever they liked."[64] On the Back Bay side, facing the Giant claims to the west, float plane docks, warehouses, and offices lined the waterfront; the east side and across the top of the peninsula was dotted with shacks, stores, and other services, including the Yellowknife Hotel. Two sparsely settled islands lay across from the camp: Latham Island (which included some Dene residents) and Jolliffe Island, which hosted the settlement's oil supplies and lumberyard.

In 1939, the Canadian government created an "administrative district" surrounding the Yellowknife camp to facilitate surveying and settlement, formalize land tenure, and other regulations, and create a government presence beyond that of the Royal Canadian Mounted Police (RCMP) and Royal Canadian Corps of Signals. Notably, the district included the claim areas of the Negus, Con, and Giant mines within its limits.[65] Otherwise, government presence remained thin on the ground, as the federal government, ruling from distant Ottawa and claiming fiscal restraint, offered little direct support to either the industry or community in the 1930s. "When it came to the industry itself," Piper notes, "the government kept its interference to a minimum."[66] The nominal regional administration, the Northwest Territories Council, was in reality dominated by Ottawa-based senior Department of Mines and Resources bureaucrats with little direct presence or influence on local affairs beyond registering mining claims, timber berths, and land titles. The council also resisted early calls for more representative and responsible local government.[67]

In spite of this rapid early growth, Yellowknife remained a remote and isolated settlement. All-season travel and freight were limited; the spring arrival of Northern Transportation Company supply barges from Hay River was a major annual event. Aviation remained the principal form of transportation for the boom, and when ice free, Yellowknife Bay buzzed with float planes from the Mackenzie Air Service, Canadian Airways, and other companies bearing passengers, mail, and freight to the new town. Starting in 1938, a winter tractor road crossed Great Slave Lake and connected Yellowknife to Grimshaw, Alberta, from there linking to the southern Canadian rail network.[68] Notably, these new transportation routes increasingly sidelined the older, water-based fur trade–era route northward through Fort Smith and Fort Resolution.

These connections, and the growing mining activity in the region, positioned Yellowknife as the hub of the industrial transformation of the Northwest Territories. In 1939, the territory produced over $2 million in precious metals and petroleum products, as well as another $2.3 million in radium-uranium concentrates from the Eldorado Mine on Great Bear Lake.[69] The non-Indigenous population of the territory more than tripled between 1931 to 1941, mainly concentrated in new mining settlements.[70] If much of this industrial activity bypassed Dene groups around Great Slave Lake, the Tatsǫt'ıné increasingly found their homelands reordered and disrupted. "The southern parts of the people's land were dotted with mining stakes and small, mostly gold, mines," recalled Elder Isadore Sangris, and this affected Yellowknives' hunting, trapping, and berry picking.[71] In spite of some casual labour and trade opportunities with the newcomers, local Dene remained at the margins of the gold boom and the emerging settlement of Yellowknife. As the lawyer Charles Perkins noted, "The Indians in the community really had little part in the Yellowknife community as such."[72] Yellowknives Dene living and working in the vicinity tended to stay in their fish camps on the east side of the bay, particularly Dettah at the southern end of Yellowknife Bay. From there, they would travel by boat or dog team across the bay for work or to trade or purchase goods, including tobacco.[73]

The outbreak of the Second World War meant Yellowknife's golden prospects dimmed somewhat. While exploration, development, and even mining continued, many miners and prospectors left for the armed services. Gold mining was briefly declared an "essential industry" in July 1940, and observers heralded Canada's ability to produce both raw materials and wealth to fund the war effort.[74] Development work initially continued at Giant, while the Thompson-Lundmark Mine (now operated by CM&S) poured its first gold bar in 1941. Both mines, however, were subsequently idled by wartime capital and labour shortages and subsequent government restrictions on gold production. Of greater consequence to Yellowknife's long-term future was the 1941 completion of the Bluefish hydroelectric dam on the Yellowknife River system, constructed by CM&S for its Con and Negus mines but which soon provided power to the town of Yellowknife.[75] These investments, along with the solid corporate presence of CM&S, signaled a future for Yellowknife beyond that of a boomtown mining camp – even before further gold discoveries at Giant spurred transformative growth in the post-war period.

Conclusion

Oftentimes, stories about mineral discoveries project an air of inevitability, even naturalness about them. Minerals, especially gold, are developed "because they are there" – geological facts awaiting discovery, needing only the heroic efforts of adventurous and knowledgeable men to reveal their presence. Unleashing their economic value, and the catalytic effects they have on local economies and ecologies, requires the pluck of explorers like C.J. Baker and the good fortune of discovery to be realized. Prospector narratives like Baker's are standard fare in mining history, but as this chapter (and other recent work on mining history) reveals, these accounts tend to obscure the complex historical and geographical context surrounding much mineral exploration and development. The discovery of gold at Yellowknife was enabled by the halting (but growing) national interest in the mineral resources of the territory that underlay Camsell's and Bell's early reconnaissance activities, the discovery of oil at Norman Wells, and the radium strike at Great Bear Lake (from which Baker's exploration teams travelled). These developments attracted increasing investment and corporate interest to the region, including that of the mining giant CM&S, which funded Nagle's exploration in the region and later founded Con Mine. Exploration parties still travelled by dog team and canoe but were just as likely to arrive via bush plane or float plane, thanks to rapidly improving aviation technology and transport infrastructure.[76]

In these ways, together Yellowknife and Giant Mine emerged as a central part of the larger, ongoing industrial colonization of Denendeh, beginning in the 1920s, and the growing numbers of settlers it attracted. Tatsǫ̀t'ıné Elder and Wıılıìdeh language expert Mary Rose Sundberg describes how Dene came to refer to the non-Dene people they encountered as "rock people," because of their peculiar interest in the local geology.[77] "It was in 1934 when we [Dene] first seen White people here in our area," recalled Elder Michel Paper. "We were scared of them because we never seen that kind of people before."[78] As many Yellowknives oral histories recount, these strangers entered a territory that was widely known, used, and cherished by Yellowknives as a rich area supporting their annual cycle of harvesting, hunting, and trapping that ranged from Wı̨ìlı̨ìcheh eastwards to the Barrenlands. This cycle was brutally disrupted by the 1928 influenza epidemic, which prompted the dispersal of surviving Tatsǫ̀t'ıné families just as the "rock people" arrived at Yellowknife Bay in growing numbers. When Dene returned to Wı̨ìlı̨ìcheh, they found their land occupied and transformed.

As the developments around Yellowknife Bay grew, Tatsǫ̀t'ıné increasingly found their valuable hunting and gathering areas overrun by miners and the rapidly growing mining camp. This displacement is remembered today with bitterness as the first of many bad experiences with mining, a negative reciprocity embodied in the story of Liza Crookedhand, the elderly woman whose exchange of a shiny rock from near Baker Creek with an unnamed prospector – perhaps Baker – sparked the "discovery" and staking of Giant Mine around these valued berrying grounds. In the years to come, the bitterness would deepen as mineral development took hold and its effects ravaged the land around Wı̨ìlı̨ìcheh.

2

Opening a Giant

The end of the war brought a renewed sense of optimism about the enormous potential of gold mining in the Yellowknife area. The cessation of wartime restrictions on gold mining activity – a policy that had, according to the *Northern Miner*, "crippled" Yellowknife – meant that the flow of workers, material, and capital into the once-burgeoning mining town could resume in earnest.[1] Con Mine, shuttered since 1943 with a skeleton crew of only thirty maintenance workers, sprung to life again in August 1946; Negus rekindled its operations in July 1945, even before the war in the Pacific was over. The gold mining industry also quickly revived or developed new satellite gold mines further afield from Yellowknife, including Discovery, opened at a site eighty-four kilometres to the north in 1950, and Thompson-Lundmark, which reopened 1947. Various companies accelerated staking, exploration, and bulk sampling activity at promising mines sites in the regions. Yellowknife's bust almost instantly became a boom as the town's settler population increased dramatically from just a few hundred during the war to three thousand by the end of 1945.[2]

No gold deposit sparked more anticipation than the Giant finds that C.J. Baker had staked a decade earlier. Preliminary work on the mine had proceeded through the late 1930s to the point where Giant Yellowknife Gold Mines had shipped small tonnages of ore and installed a twenty-five-ton mill. As with other mines in the region, however, the company shuttered the site by 1942, so indifferent that the lone caretaker at the mine,

Peter Jensen, departed after complaining to the RCMP that he was not being paid or provided with food.[3] The abandonment of Giant Mine was short lived: the Frobisher Exploration Company bought a controlling share of Giant Yellowknife Gold Mines in 1943 and proceeded with a major exploration program until they discovered a stunning high-grade shear zone beneath the Baker Creek valley. In March the *Northern Miner* declared, "what is happening in the Great Slave Lake area is a bright sign of the big and glowing things that are ahead for the mining industry when times and taxes are normal."[4]

Even as the war continued to grind on, big things started to happen at Giant Mine. In November 1944, Giant Yellowknife Gold Mines declared that it would raise $1.8 million on the stock market to finance a development program, work that *Saturday Night* magazine described in militaristic terms as a "widespread underground attack slated to follow the greatest diamond-drilling boom in the Dominion's history."[5] Some skeptics noted the difficulty of providing adequate supplies of timber and hydro power to the new development, but even more investment capital poured into the mine after the war – $3.9 million in the nine months prior to the end of January 1946.[6] Giant solved the power development problem in July 1946 when the Canadian government agreed to build a hydro generation facility on the Snare River.[7] The ever-optimistic *Northern Miner* suggested that the immediate need for 750,00 board feet of timber could be solved by mobilizing the "abundance of local spruce," a suggestion that Giant Mine pursued vigorously, cutting several thousand cords (near the mine and through a contractor at Jennejohn Lake, east of Yellowknife) in the winter of 1946 for firewood and construction.[8]

Giant's promoters rarely engaged in the nation-building rhetoric that came to dominate the discourse surrounding northern development by the late 1950s (distilled by John Diefenbaker's Northern Vision of the 1958 election campaign). But the company's pitch to the government for hydro development in the region suggested that a publicly owned power plant "would be a major step in the development of the Northwest Territories which are entirely under Dominion jurisdiction." And because a good portion of the workforce would be "returned men," Giant Mine "can be regarded as a Reconstruction measure of the first magnitude."[9] Such logic – and considerable momentum – was clearly on the side of Giant Mine. The development and construction program accelerated between 1946 and

1948, the federal government's Snare River Power Development was ready for hookup in October 1948, the total workforce jumped from roughly 140 to 250 miners between 1946 and 1948, and the mine celebrated the pouring of its first gold brick on 24 August 1948.[10] With a milling rate of 250 tons daily (an amount set to double the following year), and gold production of 42,562 ounces during its first full year, Giant Mine had begun to fulfill its promise as the most important gold mine in the Yellowknife region.[11]

For all this optimism, government and company officials were well aware from the early stages of the mine's development of the toxic threat posed by Giant Mine. In July 1944 Mackay Meikle, the district administrator for the Mackenzie region, reported in an inspection trip that Giant Mine's ore body was largely made up of arsenopyrite formations that would require roasting.[12] Gold-bearing ore mined underground would first be crushed extremely finely, then undergo flotation using reagents to separate ore-bearing rock from waste.[13] Recovery of "refractory" gold from the remaining ore remained problematic; a year later, the federal Department of Mines and Resources conducted laboratory work confirming that cyanide leaching (the standard method for gold recovery) by itself "yielded unsatisfactory results" with the Giant Mine ore because arsenic and sulfides effectively blocked the cyanide from separating out pure gold from the ore body. As a result, after first putting the ore through a standard flotation circuit to concentrate the gold-bearing ore, the company then had to roast the remaining solids at high temperatures to oxidize, or burn off, sulfides, arsenic, and other minerals. Only then could the remaining ore concentrate be treated with cyanide to extract pure gold.[14]

Ore roasting was not only essential to gold recovery at Giant; it was also the primary cause of the most severe pollution problem at the mine. It was common knowledge in mining circles that the roasting process produced large amounts of the highly toxic substance arsenic trioxide, which entered the roaster stack as a gas and, as it cooled, became a fine dust that would eventually settle on the land surrounding the mine. Roy A. Gibson, the deputy commissioner of the unelected Northwest Territories Council, did seek advice about the possible impacts of airborne arsenic from C.S. Parsons, chief of the Bureau of Mines. Parsons argued that, based on ore roasting operations at mines near Geraldton, Ontario, "this problem should cause no great concern provided reasonable precautions are taken such as the impounding of tailings and the building of a stack sufficiently high to disperse fumes such as arsenic and sulphur."[15] Gibson, satisfied with this haphazard form of analysis, advised the two mine inspectors in the region, Fred Fraser and K.J. Christie, to be "on guard against the dangers from both fumes and tailings when considering the plans for the opening up of new mines and mills or the enlargement or alteration of existing ones."[16]

Gibson's cursory approach to the environmental and health risks of gold roasting was emblematic of a broader negligence among the federal northern administration (which was comprised of the Department of Mines and Resources and the Northwest Territories Council) toward the dire health and environmental consequences of arsenic trioxide pollution for people and wildlife in the Yellowknife region. While environmental assessments were non-existent in this period, the dangers of arsenic trioxide – the world's oldest poison – were common knowledge. So was the risk associated with roasting and smelting ore. Indeed, disputes between farmers and smelter operators over the damaging effects of smelter emissions were relatively common in the early decades of the twentieth century. In 1905, farmers in Montana pursued an unsuccessful lawsuit aimed at the Anaconda Copper Mining Company's smelter at Washoe. Farmers near Sudbury also took legal action against the Canadian Copper Company in 1916 regarding the impact on crops of sulphur dioxide (also a by-product of the refractory ore roasting process at Giant). In 1938, an international tribunal forced CM&S (the owner of Con Mine in Yellowknife) to compensate American farmers for damages to crops and livestock from its smelter at Trail, British Columbia. Often in response to legal action, mining companies employed various forms of technology (i.e., scrubbers, baghouses, and the Cottrell electrostatic precipitator) to reduce smelter pollution, or they built very large smokestacks to disperse toxic material and minimize its most acute impacts.[17] Although Gibson had alluded to the need for a taller smokestack at Giant Mine, neither the Northwest Territories Council nor the Department of Mines imposed a requirement to build one. The smokestack attached to the first roasting facility at Giant Mine was a comparatively short 150 feet, and at Con it was only 100 feet; neither was high enough, as it turned out, to disperse arsenic a safe distance from Yellowknife.[18] Nor did the Northwest Territories Council demand the installation of any pollution control equipment on the stack when gold roasting commenced in 1949.

Instead, the resurgence of gold mining in post-war Yellowknife proceeded in a kind of regulatory Wild West. Con Mine, which restarted its ore roasting operation in 1948, actively contributed to the local arsenic problem, though much less so than Giant Mine because only 20 per cent of its ore was contained in arsenopyrite (as opposed to 80 per cent at Giant). Neither operation had voluntarily installed any pollution controls when ore roasting commenced. As a consequence, together both mines pumped up to 11 tons (22,000 pounds) of arsenic through their smokestacks and into the local environment *every day* (approximately 16,000 pounds of this from Giant Mine) between 1949 and 1951, an immense amount of toxic loading that carried considerable risk to local wildlife and people, especially the Tatsǫ̨t'ıné.[19] Amid the feverish race to get Giant Mine into production, the Department of Mines and Resources not only disregarded the obvious warning signs of sickness and death among local people and animals, but also ignored internal warnings from the federal government's own Department of National Health and Welfare that gold roasting posed an unacceptable health risk in the Yellowknife region.

The advent of gold ore roasting also greatly accelerated the process of colonial dispossession of the Tatsǫ̨t'ıné that began in the earlier exploration period. The rapid expansion of mining operations and the urban footprint of Yellowknife displaced the Tatsǫ̨t'ıné from traditional hunting, gathering, and fishing places. As mentioned in the previous chapter, the Tatsǫ̨t'ıné revered the flatlands where the town was located as a moose and caribou hunting area, while the Giant Mine site was important for blueberry gathering and fishing in Baker Creek.[20] Although increasing numbers of Dene settled on Latham Island (across Back Bay from Giant) and Dettah (across Yellowknife Bay to the southeast), by the early 1950s, arsenic pollution made the very notion of living off the land seem risky. Unlike settler farmers in other parts of North America, however, in the 1950s the Tatsǫ̨t'ıné lacked the legal standing (as wards of the state) and economic clout (as mere subsistence hunters in the eyes of the state) to press any claims for damages in the courts. Tatsǫ̨t'ıné voices thus went largely unheard (and unrecorded in the available archival record) during the post-war resurgence of gold mining in Yellowknife; government and industry were largely indifferent to the grim consequences that gold mining brought to them.

Toxic Town

By the time the Giant and Con mines started spewing arsenic trioxide into the local atmosphere surrounding Yellowknife, medical researchers and even the general public had a very good (if somewhat incomplete) knowledge of the health risks associated with the substance. Because it is tasteless and odourless, living beings have almost no way to avoid arsenic ingestion, a fact that accounts for its popular use as a poison dating back to the ancient world. It was common knowledge in 1949 that a dose of 70 to 180 milligrams was likely to be fatal to a human being. Such a lethal dose is only a tiny amount of material, given that 100 milligrams of arsenic trioxide is equal to one-twentieth of a teaspoon. Medical research and common experience had also established toxic effects below this fatal threshold, particularly as people were exposed to arsenic trioxide through its use as a pesticide and a component of pigments (particularly for wallpaper) in the early twentieth century, and its problematic use as a medical therapeutic (for syphilis, malaria, asthma, cancer, and other conditions). At a dosage level just below fatal, arsenic trioxide can cause vomiting, diarrhea, abdominal pain, a burning or tingling sensation in the extremities (paresthesia), skin rashes, and a thickening of the skin on the hands and feet (keratosis). Long-term exposure over many years may also produce symptoms such as hyperpigmentation, which manifests as black spots on the skin, an arrhythmic heart, poor blood vessel circulation, and possible impairments to kidney and brain functions. What was not well understood in 1949 is that extended exposure to arsenic may also produce potentially fatal cancers of the bladder, liver, and lungs. Based on the plethora of known risks, however, the United States adopted a drinking water standard of 0.05 milligrams per litre (or 0.05 parts per million) in 1942, while Canada's Food and Drug Laboratory maintained a slightly higher standard of 0.075 parts per million. More recently, governments in the United States (in 2001) and Canada (in 2006) have reduced the drinking water standard for arsenic to 0.01 parts per million as researchers unveiled the carcinogenic effects of long-term, low-dose ingestion (with many suggesting there really is no safe level of arsenic ingestion over longer periods of time). Although these longer-term impacts are more difficult to trace in the archival record (owing to a lack of any records or research tracking the effects of long-term exposure), there is no doubt that in the late 1940s and early 1950s, the gold mining industry exposed humans and animals in and near Yellowknife to arsenic levels that were acutely dangerous, and lower doses that were likely a long-term threat to health over subsequent decades.[21]

Not long after ore roasting began at Yellowknife, the adverse impacts of arsenic trioxide on health and the local environment became plain to see. Con Mine restarted its roasting plant (after a six-year hiatus) in July 1948, while Giant Mine fired up its first roasting facility in January 1949. Very quickly in February, two watchmen who had melted snow for drinking water at the Akaitcho mine property north of Giant became sick and hospitalized due to gastro-intestinal symptoms associated with arsenic poisoning.[22] While both men survived, mortality among animals in the region gave a clearer indication that something was seriously amiss. In May 1949 at least six cattle died on the Bevan farm from drinking spring runoff that was heavily contaminated with arsenic due to daily accumulation in snow over the long northern winter. The problem was likely compounded by the fact that, in order to create a watering hole for the cattle, Mr Bevan had dammed a stream running from Kam Lake, a body of water close to Con Mine and likely subject to heavy arsenic deposition on snow and ice that was then flushed through the drainage system during spring runoff.[23] The Bevan farm was the primary source of milk for the settler population in Yellowknife, and resident Barbara Bromley remembered that deliveries came to an end in 1951 as a result of arsenic poisoning. Similarly, the farm hand Helen Kilkenney remembered that the arsenic poisoning eventually killed every head of cattle in the area: "we watered the cows from Kam Lake about 500 yards from the barn. In winter we would cut a hole in the ice for the cows to drink. In the summer the cows would feed along the road and in the grassy places in the rocks. But after four years the cows got arsenic poisoning and they all died."[24] Con Mine compensated the Bevans with $20,000, but that did not prevent arsenic from continuing to wreak havoc in Yellowknife. In that same spring of 1949, two horses died in the city limits and local dogs showed symptoms of arsenic poisoning, including mouth ulcers, hair loss, gastrointestinal symptoms, and soreness in the feet. Local people also observed fatal poisoning of wildlife, including foxes, squirrels, and birds.[25] Although the signs of danger were everywhere, a local mining inspector, Steve Homulos, wrote that he was "not too alarmed" about the situation because both mining companies were "doing their utmost to solve the problem," consulting experts within their own companies and at the Geraldton mines in an effort to combat the arsenic menace.[26]

Contrary to Homulos's view, the mining companies' response was scandalously slow and largely ineffective for almost two years. W.G. Jewitt, the mine manager at Con, recalled that the company had contemplated installing a baghouse when constructing the roaster in 1941, but rejected the idea owing to the apparent absence of health issues from similar roasting facilities at Geraldton, the sparse population of Yellowknife, the apparent windiness of the surrounding area (a questionable assertion), and the challenge of safely storing the captured arsenic. As for the crisis at hand, Jewitt wrote that "we have hesitated to shut down the plant since such action on our part would probably embarrass Giant, who depend on flotation and roasting to recover almost all of their gold." While Jewitt assured Deputy Commissioner Gibson that the company was looking into the problem, he argued that "there is no need for the people of Yellowknife to be concerned about the matter."[27]

Con did install a wet scrubber (also called an impinger) on its stack in August 1949, which meant that the roaster fumes passed through cones seated in water, removing between 88 to 98.5 per cent of the arsenic content. While these numbers are impressive, the impinger, as with so many pollution-control technologies, created a new problem: what to do with contaminated material captured at the end of the pipe. In fact, Con Mine's technological approach essentially traded an air pollution problem for a water contamination issue, as the mine dumped liquid sludge from the impinger, containing approximately 50 to 60 per cent arsenic content by weight, into its tailings area. The sludge drained into nearby waterbodies such as Pud Lake and Kam Lake, setting off alarm bells about the danger that the contaminated water posed to the public.[28] Nonetheless, at least Con Mine's managers were trying to do something to solve the air pollution problem. A.K. Muir, Giant Mine's manager, reported that the company had been quoted a price of $200,000 to $300,000 (about $2.3 million to $3.4 million in 2023 dollars) for a Cottrell electrostatic precipitator (which used static electrical current to capture arsenic particles), and as a result was waiting to see how well Con's much cheaper impinger method worked before taking any action.[29]

Sounding the Alarm

In contrast to Giant mine's foot dragging, the federal government's Department of National Health and Welfare adopted a no-holds-barred approach to combating arsenic pollution in Yellowknife. At the forefront of these efforts was Dr Kingsley Kay, chief of the department's Industrial Health Laboratory, whose passionate engagement on the arsenic issue belonged to best traditions of advocacy within the field of industrial hygiene, and foreshadowed his later distinguished career working on toxins and occupational health with the World Health Organization, the International Labour Office, and the Mount Sinai School for environmental medicine.[30] Kay first travelled to Yellowknife at the end of November 1949, where he interviewed local mine and government officials. He collected reports from the mines and local health officials of high arsenic content in snow near Yellowknife, on vegetation near Kam Lake (260 parts per million where 1 parts per million was deemed safe on foods), and as water pollution in hot spots in Pud Lake (an astonishing 13 parts per million), in Yellowknife Bay (0.2 parts per million), and in puddle water on the Bevan farm (1.2 parts per million). Kay also noted with alarm the many reports that arsenic pollution had caused sickness in humans and death among animals. The only solution, Kay wrote, was that "roasting should be stopped and flotation concentrate stockpiled until these companies have installed the equipment necessary to prevent further environmental pollution." Furthermore, Kay believed that, in order to address the emergent water pollution problem, "the impinger method should be experimented with in a laboratory, not in an organized community."[31] Far from being a lone wolf on the issue, Kay received full support from his superiors (Dr Kenneth Charron, chief of the Industrial Division, and Dr Donald Cameron, deputy minister of Health and Welfare) for his recommendation to shut the roaster down. On 14 December 1949, Cameron informed Roy Gibson of his department's position:

> After careful consideration with my officers and having in mind the effects on human and animal life already observed, I have no alternative but to recommend strongly to you that roaster operations be stopped forthwith and that they remain so until proper arsenic collection and disposal practices which will entirely eliminate the health hazard, have been placed in operation.[32]

Cameron's recommendation struck like a dagger at the heart of the development dream that had accompanied the rebirth of gold mining in the Yellowknife region, and pitted the public health advocates in the Department of National Health and Welfare against the pro-development civil servants in the Department of Mines and Resources and on the Northwest Territories Council. The local mining inspector, K.J. Christie, summed up the prevailing sentiment in his department when he described Health and Welfare's recommendations as "drastic."[33] At the December meeting of the Northwest Territories Council, Kay, Charron, and Parsons from Health and Welfare presented their findings on the severity of the arsenic pollution at Yellowknife, arguing that the problem would only worsen over time. The meeting minutes suggested that the council would adopt a tough approach, with Gibson announcing that "when it is a case of weighing possible injury to human life against the possible profits of mining enterprises, Council must protect human life."[34] F.S. Parney, who attended the meeting as a representative of Health and Welfare, offered a somewhat different perspective, hinting there was some impatience with Kay's presentation on the part of Hugh Keenleyside, deputy minister of Mines and Resources and commissioner of the Northwest Territories, who had interrupted, demanded a quick summary, and then left the meeting. Kay's assessment was more blunt: he felt that Keenleyside had "dismissed" him and was angry that the commissioner had cut him off and told him to submit a written version of his remarks to the recording secretary. Noting with unease the focus on technological solutions to the pollution issue, Parney wrote, "for some reason or other, all three of us on the delegation came away from the meeting with the feeling that the Council did not have a full realization of the seriousness of the problem or the urgency for stopping forthwith the roaster process."[35]

The comment proved prescient, as Keenleyside informed Cameron that the council would not order an end to roasting because Giant Mine's managers had committed to immediate action to eliminate arsenic fumes, while Con had already removed 98 per cent of the arsenic pollution from its stack emissions.[36] As the administrative and political czar of the Northwest Territories, Keenleyside sat on the left of the political spectrum, and promoted an activist and interventionist administration when appointed as commissioner in 1947 (an approach that often put him at odds with local government officials seeking more autonomy for Yellowknife).[37] While he was not philosophically opposed to regulating industry, his vision for social advancement in Northern Canada was founded on a pillar of rapid economic development. At the January 1950 meeting of the Northwest Territories Council, Keenleyside and the other members insisted that keeping the territory's burgeoning gold mining industry running was more important than a roasting ban. Stop the roasting, they reasoned, and the result would be closure of the mines and "economic disaster" for Yellowknife.[38]

The day before the Northwest Territories Council meeting, Gibson invited Kay and Charron to his office to meet with two officials from Giant Mine, including the manager A.K. Muir, along with three other civil servants from various departments. Muir told the group that Giant was now committed to purchasing an electrostatic precipitator and finding a suitable storage method for the arsenic that the new equipment would capture. Gibson then asked Kay and Charron to withdraw their recommendation for a roasting ban.[39] The two doctors refused to budge, and their department maintained as official policy a recommendation for a roaster ban, conceding only that "if, despite this recommendation, Council are prepared to take the *calculated risk*, then we would be prepared, on request, to assist in reducing this threat to a minimum."[40]

For its decision to reject Health and Welfare's advice, the Northwest Territories Council relied heavily on the advice of Oliver Stanton, the local medical officer of health for Yellowknife, and the first and only doctor in the region until the construction of Yellowknife's hospital (now named for him) in 1948. Throughout the arsenic crisis, Stanton continually downplayed the toxic threat, and described Health and Welfare's recommended roaster ban as "rather drastic."[41] When Con Mine contemplated shutting down its roaster plant and relying on its supplies of non-refractory ore, Stanton told the company not to bother because there was no risk to the general public.[42] Although he had treated patients with arsenic poisoning, Stanton repeatedly asserted (to Charron and to the February meeting of Northwest Territories Council) that the pollution threat was confined to the spring months, and presented no danger so long as people did not use snow for water and washed all berries and locally grown produce. Stanton repeatedly argued that the warning signs

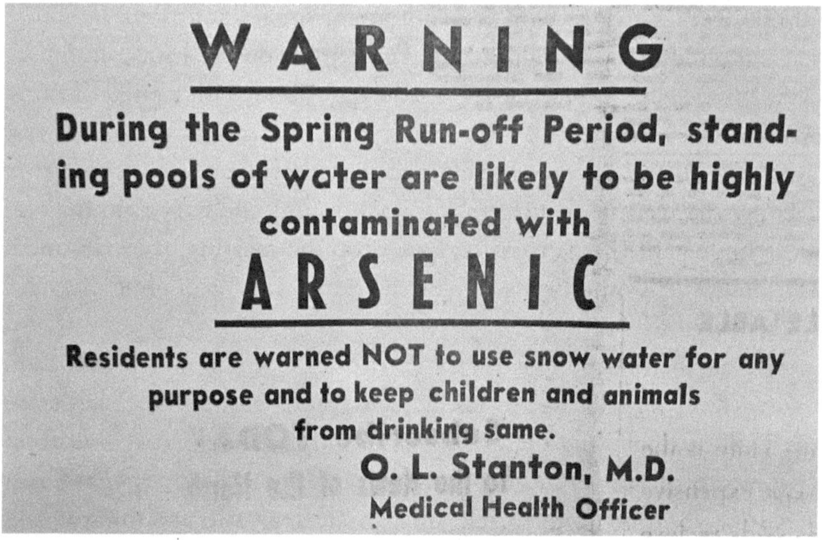

WARNING

During the Spring Run-off Period, standing pools of water are likely to be highly contaminated with

ARSENIC

Residents are warned NOT to use snow water for any purpose and to keep children and animals from drinking same.

O. L. Stanton, M.D.
Medical Health Officer

Figure 2.1

Arsenic pollution warning published in *News of the North*, April 1951, on behalf of Dr O.L. Stanton, medical health officer for Yellowknife. In spite of public warnings, at least one Dene child died from ingesting arsenic-laden snowmelt water.

he ordered posted at local lakes and advertisements he had submitted to the local press ought to be enough to guard public health.[43] The Northwest Territories Council prefaced its decision not to ban ore roasting with the suggestion that Stanton, as chief medical officer of health and the chair of the local municipal government (the trustee board), could work with Health and Welfare on ongoing efforts to mitigate the arsenic problem.[44] As a man who wore many hats, Stanton was not a completely disinterested medical practitioner: he had served as the company doctor at the Con Mine hospital from 1937 to 1948 and his role in local government likely made him more aware than doctors in Ottawa of mining industry interests.[45] While it is hard to assess Stanton's motivations from his official correspondence, he was certainly the least concerned among the medical professionals who offered advice on the arsenic issue, consistently telling mine managers and federal officials that there was no real danger on the ground.

Despite Stanton's assurances, the Department of National Health and Welfare continued to raise the alarm about the acute danger of arsenic toxicity near Yellowknife. In January 1950, Cameron reminded Keenleyside that the water in Kam Lake was "considered polluted and dangerous," a matter of grave concern because the lake was a secondary water supply for the town of Yellowknife and the primary supply for the Bevan farm (the latter of whom, Charron suggested, shockingly, had not yet been informed of the high pollution levels). He suggested that all locally grown produce should be kept out of market pending further study because of high arsenic levels on a small sample of vegetables.[46] Kay was much more forthright in internal departmental correspondence, as his frustration with inaction in the face of danger began to boil over. Commenting on Con Mine, he wrote:

> I think it simply incredible that this company, in full knowledge of cause and effect, has gone on month after month saturating the Yellowknife community with effluent from their operations. Having reduced pollution by air on the 19th of August, they turn to the rapid pollution of Pud Lake and adjoining waterbodies with all the insouciance of 19th century industrialists.
>
> The further pollution data, taken with Mr. Bevan's new plight … strengthens my conviction that our recommendations to Mr. Gibson should never have been ignored.[47]

Kay remained concerned that water samples from local lakes continued to show disturbingly high arsenic levels through 1950.[48]

Yellowknifers also continued to report deaths among domestic animals – clear evidence that arsenic persisted at dangerous levels in the local environment. In May 1950 Bonniface Bourke, a teamster, turned his two horses loose to forage on Latham Island (separated from Yellowknife by a very narrow channel and a bridge built in 1945), where they died after grazing and drinking from stagnant pools.[49] In a local oral history study, Laurie Cinnamon recalled that her father's horse team, which he used to move cordwood, died that same spring because the animals "got arsenic poisoning from drinking the spring run-off water lying about in puddles."[50]

Figure 2.2

View of the roaster stack at Giant Mine, August 1955. By this time, some arsenic was being recovered, but a significant amount was still being emitted from the stack.

None of this is surprising because Con Mine continued to pollute local waterways with arsenic, while Giant Mine, the much larger source of airborne arsenic pollution, continued to pump untreated emissions from its roaster stack as rail strikes and flooding prevented the delivery of its Cottrell electrostatic precipitator.[51] For all the meetings and bureaucratic discussion of the issue, government and industry had done little to curb arsenic levels that were severe enough to kill large animals, and thus also potentially a human being.

The Tatsǫ̨t'ıné and Arsenic

Winter typically comes early in the Yellowknife area, with freezing temperatures and snow arriving during the time of year that southern Canadians consider to be autumn. In 1950, bitter cold descended on Yellowknife in October, with temperatures reaching a low of minus eighteen degrees Celsius and Yellowknife Bay freezing over on the twenty-seventh day of the month. Sub-freezing temperatures did not relinquish their grip on the region until March 1951, and then only to a maximum temperature of 2.8 degrees Celsius. For the better part of five months, thousands of pounds of arsenic trioxide dust settled into the snowpack each day in the Yellowknife area (most of it from the Giant Mine smokestack), with no rain or runoff to dilute the accumulating toxic material. In April, however, the seasons began to turn. Although temperatures fluctuated between freeze and thaw, they reached a spring-like high of 14.4 degrees Celsius during the month, and for the first time since October, rain fell, albeit only 2.5 millimetres. In May, temperatures reached a daily average high of 9.9 degrees Celsius and rainfall amounted to 12.7 millimetres, enough to melt considerable amounts of toxic snow and mobilize large amounts of arsenic in local watersheds.[52]

Signs of the looming danger from arsenic were readily apparent by April. Local representatives of the Department of Resources and Development noted that snow samples in winter 1950 to 1951 had revealed that "heavy concentrations of arsenic existed in the Yellowknife regions, particularly at the north end of Latham Island," the very same area where arsenic had killed Bonniface Bourke's horse team a year earlier. On 14 April the department implored Stanton to warn people that they should take "certain precautions" during spring runoff and told the local Indian agent to warn the Chief of the Tatsǫ̨t'ıné, who lived on Latham Island.[53] As mentioned in the previous chapter, this small group of Tatsǫ̨t'ıné had only settled on the island since the mid-1940s, after the Department of Indian Affairs had encouraged them to move to a more centralized village (now called Ndilǫ) for ease of service provision (schools, housing, etc.) and so that they could more easily obtain jobs at the mines. Indian Affairs also created the village as a kind of unofficial reserve that segregated Tatsǫ̨t'ıné from the settler population, many of whom objected to the fact that some "Indians" had drifted into town.[54] Only the open water of Back Bay separated the village from Giant Mine, located approximately two kilometres to the northwest, with no natural barriers to divert arsenic from settling on Latham Island when the wind was from the north. Despite the obvious danger, one key service that Indian Affairs neglected to provide to Latham Island settlements was a supply of clean water so they did not have to rely on lake water and snowmelt that the government knew was heavily contaminated with arsenic. As a result, during the spring runoff season of 1951, several Tatsǫ̨t'ıné became acutely sick and some went to hospital. Then, on 14 May, Frank Abel, a two-year-old who drank contaminated water, probably from snowmelt and an ice hole in Yellowknife Bay, died of acute gastroenteritis after failing to respond to treatment in hospital.[55] His death was the fulfillment of everything Kay and his colleagues had feared, the culmination of two years of "calculated risk" that the Northwest Territories Council and the mining companies had been willing to take with arsenic pollution.

As word of the child's death spread through the government, the Department of Resources and Development and local health officials immediately sought to absolve themselves of responsibility. G.E.B. Sinclair, director of the Northern Administration and Lands Branch, emphasized the warnings and other precautionary measures that were taken in response to high arsenic levels.[56] Stanton essentially blamed Abel's family for the death, noting that "this family was either using snow and ice melted down or scooping up runoff water from the surface of the ice despite being warned against it." Stanton went on to highlight all the preventative actions he had taken, including the placement of warning signs around town, placing "large" advertisements in the newspaper (see figure 2.1), and communicating the danger to the Indian agent I.F. Kirkby.[57] Stanton did indeed place fairly large ads in *News of the North*, one on 13 April, one on 20 April, and another on 13 July, though how many signs were posted and their locations remains unknown.[58] Regardless, barriers of language and literacy would have prevented many, if not most Tatsǫ̨t'ıné from reading the warnings. Even if the Indian agent did warn the Chief on Latham Island, many Tatsǫ̨t'ıné had no alternative other than to drink water from the bay or from melted snow because there simply was no other source available to them. It was only after the death of Frank Abel that the government trucked in barrels of water from the town supply for the Tatsǫ̨t'ıné.[59]

Figure 2.3

Aerial view of Giant Mine, looking southeast, 1954. The plume from the stack carried arsenic into the surrounding environment and communities.

In addition to water deliveries, a meeting of federal officials and mine managers in June 1951 proposed a multi-pronged response to Abel's death, including the placement of more warning signs at all polluted lakes, clinical exams of the local population to assess the effect of ingesting arsenic, and testing for arsenic in the Yellowknife water supply, in local lakes, in soil, and on local produce. Remarkably, A.K. Muir, Giant Mine's manager, reported to the meeting that the Cottrell electrostatic precipitator was not yet installed; the mine was nevertheless permitted to continue with emissions of untreated roaster fumes for more than four months after Abel's death.[60] As for Abel's family, Giant Yellowknife Gold Mines quietly paid them $750 in compensation for the loss of their child, far less than the $20,000 the Bevans received from Con Mine for the death of their cattle.[61]

The poisoning of the Latham Island community carried broader consequences for the Tatsǫ̨́t'ıné. Oral testimony from Yellownives Dene Elders in Ndilǫ (on Latham Island) and Dettah (the Dene village on the east side of Yellowknife Bay) recounts the many ways that arsenic poisoning undermined the local subsistence economy and severed close cultural ties to the land, accentuating the jarring adjustments brought by relocation from seasonal camps into the villages. The Tatsǫ̨́t'ıné grew wary of hunting, fishing, berry picking, and gathering medicinal plants in contaminated areas, and some plant and animal species became less abundant in the Yellowknife regions. Many community members also remember the immediate impacts of arsenic poisoning on humans being more severe than the archival record acknowledges. Most Tatsǫ̨́t'ıné claim, for instance, that more than one child died and that acute sickness was more widespread than official reports suggested. The Elder Therese Sangris captured many of these themes in an undated interview recording:

> The people were never warned about the impacts and risks of living near mines. In late December of 1949, a massive emission from the Giant Mine dispersed huge amounts of arsenic into the air, settling into the ice and snow. Melting snow in the spring of the following two years was so toxic that notices were printed in Yellowknife newspapers warning people not to drink or use the meltwater. Few Weledeh Yellowknives Dene could read the notices. Anyone who washed their hair with arsenic-laden meltwater in the next two springs went bald. ... But the greatest tragedy occurred in spring 1951: four children in family camps in Ndilǫ died. The mine owners gave their parents some money, as if it could compensate for the loss. Women stopped picking medicine plants and berries, which used to grow thickly in the area of Giant Mine. The people moved away, avoiding the mine area for some years, although it had once been so important to them.[62]

During a recent traditional knowledge study, another Elder (who maintained anonymity) described the impacts on berries and terrestrial animals, and also fish:

> Eventually people started to realize that area, that's not safe to pick berry or go hunting in that area, or trap in that area. Because it's all the smell from the chemical they use. So, they kind of destroyed hunting and trapping in that area. They put it in the water eventually, so the fish, they used that area and now it's no longer used after all the pollution they put into the water. So, they know that the fish got deformed, some of them. People have nets in that area said the fish weren't... the muskrats all kind of disappeared, and beavers, muskrats, rabbits, you know. They all kind of faded away in that area.[63]

Rachel Crapeau described the devastating impacts of arsenic, not only on people but also on their dog teams, recalling,

> Before the Yellowknives Dene understood what arsenic was, they were aware of changes that made them wary of the water, fish, berries, and plants near the mine sites. When land users took their sled dogs through the tailings ponds that crossed their traditional trails, the dogs would lose the fur on their paws within a day or two. The Elders can recall people falling off their sled into the tailings ponds, which stayed open year-round, and becoming ill, losing their hair soon after. After many of their sled dogs died without obvious cause, dog owners stopped feeding them fish from Weledeh. People, too, started dying from cancer at a rate previously unknown to Yellowknives Dene.[64]

In turn, the poisoning of dog teams affected the Tatsǫt'ıné's ability to travel, due not only to the loss of dog teams but also to the avoidance of travel routes near the mines. As one (anonymous) Elder described it:

> People used to travel on dog teams a lot, and dogs got sick too. Kind of hard for people to travel through there; dogs get sick, it gets lots of hardship on people because they need dogs for survival, a long time ago. It was pretty harsh for a while there. Lots of people travel all kinds of different places; they stayed away. People just stayed further away, even further away from these guys because there is just lots of noise pollution and everything.[65]

The manner in which mining companies and the government used the Yellowknife area as a dumping ground for atmospheric arsenic pollution was ultimately a colonial act that displaced Indigenous people from crucial social and ecological relationships they maintained with the land. In this sense, the impact was not unlike the callous slaughter of Inuit sled dogs by the RCMP during this period, with devastating effects on Inuit mobility and culture.[66] Even though Tatsǫ̨t'ıné subsistence land uses had been displaced to areas far beyond the Giant mine site itself, extensive pollution from the mine had rendered a much broader landscape a toxic threat.

The mining industry provided some opportunities in the new industrial economy. Approximately fifty Tatsǫ̨t'ıné men found mine employment in Yellowknife or at other nearby mines by the late 1950s, a small share of the total wealth being extracted from their traditional lands.[67] But the costs of industrial development were high: the "wastelanding" of the Tatsǫ̨t'ıné's traditional territories severed the Tatsǫ̨t'ıné's relationship to local landscapes and pushed their hunting and gathering activities further and further from the communities, making it more difficult to engage in subsistence practices.[68] The Elder Isadore Sangris described the process in this way:

> As a result of the mines in the area, the land has been wasted, destroyed, and contaminated. Mining has occurred for more than 50 years and a lot of damage has occurred. The water is contaminated; rabbits and grouse are contaminated; the Dene people have become very cautious of eating traditional foods because of the heavy contaminants in the water, land, and air. The contamination even destroys trees, marshes, habitat, and wild berries. All things that the Dene people want to use but cannot anymore. The land here cannot sustain them anymore. The Weledeh do not fish in the bay anymore; instead, they go to Wool Bay, they have to go to communities far from the mines to get their fish and water fowl.[69]

Giant Mine's and Con Mine's release of arsenic pollution brought blatant environmental injustices to the Tatsǫ̨t'ıné in the form of sickness and death. It was also a key contributor to the colonization of the area inaugurated by mining activity and settlement itself, a pollution-induced form of displacement that alienated the Tatsǫt'ıné from lands that had sustained them for generations.

The Aftermath

The long-awaited installation of Giant Mine's Cottrell electrostatic precipitator in October 1951 did not, contrary to the hopes of government and industry, eliminate the arsenic pollution problem at Yellowknife. The most immediate issue was that the Cottrell was not particularly efficient at capturing arsenic trioxide. Remarkably, sampling of stack emissions for arsenic only began in 1954, and the first year's results revealed that the Cottrell only prevented 41.8 per cent of the arsenic from escaping the roaster stack, meaning that 11,980 pounds per day of arsenic had still been emitted (Con's impinger operated at 97.8 per cent efficiency and thus the company's roaster added another 147 pounds per day). Giant Mine managed to reduce the daily arsenic load to 7,400 pounds in 1955 with the installation of a second Cottrell unit, but pollution amounts actually rose in the subsequent two years (to 9,600 pounds per day in 1956 and 9,420 pounds per day in 1957) because of decreasing efficiency of the pollution controls and an increase in ore tonnage processed. Giant Yellowknife Gold Mines did not, in fact, put a significant dent in its arsenic emissions until 1958, when the installation of a baghouse (a large fabric filter that further captures arsenic dust from the roaster emissions) reduced the amount of pollution to 115 pounds per day in 1959, which was for the first time less than Con's total of 151 pounds per day.[70]

Government officials were well aware that high levels of arsenic persisted in the Yellowknife area during the early 1950s. Kay led an ongoing arsenic monitoring survey beginning in 1951 and requested additional funds to continue the survey in 1954 because "we are not yet satisfied that arsenic contamination has reached a consistently low level."[71] Stanton continued to advertise locally about the dangers of arsenic in the spring, writing in June 1954 that "the season was prolonged this year and I felt it wise to advertise until I considered the danger past."[72] The government had obviously adopted the "dose makes the poison" approach to regulating contaminants that prevailed during this period, reasoning that small amounts of arsenic ingestion could be safe, without considering that low-dose, long-term exposure to arsenic also carried health risks.[73] Regardless, Yellowknife's water supply (drawn from Back Bay) frequently exceeded "safe" limits, often climbing above the arsenic limit of 0.05 parts per million that the Northwest Territories Council had adopted as a drinking water standard in 1951. As late as the summer of 1959, arsenic levels reached a high of 0.14 parts per million in Yellowknife's tap water, while Giant Mine's own tap water supply contained a shockingly high level of arsenic at 0.25 parts per million.[74] One retrospective report on the Yellowknife water supply claimed that arsenic levels rose above the acceptable limit of 0.05 parts per million approximately 15 per cent of the time between 1951 and 1960.[75] While the short- and long-term health impacts from this low-level poisoning are unknown, in 1953 the Department of Indian Affairs did suggest that a non-status Indigenous man who lived in Yellowknife, Henry Lafferty, was likely sick because of arsenic.[76] A clinical study from 1975 mentioned that in 1954, several participants (mostly millworkers from Giant) had experienced sub-acute and acute symptoms of arsenic poisoning owing to workplace exposure.[77] Despite calls to action after the death of Frank Abel, the mining industry continued, throughout the 1950s, to saturate the local environment with arsenic in a manner that presented clear health risks to the local population.

To make things worse, the mining companies' attempts to reduce arsenic pollution often created as many problems as they solved. A great deal of pollution control equipment during this period amounted to little more than "high tech" barrier methods, merely blocking and collecting toxic waste without chemically altering it to a less dangerous form. Always the problem of final disposal and safe containment loomed large. As noted previously, the Con impinger may have prevented air pollution, but it threatened local watersheds due to the production of arsenic-laden sludge. Kay somewhat reluctantly approved the construction of a new disposal area for the sludge in the nearby Crank Lake in June 1950 after Con Mine maintained that the rock basin of the pond was impermeable. While this may have been true, previous dumping of sludge continued to contaminate Pud Lake and adjacent Kam Lake.[78] Con officials also raised concerns about Rat Lake, also heavily contaminated (primarily because of airborne deposition of arsenic, according to Con) and only 100 feet from a town pumping station that pulled water from Great Slave Lake.[79] Adding to concerns about surface contamination, the Department of Resources and Development quite remarkably permitted the adjacent Negus Mine to install a roasting facility using the impinger method in 1951, reasoning that it was unfair to demand a different approach than that used at Con, despite concerns that the proposed Negus pond might leak into Great Slave Lake.[80] Negus's roaster eventually failed to operate properly, leading to the collapse of the company (because it could not process vital stockpiled ore) and allowing CM&S to swoop in and take over the property in 1953.[81] Over the next fifty years, CM&S dumped 30,000 tonnes of arsenic sludge into Con Pond (the storage pond adjacent to Crank Lake) and Negus Pond, all of which required treatment in an autoclave between 2003 and 2007 to reduce it to a less toxic state. With tons of arsenic-laden tailings also dumped in the Pud Lake and Crank Lake areas, local lakes such as Kam, Meg, Keg, and Peg (all connected to Pud) remain heavily polluted with arsenic, exceeding current guidelines for drinking water and the protection of aquatic life. Recent scientific studies suggest that the recovery of ecosystems in these lakes is slow, while public warnings not to drink the water or eat the fish serve as a constant reminder of Con Mine's pollution legacy.[82]

The problems at Con Mine paled in comparison to those at Giant Mine. Ironically, however, it was the water pollution from Con that prompted the northern administration to reject the idea of storing the arsenic captured in Giant's Cottrell at the surface. In June 1950, for instance, Kay recommended against Giant's proposal to dump the arsenic in an area near Veronica Lake (named Pocket Lake today), adjacent to the Yellowknife golf course, arguing that the material was likely to seep into local groundwater.[83] Giant Yellowknife Gold Mines investigated a number of options, including wood vats (too leaky), metal storage containers (too subject to corrosion), or large concrete containers (reasonably safe but too expensive).[84] In July 1950, Roy Gibson argued that storage in concrete tanks was the safest option, but "the Departments concerned do not desire to put the mining companies to unnecessary expense."[85]

In February 1951 Giant's manager A.K. Muir declared that Giant would store all the arsenic dust from the soon to be installed Cottrell in underground chambers, arguing that once mining ceased, natural permafrost would entomb the toxic material in an impermeable barrier, "and that it should remain perfectly dry and stable in permanently frozen ground."[86] As director of the northern administration, Sinclair had sought advice from A.O. Dufresne, Quebec's deputy minister of mines, on best practices for storing arsenic at mines in that province (they actually managed to sell the relatively small amounts produced at two mines). Dufresne recommended against underground storage because "mine waters tend to circulate even through 'non-porous' rocks, and very close control would have to be kept to ensure that mine water does not become highly contaminated."[87] The northern administration applied Dufresne's logic to the proposal at Negus for underground storage, asserting that "the excavation chamber might open up if the mine were to be abandoned and allowed to flood, thus producing a circulation of underground water directly connected to Yellowknife Bay."[88] In November 1950, one of Giant Mine's own engineers, W.M. Gilchrist, recommend against underground storage because "the advantage ... is not marked enough to warrant it when the possible effects of years of operation in the area and the lack of control over the material once it is placed in an underground chamber are considered."[89] Regardless, the northern administration embraced the short-term expediency of preventing arsenic contamination on the surface, adopting the consensus position that "the Cottrell collection plant and disposal of dry arsenic tri-oxide in an underground permafrost area, as adopted by Giant, offered the least objection from a public health standpoint."[90] It was a position endorsed by Stanton as well, who assured Sinclair that "unless some very definite contra-indication can be pointed out [underground storage] has my complete approval."[91] And so, after the Cottrell was finally installed, Giant Yellowknife Gold Mines began to pump arsenic dust into rock chambers under the ground: day after day, tonne after tonne, for half a century, leaving a massive deposit of toxic material for another generation of Yellowknifers to reckon with (a story we will return to in the last chapter).

In the shorter term, major reductions in airborne arsenic from Giant Mine after the installation of the baghouse in 1958 seemed to have pushed the pollution issues to the sidelines in Yellowknife. The federal government stepped back from the issue, Kay ceased his monitoring studies by the mid-1950s, and there is very little correspondence on the issue in the relevant archival files in the decade between 1954 and 1964.[92] The local Yellowknife newspaper (the unreservedly pro-mining *News of the North*) published only

Figure 2.4

Latham Island in 1950 (now Ndilǫ), looking west across Back Bay toward Giant Mine. Note the vegetable gardens beside the houses.

one article on arsenic between 1949 and 1951 (about how well Giant's Cottrell and Con's impinger were performing), failing even to report on the poisoning death of Frank Abel. The newspaper did not follow the arsenic issue in any meaningful way until the 1970s.[93] With no critical press coverage, many Yellowknifers likely took comfort from Stanton's proclamations that the dangers associated with arsenic were easily avoided by washing one's vegetables and by not drinking snowmelt water. Giant Yellowknife Gold Mines had, in many respects, buried the arsenic problem from public view after the installation of the Cottrell electrostatic precipitator and the baghouse. Out of sight and out of mind, the arsenic issue slipped off the public agenda by the end of the 1950s as the federal government and industry thought they had solved the problem for good.

Conclusion

During the early years of Giant Mine, several basic approaches to managing arsenic trioxide were established that would hold for the next five decades. The first of these was that threats to public health, no matter how severe, would always play second fiddle to ensuring that the mine could operate at full capacity. Neither the company nor the federal northern administration would entertain pauses or slowdowns in production, even when federal health officials recommended such actions. Nor would industry or government consider a search for less risky ore bodies, or less polluting methods of mining precious metals, so long as gold reserves lay ripe for exploitation. Another principle of pollution control was that company efforts would be voluntary, not subject to any specific pollution limits linked to clear public health and environmental criteria. Federal regulators essentially told the mining companies to adopt whatever techno-fix was available and hope for the best. Nobody really wrestled with the problems of abatement technologies failing to capture all of the arsenic trioxide emissions, or the fact that these technologies produced new pollution problems in the short term (water pollution at Con) and for the distant future (underground storage at Giant Mine). Some federal officials, notably Kay and others in his department, tried to convince their colleagues in Northern Affairs to adopt a more precautionary approach, but they were effectively silenced.

The absence of strong regulatory action is also implicated in another tenet of arsenic management at Yellowknife: people living in the area were largely left to their own devices. Indeed, the efforts of local officials to post warning signs and place newspaper ads in a language many Indigenous people would not understand, and then blame people for not following their advice, underscores the piecemeal public health response to the arsenic threat. The failure to provide a source of clean drinking water to Tatsǫ̨t'ıné on Latham Island and surrounding communities in the immediate aftermath of acute arsenic contamination in 1951 meant that people were left with no alternative to contaminated sources until the local government arranged for water to be trucked in to the community. Even as the local population continued to be exposed to arsenic, the mining companies and federal regulators assumed, without much evidence, that the emission reductions they had achieved were enough to protect public health. Giant Yellowknife Gold Mines believed it had put the lid back on the arsenic problem at Giant Mine, and, for a time, public and regulatory concern for the issue melted away.

3

Hiding Poison

The years between 1960 and 1975 represented a period of heady growth and political development for Yellowknife. Production rates at Con and Giant rose steadily, peaking at over 900,000 ounces in 1960 and remaining high until a sharp drop to approximately 300,000 ounces in 1975. While employment remained somewhat stagnant at Giant Mine, fluctuating between 350 and 400 workers over this period, the population of the town nearly doubled, from over 3,245 in 1961 to 6,122 residents a decade later, making it by far the largest urban area in the Northwest Territories.[1] In part this was because a new highway link to Edmonton was completed in 1960, meaning that residents could finally drive to the rest of Canada and import goods overland (albeit along a dirt road on the northerly segment of the route that was not fully paved until 2006). The new road, along with existing airport and floatplane infrastructure, solidified Yellowknife's position as a service and trans-shipment centre for mineral exploration and remote mines such as Discovery Mine, which operated (complete with a small town) in the taiga to the northeast from 1950 to 1969, and Tundra Mine, even further north, which operated from 1962 to 1968.

As Yellowknife grew, the town slowly began to gain more political autonomy from Ottawa. In part this was because of the agitation of local residents, most prominently Jock McMeekan, editor of the local newsletter, the *Yellowknife Blade*, who resented the interference of Ottawa's bureaucrats in local affairs. McMeekan and other residents argued that a growing settlement ought to be granted the same political autonomy and democratic institutions as those in southern Canada. Although Ottawa was reluctant to abandon its paternalistic role, Yellowknife achieved municipal status in 1953 (with the former mill manager at Negus, Jock McNiven, elected as the first mayor) and then full incorporation as a city in 1970. Most importantly, Yellowknife was named the capital of the Northwest Territories in 1967 at the same time as the federal government began to devolve power to an elected territorial government. What had been a gold mining camp on the North Arm of Great Slave Lake just a few decades earlier now had a legislature, a growing territorial bureaucracy, and a more diversified economy than in the early days. A federal government report from 1963 expressed some concern about Yellowknife's economic dependence on gold mining but noted its potential as a permanent regional service centre and administrative hub.[2]

If the future seemed to belong to Yellowknife, the town remained haunted by its past. By the early 1960s federal officials realized that, despite major reductions in airborne arsenic pollution, problems persisted with the contamination of local waterways. While the small lakes near Con Mine attracted much of the regulatory attention in the earliest years of the arsenic crisis, by the 1960s the problem of pollution in Yellowknife's drinking water came to a head as local people realized that surface runoff from Giant Mine's arsenic-laden tailings and waste rock had contaminated the city's main water source in Back Bay. Nor had the air pollution problem completely disappeared: emissions from Giant and Con crept back up from a low of 549 pounds per day in 1959 to 894 pounds per day in 1969 because of variability in production rates and the overall efficiency of the arsenic collection system.[3] For all the application of expensive technology to solve the problem prior to 1960, the persistence of arsenic on land and in water became a key public health concern once again over the next two decades, even if a rotating cast of public officials routinely disagreed about its severity. This time around, the government largely confined the arsenic debate to bureaucratic back rooms and clamped down on criticism from within, but only until the early 1970s. At this point, the arsenic issue exploded into public view in Yellowknife once again, owing to new scientific study of the issue, increased media attention, and a high-profile tailings spill. As public knowledge of Giant Mine's environmental problems increased, the issue became caught in a rising tide of Indigenous anti-colonialism, occupational health activism among organized labour, and the growing anti-pollution agenda of the environmental movement raising vital questions about the environmental injustices that had accompanied industrial development in Canada's northern territories.

Enduring Problems

In 1963, Jack Grainge, an engineer with the Department of National Health and Welfare, reported on an experiment he had performed to see if there were any arsenic-free sources of water in Yellowknife Bay that could be used as a source of drinking water for the adjacent city. Grainge also hoped to find a current that might be used as a free-flowing dump to carry away arsenic-laden effluent from Giant and Con. He thus poured red dye into the water at various locations but found that currents moved in every direction, round and round on a horizontal plane and up and down vertically. Everywhere, the red dye mixed evenly with the larger body of water, dashing hopes that somewhere, somehow, a stream of water pulsed through the bay unaffected by arsenic pollution. The report noted that arsenic levels in the bay ranged from 0.02 parts per million to a quite high 0.2 parts per million. Grainge recommended bringing Yellowknife Bay's arsenic levels in line with drinking water standards imposed a year earlier in the United States, which set 0.05 parts per million as the absolute limit, but he also advised that a new source of water should be sought when concentrations consistently exceeded 0.01 parts per million. Grainge's report also noted the increasing evidence demonstrating a link between arsenic ingestion and various forms of skin cancer (a connection also cited by US public health officials in their report on new drinking water standards). He recommended that Giant Yellowknife Mines (the company had dropped "gold" from its name in 1960) discharge tailings effluent at the narrows, further from the city's water intake, but town officials deemed the potential deposit of sediment to be objectionable. Grainge maintained years later that the water in Yellowknife Bay was safe most of the time, but his report in 1963 was the first in many years to sound an alarm about the presence of arsenic in the Yellowknife environment.[4]

Mine workers faced the dual threat of arsenic exposure in the community and in the workplace. Local 802 of the International Union of Mine, Mill and Smelter Workers (which represented workers at the mine from 1949 until the union merged with the United Steelworkers of America in 1968) first made the issue a bargaining priority in 1955, a year after arsenic gas poisoning in the treatment plant led to the hospitalization of twenty-one mine employees. The union continued to press the issue during bargaining in 1958, when the company implicitly recognized the dangers associated with workplace arsenic exposure by granting a twenty-five-cent-per-hour wage premium for certain high-risk jobs in the treatment plant. In 1962, the company again responded to union demands on the arsenic issue with a full schedule of premium pay rates for certain jobs in the arsenic-infused environment of the roaster facility.[5] While the issuance of "danger pay" may have compensated workers for additional risk, the extra money did nothing to reduce the exposure to arsenic that the miners faced every day.

Beyond the mine, additional signs pointed to the accumulation of arsenic throughout the Yellowknife environment. In 1965 an unnamed official (identified as "M17") from the Indian and Northern Health Services division declared, "I have recently discovered that the problem of arsenic pollution at Yellowknife is far from solved." The official was alarmed at the fact that Giant and Con were each still pumping three hundred to four hundred pounds of arsenic dust every day from their roasters. Recent sampling of locally grown lettuce and cabbage revealed arsenic contamination levels at forty to fifty parts per million, well above the recommended limit of one part per million. Ten days later, the same official reported on a meeting in which "it was agreed that a definite problem exists," and that plans should be drawn up in the coming year for a clinical study of the local population, a roaster stack emissions and fallout study, and possibly a wildlife survey.[6]

In response to Grainge's report, Health and Welfare began an intensive water monitoring program beginning in 1966, one that revealed that arsenic pollution levels in Yellowknife Bay remained high despite some attempts to divert tailings runoff at Giant Mine. In November, Gordon Butler, the chief medical and health officer for Yellowknife (a position now under the authority of the federal Department of National Health and Welfare), declared that he was "very concerned about the increasing amount of arsenic

Table 3.1 • Estimated daily arsenic emissions from Giant Mine and Con Mine, 1954–1969

Year	Giant Mine (lbs. /day)	Con Mine (lbs./day)	Total (lbs./day)
1954	11,980	395 (147)	12,375 (12,127)
1955	6,392 (7,400)	421 (113)	6,813 (7.513)
1956	5,998 (9,600)	412 (172)	6.410 (9,772)
1957	6,544 (9,420)	401	6,945
1958	3,330	385	3,715
1959	115	434 (151)	549 (266)
1960	165	586 (255)	751 (420)
1961	330	440	770
1962	330	440	770
1963	330	440	770
1964	496	294	790
1965	372	369	790
1966	247	309	556
1967	124	340	464
1968	256	337	593
1969	466	428	894

Note: Because sampling data was not consistent across sources, cells with numbers in parentheses show the contrasting emissions rates.

Soure: De Villiers and Baker, *Investigation into the Health Status*, 5. Alternative emissions data (in parentheses) comes from J.P. Windash, industrial hygienist, Occupational Health Division, to A.T. Jordan, Chief Mining Engineers, Department of Northern Affairs and National Resources, 24 November 1960. RG 29, vol. 2977, file 851-5-2, pt 1, LAC.

pollution in Yellowknife Bay" – with good reason, as monitoring data for city tap water in 1966 to 1967 showed plenty of readings above the 0.05 parts per million threshold, including frequent spikes between 0.15 and 0.2 parts per million and one astonishing reading of 2.92 parts per million on 16 June 1966.[7] In August 1967, Butler alerted his colleagues to evidence of serious health impacts from arsenic pollution. Yellowknife doctors were reporting high rates of anemia among female patients who had only recently arrived in the city, a possible indicator of low-level arsenic poisoning.[8] To all appearances, the respite in Yellowknife's arsenic crisis was officially over and an urgent response was needed.

Nonetheless, few individual officials within the Department of National Health and Welfare saw the need to act. Butler pressed his superiors on the arsenic issue, but in contrast to the top-level support that Kay received in the 1950s, senior bureaucrats in Health and Welfare tended to downplay the issue in the 1960s. On one occasion, H.A. Procter, director general of medical services, mused that a contaminated water supply might not be much of a threat to people in a cold climate because they were less inclined to drink a lot of water. In a cheeky response, Butler assured his superior that this was not the case, arguing that "the high consumption of liquor (usually with a water mix), tea and coffee, in the north, together with the very dry climate, would appear to negate any suggestion that there is less water consumption per capita."[9] According to Butler, people in Northern Canada were just as thirsty as anywhere else, so the focus on individual consumption habits was a distraction from the widespread public health threat of arsenic contamination in local drinking water.

The local government in Yellowknife certainly understood the threat. In 1967, local officials pushed for funding from the federal government and the mining companies to move the town's water intake upstream from the arsenic runoff from Giant Mine (from Yellowknife Bay to the mouth of the Yellowknife River). Butler expressed several concerns about this approach. He wrote to A.B. Yates, assistant director of Indian Affairs and Northern Development, about his fear that arsenic might still enter the water supply from several nearby sources, including contaminated lakes, soils, and heavily polluted areas in Back Bay. At this point, however, Butler's superiors clearly saw him as having gone rogue, and tensions over his arsenic advocacy boiled over. Procter first reprimanded Butler for contacting Indian Affairs without clearing it through his office. He then told Butler that it was pointless to raise concerns about a plan that had not been finalized. Butler, clearly piqued, claimed that his attentiveness to the issue had done some good, convincing the local government to move the water intake much further up the Yellowknife River and away from the most potent sources of arsenic pollution. More pointedly, Butler resented his superior's interference with his responsibilities as a public health official. He told Procter that he was "most concerned that I should be reprimanded as Chief Medical Officer for raising a query which has resulted in changes being made in the recommendations re. water intake point and which if these changes had not been made, would have resulted in a contaminated water supply even after the expenditure of over 1 million dollars."[10]

Butler continued to be outspoken about the threat of arsenic contamination in Yellowknife for several years, although the reprimands began to take their toll. In September 1970, Butler wrote a somewhat desperate memo to the new director general of medical services, J.H. Wiebe, highlighting the fact that combined airborne arsenic emissions from the two mines had increased to 967 pounds per day. He pointed out that local vegetables, especially carrots, beet leaves, lettuce, and chard, had arsenic levels approximately two to four times the allowable limit of one part per million (even if the amounts had been greatly reduced from the arsenic contamination found in 1965). Butler declared, "it is evident that a major problem of arsenic pollution of the atmosphere and terrain still exists at Yellowknife," and "I must now make a public statement warning the residents of Yellowknife that they should not consume vegetables grown in the area and this is likely to hit the headlines." He went on to recommend a "full and detailed study and immediate action," objectives Butler said he would pursue with the help of universities or provincial governments if his department would not act.[11]

Instead of action, however, various officials in the federal and brand-new territorial government directed their energy toward muzzling Yellowknife's chief medical and health officer. Stuart Hodgson, the first commissioner of the Northwest Territories to reside in the region, wrote to Jean Chrétien, minister of Indian Affairs and Northern Development, to suggest that "irreparable harm" would result from any public announcement about arsenic, and that the mines should be consulted "before allowing this problem to be blown out of proportion."[12] Chrétien quickly contacted his ministerial counterpart at Health and Welfare, John Munro, imploring him to cut off authorization for any public statement that Butler might make.[13] For his part, Munro suggested that market gardening was no longer practised in Yellowknife, so the amount of local produce consumed was negligible. Munro ignored the issue of household gardening, widely practised in Yellowknife, or the possibility that wild berry crops might be contaminated, a pollution vector that would have serious implications for the Tatsǫ̨t'ıné. Instead, he pointed to the reductions in arsenic on local produce as something to celebrate, regardless of whether current arsenic levels remained above levels considered safe.[14] He ordered Butler not to issue any "alarming announcement" about the issue of contaminated produce.[15] Chastened, Butler answered a query from the Consumers' Association of Canada in November with the claim that "the situation as regards arsenic in water and vegetables is now under good control and ... there is no danger to the health of the public."[16] Clearly, secrecy and denial were the order of the day, as federal officials believed that the threat of public alarm was greater than the threat of arsenic to public health.

The federal government did take some steps to address the resurgent concern over arsenic in the 1960s, relying on the same combination of engineering solutions and further study that had marked the mitigation programs in the 1950s. Undoubtedly the most important step was, as Butler had suggested, the movement of Yellowknife's water intake, a project completed in 1969, with Con and Giant each paying one-third of the cost at the behest of the federal government. The impact on the town's water was immediate. Butler reported in November 1970 that "the amount of arsenic in circulation has been reduced considerably," and measurements from a month later detected no arsenic whatsoever in the water.[17] Giant Mine also brought about major reductions to arsenic levels in its own tap water system (which still drew water directly from Yellowknife Bay), so the threat of contaminated drinking water was removed – at least for the settler population in Yellowknife.

The federal government also responded to the renewed concern over arsenic with a comprehensive environmental and medical survey. Health and Welfare appointed A.J. de Villiers and P.M. Baker, both with the department's Occupational Health Division, to conduct work on the issue between 1966 and 1969. De Villiers was no stranger to occupational dangers associated with mining. In 1964, he co-authored a bombshell report that linked high rates of lung cancer in St Lawrence, Newfoundland, to underground radon exposure in the town's fluorspar mines, a shocking revelation that prompted a royal commission five years later to make recommendations on mine safety and compensation.[18] De Villiers and Baker's work on Yellowknife's arsenic problem contained nothing quite so alarming as the St Lawrence case, but still revealed cause for concern. From June to August 1966, they and a team of medical students and Indian Affairs health officers scoured through medical records and distributed a health survey door-to-door. They arranged clinical exams for residents who reported symptoms of arsenic exposure, workers exposed to arsenic on the job, and any person who had lived in Yellowknife for more than ten years. Their report found high incidences of skin cancer, respiratory illness, and electrocardiographic irregularities, but could not definitively link such conditions to arsenic exposure (noting, for instance, that respiratory disease could also have arisen from smoking). But neither did it rule out a possible connection, noting that the scientific literature had in recent years established clear links between arsenic and skin cancer (among the other known impacts of arsenic). In Yellowknife, incidences of skin ailments and respiratory conditions had definitely increased among workers exposed to arsenic.[19]

De Villiers and Baker also noted the conundrum of tracking the medical impacts of chronic, long-term arsenic exposure in a town where many workers left after several years of working in the mine and mill. So, a precise picture of the medical impacts of arsenic exposure remained elusive in Yellowknife. More definitively, the two doctors confirmed that arsenic was still prevalent in the local environment, noting that the city's water supply (prior to the movement of the intake) was within the acceptable limit of 0.01 parts per million less than 16 per cent of the time and above the maximum level of 0.05 parts per million 15 per cent of the time. They also noted that about two pounds of arsenic trioxide fell each year on every acre of land in the city. The mining operations still exposed Yellowknifers to arsenic on a daily basis – in the water they drank, in the air they breathed, and in their places of work. Nonetheless, de Villiers and Baker's survey provided only hints of what the long-term impacts of such exposure might be.[20]

As important as these findings were, Health and Welfare did not make any attempt to distribute the report. In fact, it remained unavailable within the halls of government for two years after the submission deadline of 1969, and remained hidden from the wider public for over five years. There were a number of issues at play: author delays, bureaucratic bungling, and, not least, the federal government's desire to keep quiet about the arsenic issue. There was certainly no shortage of people interested in the results. Between 1969 and 1975, repeated requests for copies flowed in: from Butler, the Yellowknife city government, the Northwest Territories Council, the Northwest Territories Water Board (a regulatory body that issued water-usage licences after the passage of the Northern Inland Waters Act in 1972), the Canadian Broadcasting Corporation (CBC), and the National Indian Brotherhood (a pan-Indigenous advocacy group formed in 1967).[21] The exasperation of those seeking access to the report often seeped through the various written requests. In September 1970, Butler asked his superior, Wiebe, "Could pressure on Environmental Health be reapplied until the report which is now three years overdue is squeezed out of them?" Two months later, Butler asked again, noting that the survey was completed three years earlier and that he was getting a lot of pressure from local radio and newspapers.[22] De Villiers offered various explanations for the delay, including staffing issues (including a transition to a new statistician) and balancing vacation time. He was also frequently away at international conferences and slow (or outright neglectful) when it came to answering correspondence.[23] In August 1972, H.L. Brett, the new regional director of the northern region, wrote, "we are well along in another 'round-robin' contest with Dr. de Villiers," and "you will recall that he set an international record of delay in preparation of his report on the arsenic survey in Yellowknife."[24]

If frustration at the delays is understandable, it is also clear that Health and Welfare possessed a draft copy of de Villiers's report, which was circulated internally as early as May 1971.[25] Although there was some discussion of the report's key findings, Health and Welfare officials, especially Otto Schaefer of the Northern Medical Research Unit, generally downplayed the results, seizing, for example, on the idea that the high incidence of respiratory conditions in Yellowknife might be related to the cold climate."[26] Health and Welfare sent a few copies of the report to the Northwest Territories commissioner in June 1971, and to the city government in 1972, but did not make it public. One retrospective memo suggested that, in the wake of the dust-up over Butler's threats to go public, the Northwest Territories commissioner and his allies in the federal bureaucracy still wanted to keep the arsenic issue from public scrutiny until further pollution controls could be implemented.[27] As we shall see, this commitment to secrecy would provoke a massive public backlash and accusations of a cover-up directed toward the Department of National Health and Welfare just a few years later.

In the meantime, Health and Welfare adopted a relatively hands-off approach to the arsenic problem. In October 1970, the Medical Services Branch did create an arsenic committee to study and monitor the situation at Yellowknife. It was hardly a multi-stakeholder initiative, however, being composed of three departmental insiders: de Villiers, A.B. Morrison of the Food and Drug Branch, and W.H. Frost of the Medical Services Branch. Perhaps in a sign of internal disarray, the committee shuffled its membership only a month after its formation (J.A. Campbell, the assistant director general of foods, replaced Morrison, while R.E. Tait of Public Health Engineering joined as a new member). The committee's first review of the situation concluded that there was no cause for alarm, particularly regarding the issue of contaminated vegetables (for which they called for more testing), a position that validated the federal government's efforts to silence Butler on the issue.[28] Frost's further review of the situation, penned just after the creation of the committee, summed up the government's laissez faire approach. As long as the mine operations trapped the lion's share of airborne arsenic and limed their tailings ponds to mitigate seepage into the surrounding environment, Frost argued, there should be no cause for concern. At any rate, Frost reiterated that the relocation of the Yellowknife water intake had solved the problem of polluted drinking water. Arsenic levels on vegetables may, in some cases, have been four times the accepted limit, but so long as they were washed and not produced in large quantities for the market, Frost reasoned that they were safe.[29] According to Wiebe, the director general of medical services, Frost's report showed there was nothing to worry about: "the general situation and the controls being exercised at Yellowknife are regarded as being satisfactory for the present."[30]

The improvement to the municipal water system was a tangible step forward in public health protection, but it did nothing to stop ongoing arsenic pollution in the local environment. Scientific studies in the early 1970s suggested that severe pollution problems remained in the area surrounding the gold mines. In 1972 a group of scientists from Iowa State University published a trace element survey that they had conducted in Yellowknife during the previous two years. The study detailed a litany of alarming results: high levels of arsenic and antimony in soil, water contamination that worsened in lakes closer to Giant Mine's roaster, contaminated snow in some areas, and higher than normal levels of mercury and arsenic in hair samples taken from human participants in the study.[31] The lead author of the study, James O'Toole, recommended to the city of Yellowknife's Board of Health that it issue a statement of concern about the high levels of contaminants in the local area, and a second statement inviting more research teams to conduct "a comprehensive evaluation of the total environmental impact of the refinery effluents on the human population and wilderness ecosystem." O'Toole understood local sensitivities well enough that he cautioned against any "emotional" appeals to shut down the mines, but there is little evidence to suggest that the report was taken seriously.[32] Indeed, after Helga Reismann, member of Ecology North (a new environmental group founded in response to the arsenic issue), wrote a letter of concern about the report, John Munro, minister of Health and Welfare, countered that study of the problem was ongoing and the situation in Yellowknife was under control.[33] In January 1973, O'Toole sent a proposal to Health and Welfare outlining the contours of a further comprehensive study of trace element contamination in Yellowknife, but none was undertaken.[34] Whether the Iowa report was ignored, buried, or forgotten, Health and Welfare was clearly not about to set off any warning sirens about the health and environmental risks of contamination in Yellowknife.

Nevertheless, some pollution problems at Giant Mine became too obvious to ignore. In March 1974, a federal fisheries officer on a routine flight noticed a mass of discoloured ice expanding from the shoreline near Giant Mine along the frozen surface of Yellowknife Bay. Giant Mine staff investigated further and found that a dyke at the south end of one of the three tailings ponds at Giant had failed. Effluent had spilled over the rocks and onto the bay for several days, forming a solid, layered deposit of contaminated ice. While a cleanup effort did remove some of this ice, in April a second dyke failure at the northeast end of the same pond resulted in a "voluminous quantity of waste" flowing down the rocky hillside to the bay.[35] This time, thin ice, and the presence of open water in some places, prevented any kind of cleanup. In July, the northeast dyke failed yet again, allowing additional large amounts of effluent to flow into the bay. Although the effluent had been contained temporarily by a dam located below the dyke, the dam overflowed and contaminated water flowed as a stream running toward the bay. The federal government's Environmental Protection Service dispatched two scientists, Ron Wallace and M.J. Hardin, to assess the damage. Their measurements indicated that the effluent had not raised arsenic levels in the city's upstream water supply, but did carry large amounts (with the totals difficult to measure) of arsenic, cyanide, and other heavy metals into Back Bay, and since these contaminants were "known to be toxic to fish and other forms of aquatic life," they "therefore pose a definite threat to them in the receiving water."[36] Wallace and Hardin's report also noted the potential long-term impact of heavy metals and chemicals accumulating in the bottom of Yellowknife Bay. The two authors claimed that their study was only one in a long line pointing to problems in the tailings containment system at Giant Mine that were resulting in pollution along the shoreline near the mine.[37]

Local reaction to the spills suggested that patience with Giant Mine's management of its tailings pond containment facilities was wearing thin. Several Yellowknife city aldermen were furious about the "snow job" from the federal government and the mine, both of which had kept the spill secret for ten days. The city council passed several motions not only condemning the failure to report the spill to the public (and also the mayor for being complicit with the secrecy), but also admonishing Giant Mine for the spill and calling on the federal government to address the chronic problem of pollution in Back Bay.[38] Local concern was enough that city officials ordered signs to be put up along the shoreline, warning of elevated arsenic levels. Edward Ristan, a federal environmental health officer, raised the issue of the signs being in English only, and not the Dogrib language (likely unaware that the majority of Tatsǫ́t'iné spoke not Dogrib but the distinct Wıìlìdeh language).[39] Environment Canada charged the company under the federal Fisheries Act with dumping a noxious substance in waters frequented by fish, and, in February 1975, a local court took a somewhat remarkable step (given Giant Mine's centrality to the local economy) of convicting the company. However, F.G. Smith, the local magistrate, imposed only the lightest of sentences, a total fine of only $2,000 (the maximum penalty was $5,000 for each day that the effluent had escaped Giant Mine, which would have added $45,000 to the fine).[40] On 17 January 1975, effluent once again broke through the tailings dam and smaller backup dams, and flowed down into Back Bay at the rate of thirty gallons per minute, a leak that took a full weekend to get under control.[41] That same month, another study of the tailings effluent situation at Giant determined that Giant's method of attempting to precipitate out arsenic by liming the tailings ponds was "almost useless."[42]

In April 1975, Giant Yellowknife Mines committed publicly to a spending program of $1.5 million to develop a new, more reliable system of tailings dams and backup dykes, coupled with research on new chemical treatment

Figure 3.1

Giant Mine tailings spill, 1975. A series of tailings spills in 1974 to 1975 raised alarms over the contamination of Back Bay.

processes to precipitate arsenic from the tailings water. The company's action plan was not entirely voluntary. The implementation of the federal Northern Inland Waters Act (1972) meant Giant Mine would have to apply for a licence from the newly created Northwest Territories Water Board to use the 900,000 gallons of water that it extracted from Back Bay each year. Indeed, the company's announcement of the tailings containment plan came only two days after a public hearing of the Water Board, in which the company received intense criticism from many who attended (see below). Although the company's plan had the potential to improve water quality in the short term, the proposal was to contain the arsenic in the sediment of the tailings ponds rather than remove it, a source of surface contamination that would remain there after the closure of the mine.[43]

The long-term risks associated with short-term techno-fixes at Giant were already becoming apparent in another area of the mine's operation. In May 1973, mining inspector Erland Bengts raised critical concerns about the arsenic trioxide collected in the Cottrell electrostatic precipitator and baghouse and stored in chambers beneath the mine. Contrary to the company's longstanding claim that permafrost would re-establish itself around the arsenic chambers, Bengts reported that seasonal thawing had penetrated to "considerable depth" in the mine, and permafrost could not be relied upon to form a containment barrier. The inspector noted the possibility that the mine might close in the near future, leaving behind a mass of arsenic trioxide underground that was projected to grow to 174,000 tons by the end of 1974. Bengts was the first person to frame the magnitude of the problem in terms of the stored arsenic's potential to "kill the world's population four times over," a common talking point that comes up in street conversations about arsenic in Yellowknife today. He also pointed out that water would have to be pumped out of the mine long after closure because the staggering amount of buried arsenic had the potential to pollute a body of water 290 miles long, 62 miles wide, and up to 330 feet deep. Since Great Slave Lake is 290 miles long, 12 to 126 miles wide, with an average depth of 135 feet, one can surmise the widespread and pervasive impacts of groundwater filling the mine and then dissolving and mobilizing thousands of tonnes of arsenic trioxide into the adjacent lake. Bengts recommended a study program to monitor the prospects for the re-establishment of permafrost around the arsenic chambers for the next two decades.[44]

An incident in July 1974 further underscored the potential threat from the underground arsenic. That month, as miners worked to expand a subdrift in the mine, they opened up two holes in an arsenic chamber, one of which leaked water. Two water samples from the leak revealed astonishingly high levels of arsenic contamination at 4,529 parts per million and 5,816 parts per million.[45] The holes were soon plugged with cement, but the incident raised concerns about the ticking time bomb of the underground arsenic. In December 1974, federal Environmental Protection Service biologist Ron Wallace argued, "this could well represent one of the most serious pollution threats in the Northwest Territories. I am therefore rather surprised, and disappointed that no government agencies have addressed themselves to the problem."[46] Wallace's fears did not resonate in the halls of the federal government, however, and no plan of action was developed until well after the closure of the mine in 2004 (see chapter 6). Instead, Giant Yellowknife Mines did everything it could to promote the soundness of its arsenic storage strategy. At the 1975 Water Board hearing, Dave Emery summed up the company's position when he stated that "all the arsenic dust is collected and pumped back underground in a dry state in a closed system into sealed chambers underground in the permafrost layer where there will be no possibility of groundwater coming into contact with it."[47] The "bury and forget" approach to arsenic pollution was, in the end, a sleeping zombie that would later come back to haunt the federal government. But for the time being, all but a few fearful critics seemed content to push the problem off to some other people at some other time in the future.

The government also continued to "bury" (at least metaphorically) the ongoing threat from arsenic pollution at the surface. In addition to the problem of tailings seepage, air pollution from the Giant stack increased from lows of 115 pounds per day in 1959 to close to 900 pounds per day of arsenic discharge between 1971 and 1973, the results of an inexperienced baghouse operator and the mining of ore that was difficult to process through the baghouse.[48] Based on survey work in 1974, a new interdepartmental arsenic committee (which met for the first time in January 1975) concluded that, while the city's drinking water supply remained safe, ongoing arsenic deposition from the mine meant that nobody should drink water from local lakes or snowmelt in the area around Latham Island and Jolliffe Island.[49] In fact, water testing near Latham Island consistently revealed arsenic levels well above the "safe" level of 0.05 parts per million, with readings in the range of 0.083 to 0.198 parts per million.[50] Although city water was trucked to the Yellowknives Dene (and some non-Dene residents) on Latham Island, the town charged $5 per month for delivery. Thus, it is likely that many low-income people continued to draw drinking water from local sources. As mentioned previously, officials who posted warning signs along the bay near Latham Island after the spills of 1974 did so in English only. The warning sign campaign may also have been intermittent and inconstant: Jack Grainge's summary report on arsenic in 1976 suggested that the warning campaigns had been subject to "interruptions," but "most people would remember from early years."[51]

Even if this were true, federal officials were not completely forthcoming with Yellowknife residents about the medical risks of arsenic exposure. In the late 1960s and early 1970s, several peer-reviewed occupational health studies suggested some links between workplace arsenic exposure and higher rates of respiratory disease and heart problems, including higher rates of lung cancer.[52] Officials in Health and Welfare and Environment Canada quietly gathered some of the emerging evidence around cancer risks associated with arsenic exposure, and the department's own de Villiers and Baker report had discussed the possible risks of skin and lung cancer due to arsenic exposure.[53] In February 1975, an internal Environment Canada memo outlined how the US-based Occupational Safety and Health Administration (OSHA) and National Institute for Occupational Safety and Health (NIOSH) had dramatically decreased the eight-hour indoor exposure limit for airborne arsenic dust from 500 to 4 micrograms per cubic metre precisely because the carcinogenic effects of arsenic had been confirmed in the scientific literature. Adopting the longstanding attitude of secrecy among federal officials, the memo stated that "it would be advisable not to release this information to the public as it may cause undue concern at this time."[54] By this point, however, a wave of public concern that had been building for several years was about to break, profoundly challenging government's and industry's attempts to control the narrative around arsenic pollution at Yellowknife.

Fighting Back

In all the archival records we consulted, evidence of local opposition, especially Indigenous opposition, to pollution from the Yellowknife gold mines is largely non-existent prior to the 1970s. We viewed thousands of pages of documents from the early period of Giant Mine's history, and they are devoid of petitions, letters, or other records of Indigenous protest. From oral testimony cited in earlier chapters, we know that the Tatsǫ̨t'ıné strongly objected to the way the gold mines appropriated and polluted important areas for hunting, fishing, and gathering, and they remember the devastating sickness and death that resulted from arsenic during the intensive period of arsenic loading in the 1950s. It is possible that the Tatsǫ̨t'ıné did send written forms of protest that federal officials did not include in the relevant archival files. Given the government's general disregard for the health risks of arsenic during this period, any protests against Giant's pollution would probably have been ignored.

It is nevertheless highly unlikely that the Tatsǫt'ıné were passive in the face of acute pollution problems. Broadly speaking, Dene communities in the Northwest Territories had engaged in various forms of anti-government protest since at least the 1920s, refusing treaty payments, forwarding petitions, or writing protest letters, often in response to the expansion of game regulations and wildlife parks.[55] Among the Yellowknives Dene, one highly respected Elder, Michel Sikyea, challenged the seasonal hunting restrictions of the federal Migratory Birds Convention Act in 1962, purposely killing a duck out of season and challenging the game laws as a violation of treaty rights to hunt. The case went all the way to the Supreme Court of Canada, and though Sikyea lost, his acts of resistance illustrate that the Yellowknives Dene were willing and able to press their rights claims, even through colonial legal processes.[56] At the same time, the Yellowknives would not have had many formal opportunities to address the arsenic threat prior to the mid-1970s because the federal government did not, as a rule, consult with local communities (Indigenous or otherwise) about resource development projects. None of the environmental assessment and licensing processes that are common today existed during this period, and neither, therefore, any public hearing transcripts and document registries (including correspondence from the public) that might capture the voices of local people. So, while the Yellowknives Dene may have engaged in vigorous forms of informal protest, challenging local officials verbally whenever the opportunity presented itself, much of this activity would be obscured by the limitations inherent to the archival record.

The protests of the Yellowknives Dene and settler communities became more visible in the 1970s due to a combination of specific local events and broader legal, administrative, and societal changes. As mentioned above, the federal government's Northern Inland Waters Act, enacted in 1972, mandated public hearings on water licence applications before the Northwest Territories Water Board. The Water Board itself emerged as part of a growing northern administrative structure following the 1967 relocation of the territorial government from Ottawa to the Northwest Territories itself (with its capital in Yellowknife). Territorial officials – themselves mainly non-Indigenous – subsequently became important actors in pollution control debates.[57] Beginning in 1974, the high-profile Mackenzie Valley Pipeline Inquiry further entrenched the notion that Northerners, and in particular northern Indigenous groups, ought to be consulted about development projects. Led by Justice Thomas Berger (whose background as an Indigenous rights lawyer meant he was inclined to take Dene concerns seriously), the inquiry featured public hearings in 1975 and 1976 that gave Dene communities a chance to describe the impacts of pollution, colonialism, and mega-developments on their subsistence economy, with ample coverage from the national media.[58] Government and industry also had to contend with new Indigenous activist groups demanding a voice in the policy process. Two of these played a major role in the arsenic controversies of the 1970s: the Indian Brotherhood of the Northwest Territories, founded in 1969 (and later named the Dene Nation), and the National Indian Brotherhood, established in 1967 to represent status and Treaty Indians across Canada.[59] For the Yellowknives Dene, these new organizations and new public forums gave them venues through which they could press their protests over the arsenic situation in Yellowknife.

The first formal evidence of Yellowknives Dene objections to arsenic pollution came in the form of a letter sent in September 1973 from Michel Sikyea to Jean Chrétien, minister of Indian Affairs and Northern Development, highlighting concerns over water pollution in Yellowknife Bay. Sikyea informed Chrétien that the Latham Island community had never been hooked up to the new city water supply that contained little arsenic. He was outraged that the town of Yellowknife had begun to charge a monthly fee for water delivery by truck, threatening to cut off anybody who could not pay. Sikyea also summarized the historical impacts of arsenic pollution on his community, writing that "in the early 1950s, our band lost four children drinking arsenic poisoned water which was ruined by the mine. Many others were sick." He went on to claim that "at that time the fish and trees were dead and I went and took Dr Stanton to see it. When he saw it I asked him to make a law that no Indians would ever pay for water again. He said, 'sure I will do that. I will fight for you.' From that time on we never paid for our water." In the past few years, however, the town had imposed a levy of five dollars per month for water, an amount that severely cut into the food budgets of those on social assistance. Sikyea was concerned that low-income residents of Latham Island would be forced to drink water from Back Bay, which was polluted not only with arsenic, he claimed, but also oil and gas from snowmobiles and aircraft. Not merely a

Figure 3.2

Rainbow Valley on Latham Island, 1972, in what is now known as Ndilǫ. This Yellowknives Dene community lacked piped water and had to pay for trucked water delivery.

practical matter, for Sikyea the issue was also political. He wrote, "others have become rich in our settlement of Yellowknife who can afford to pay for clear water which comes out of their taps, but we, the owners of the land have only barrel water delivered to count on."[60] For Sikyea, then, the issue was about more than the delivery of sub-standard municipal services; it stemmed from fundamental injustices associated with resource theft, colonialism, and land dispossession.

Yellowknives Dene representatives raised similar issues at the public hearing on Giant Mine's first water licence application in October 1974. While the Yellowknives Dene Indian Band (as it was called at the time) and the Indian Brotherhood of the Northwest Territories shared legal representation at the hearing, their lawyer, Jerry Sutton, focused mostly on procedural questions and wisely left the substantive comments to Chief Joe Charlo. The Chief recalled the days before the mines when the Tatsǫ̨t'ıné could set nets and pull plenty of fish out of the bay, or hunt from camps up and down the bay while drawing cool, clean water directly from Great Slave Lake (the absence of which would have made it much harder to spend large amounts of time on the land, given the difficulty of packing bulk water to remote camps). Since the advent of mining at Giant, arsenic pollution had "spoiled" the water, according to Charlo, and made the fish in Yellowknife Bay taste strange. As did Sikyea, Charlo (speaking through a translator) argued that his people, as original owners of the land, should not have to pay for water:

> And now, he says, that these two mines, ever since they put a mine in Yellowknife they probably both made so many money, probably millions and millions of dollars and here they are right at our doorstep and we don't ask them for any help at all. And now, he says, that they are using our own land, they are using our water, and now, he says, we have to turn around and if we get a water delivery we pay for it – why should we pay for our water? Actually, he says, I would sure like to see both mines pay the water for us.[61]

Charlo further reported that water trucks were simply bypassing the houses of people who had not paid their bill, so older pensioners and low-income families had begun to draw water from the polluted bay.[62] Despite Charlo's plea for help, there was no response to his comments from Giant Mine or members of the Water Board, as the chair abruptly switched to procedural questions surrounding board membership. One city official asked Charlo whether he knew if the monthly water payments went to the city or the Department of Indian and Northern Affairs, and then after some muddled conversation, the hearing abruptly adjourned until a later date.[63] Sikyea's letter and Charlo's comments before the Water Board were a signal, however, that a new period of Dene assertiveness and activism over the arsenic issue was about to begin.

A rising tide of concern was also building among the settler population at Yellowknife. The charges and the fine over the tailings leaks at Giant Mine in 1974 were the first ever taken against the company, and the incident prompted local media (made up of the local CBC radio and television, and two generally pro-mining newspapers, *News of the North* and *The Yellowknifer*) to report widely for the first time on pollution issues associated with the gold mines. The frustrations of Yellowknife city council over the tailings spills suggests that the golden sheen associated with Giant Mine was starting to dim somewhat, even if the mine remained one of the town's largest employers. The main union at Giant Mine, the United Steelworkers of America (USWA), had adopted strong anti-pollution and occupational health positions since the 1950s and became a focal point for the settler community's critics of the mining industry's environmental and occupational health record. In 1967 the USWA formed a Northwest Territories Area Council and began to advocate for mining safety ordinances that included a right to refuse unsafe work, the proper storage and labelling of hazardous chemicals, and the enforcement of maximum threshold limit values for toxic substances in the workplace.[64] The resurgent activism among organized labour was consistent with a new era of anti-pollution activism among the broader public in the early 1970s, which was manifest locally in Yellowknife through the formation of environmental groups such as Ecology North and the Canadian Arctic Resources Committee, both established in 1971. By the middle of the decade, Giant Mine's pollution issues were tightly woven into the political struggles of the Yellowknives, organized labour, the city government, and local environmental groups, a coalescence of interests that soon became formidable opponents to the company and its promoters within government.

Conclusion

The attempts of the government and the mining company to quietly manage the arsenic problem had clearly failed by the early 1970s. The general public was obviously aware that the arsenic pollution problems at Giant Mine had not been fully addressed. The growth in grassroots anti-pollution activism in the Dene communities, and among labour and environmental organizations, meant that arsenic emissions would no longer remain solely an issue for government experts. With a growing number of public venues in which to air grievances, it was increasingly difficult for those in positions of responsibility to evade tough questions about arsenic pollution. After the highly visible effluent spills in Back Bay, Yellowknife residents started to openly wonder whether arsenic exposure was a price worth paying to make a living and maintain their economy. The Yellowknives Dene demanded to know why they faced the unpalatable choice of effectively paying for water delivery (a service that really ought to have been the responsibility of the polluter) or consuming water that experience had taught them was dangerous and possibly deadly. For them, nothing reflected the colonial nature of gold mining in their territory more than the mining companies using local lakes as a pollution sink while passing the bill to their communities, even as very little economic benefit flowed to the Yellowknives Dene First Nation. If the federal government thought it could sweep the arsenic problem under the rug by silencing internal critics such as Butler, holding back health and environmental surveys from the public, and downplaying the threat of exposure, it underestimated the anger smouldering beneath the surface of Yellowknife's communities. If the arsenic issue still needed some oxygen and a spark to push flames of discontent into the open, that soon came in the form of a radio program that put Yellowknife's pollution issues at the forefront of local and national politics.

4

Arsenic and Red Tape

On the evening of 8 January 1975, just after the supper hour, the familiar jazzy opening theme music for CBC Radio's current affairs program *As It Happens* beamed into cars, kitchens, and living rooms across Canada. The program was (and remains) a flagship of the CBC's national broadcast lineup, a nightly array of interviews that range from quirky to hard-hitting investigative journalism. On this particular night, a segment of the program featured an exposé that vaulted the issue of arsenic exposure in Yellowknife to national prominence, reaching not only major media outlets but as far as the floor of the House of Commons in Ottawa.[1] The story was shocking enough, featuring lengthy interviews with Tatsǫt'ıné who described the history of arsenic poisoning in their community and their ongoing challenges with access to drinking water. Thousands of Canadians also heard, for the first time, from scientific experts who highlighted the dangers of arsenic, and also from two muckraking journalists who accused the federal government of a (apropos for the time period) Watergate-style cover-up of Yellowknife's arsenic problems, allegations that stemmed from the apparent suppression of the de Villiers and Baker health and environmental survey. The *As It Happens* program was a major public relations disaster for the federal government, provoking outrage in Yellowknife and across the country, and shedding an unflattering light on a pollution controversy that the northern administration sought to downplay. But now it was all out in the open for everyone to see.

The growing controversy over community health, environmental pollution, and Indigenous rights in Yellowknife played out alongside a broader tectonic shift in public attitudes on these issues in the 1970s. As in the United States, this period saw the rise of environmentalism in Canada, with emerging groups like the University of Toronto's Pollution Probe and Vancouver's Society for Pollution and Environmental Control protesting issues such as phosphate loading in the Great Lakes, urban air pollution, and industrial emissions.[2] As the public clamoured for environmental protection, federal and provincial governments created new environment departments and issued regulations aimed at curbing pollution, including the federal Arctic Waters Pollution Prevention Act of 1970 (similar to the Northern Inland Waters Act but applied to more northerly latitudes). However, widespread skepticism around the health and environmental policies of industry and government persisted, especially in Indigenous communities, fuelled by controversies such as the discovery in 1970 of mercury poisoning from pulp and paper waste in the Anishinaabe community of Grassy Narrows in northwestern Ontario, or the objections of Anishinaabe on the Seine River Reserve (near Atikokan, Ontario) over potential sulphur dioxide and mercury pollution from the proposed Marmion Lake generating station.[3] Yellowknife's arsenic issue also intersected with the heightened concerns of southern Canadians over the environmental impacts of northern development. As noted in chapter 3, in the 1970s the arsenic controversy frequently shared local and national headlines with Justice Thomas Berger's high-profile inquiry into the proposed Mackenzie Valley Pipeline, which highlighted Dene and environmentalist criticisms of resource development and environmental destruction.[4] This period also coincided with insurgent Dene and Inuit activism and legal demands for rights recognition in the face of hostile federal and territorial Indigenous policies.

In Yellowknife itself, the arsenic controversy that erupted after the *As It Happens* coverage solidified a unique, emerging coalition of local environmentalists, Indigenous communities, and labour/occupational health activists, who came together between 1975 and 1978 to challenge government declarations that pollution levels remained safe in the community. The federal government (and a newly assertive territorial government) continued to manage the arsenic issue through internal studies and expert committees aimed at mollifying rather than confronting public concerns.

Local critics challenged this attempt to swaddle the arsenic question in red tape, conducting their own community-informed scientific research and challenging at every turn the government's insistence that arsenic exposure levels remained safe.

As It Happened

If the northern administration had known who was behind the arsenic segment of *As It Happens*, they might have known trouble was on the way. One of the show's producers in 1974 was Lloyd Tataryn, a journalist and labour activist who later published *Dying for a Living*, a popular book that highlighted occupational health controversies throughout Canada, including asbestos exposure at Quebec's Thetford Mines, radiation exposure in the uranium mines at Elliot Lake, the dousing of mine workers with aluminum powder as a preventive for silicosis (leading to high rates of neurological disease), and a full chapter devoted to Yellowknife's arsenic controversy.[5] According to Tataryn, he and another journalist, Michael McLoughlin, became interested in the arsenic issue and requested a copy of the de Villiers and Baker report for investigative purposes, only to be informed by René Mercier, Health and Welfare's chief information officer, that it was an "internal document." The two journalists eventually managed to obtain a copy through a back channel, which they sent to three experts for review: Tom Hutchison, a professor of biology at the University of Toronto, Bernard Carnow, the head of occupational and environmental medicine at the University of Illinois, and none other than Kingsley Kay, now a researcher at Mount Sinai School of Medicine and the US National Cancer Institute. All three experts eventually appeared on the *As It Happens* broadcast and raised concerns about possible links between arsenic and the relatively high rates of leukemia, respiratory disease, lymphatic tumors, and heart disease noted in the de Villiers and Baker report (which had come to no definitive conclusion on causality but did call for more research). While arsenic had more recently been linked to lung and skin cancers, Carnow emphasized the knowledge gaps about the health impacts of arsenic. He argued that health authorities should assume that there was no safe level for arsenic because it could take two or three decades for cancers to develop after chronic exposure to very low levels. As one might expect, the biologist Hutchison raised the issue of arsenic contamination in the broader aquatic and terrestrial food chains. It was Kay, however, who levelled the most stinging indictment at the government, describing the ongoing exposure of the Yellowknife population as an "experiment" with unknown consequences. Drawing on his previous experience in Yellowknife, Kay did not pull any punches in response to a question from hosts Barbara Frum and Alan Maitland about the suppression of the de Villiers and Baker report:

> Well, I'm not surprised they haven't made it public because they weren't very keen about what I did in the 1950s. I think that's what these two studies show. That's why I regard it as a human experiment – an experiment in which you make measurements, how much people are exposed to, and you're waiting to see what will happen to those people.

Kay compared the quarter century of arsenic exposure at Yellowknife to the Tuskegee syphilis experiments that began in 1932, a notorious case that involved the decades-long denial of medical treatment for syphilis to a control group of Black men. If the analogy was somewhat strained (the pollution problems at Yellowknife were tied to broad-scale pollution from an industrial development rather than a targeted, unethical research project), Kay's comments underscored the idea that the federal government's casual approach to regulating arsenic pollution represented the antithesis of a precautionary approach. Ominously, he suggested that it was unlikely that many types of cancer associated with arsenic exposure would have developed by 1966, the year de Villiers and Baker began their study, and just seventeen years after roasting operations began – but by 1975, after nearly ten more years had passed since the study, there was likely to be a higher incidence of cancer.[6]

The *As It Happens* segment concluded with an interview featuring Michel Sikyea and another member of the Latham Island community, Marion Betsina. Asked about drinking water, Sikyea highlighted the same issue he had raised in his letter to Jean Chrétien (see chapter 3): he and many of the Elders on Latham Island took ice from the bay to make water because they could not afford the monthly charge for water delivery. Sikyea also highlighted the changes in the texture and taste of fish from Yellowknife Bay and his community's fears about swimming in the lake, noting

Figure 4.1

A warning sign posted by the City of Yellowknife, which reads, "Warning: Drinking of or bathing in this water may be dangerous to your health." Likely taken from Sikyea Tili or Tililo Tili in Ndilǫ in 1978.

that none of these problems existed prior to the advent of gold mining. Asked about the recent death of Elder Elizabeth Drygeese, Sikyea said she had poor lungs near the end of her life and the doctors had said that "she had some arsenic in her body." Betsina mentioned that warning signs around the bay had only recently been posted in Indigenous languages. Sikyea concluded that the arsenic threat was getting worse, and Betsina said that the people in her community were "afraid" because of the ongoing pollution. Although it was only a brief interview, for the first time, two members of the Latham Island community had the opportunity to tell the story of their community's unwanted encounter with arsenic to a national audience.[7]

The reaction to the *As It Happens* report was swift and heated. The Indian Brotherhood of the Northwest Territories issued a press release calling for the release of the de Villiers and Baker study, and the free delivery of water to Latham Island, which, the release noted, would only cost $300 to $400 per month to supply to the roughly 140 people who could not afford it, far less than the $1.5 million the federal government had spent on moving the city's pipeline. The Brotherhood concluded with the following statement:

> We are especially outraged that the knowledge and complaints of the native people of the area affected have been ignored for years at great cost to our own health and lives. It is an object lesson in politics that the native people should have to wait until it became obvious to white people that their health is also endangered before the situation reaches scandalous proportions.[8]

As with Sikyea and Betsina, the Brotherhood framed the water issue as essentially a product of colonialism: "the most important lesson to be learned from this is that native people cannot rely on the government to protect their land and rights."[9]

Anger over the apparent suppression of the de Villiers and Baker report was also palpable among the settler community. Fred Henne, the former mayor of Yellowknife, told local media that he had actually participated in the de Villiers and Baker study, gathering water samples from the bay as a private citizen. Despite his status and close connection to the study, Henne said he could not get his hands on the report, even after he became mayor in 1968. He suggested, "We never got any real cooperation from Health and Welfare and there was more kept under the blanket than anybody knows."[10] With similar outrage, Wally Firth, the member of Parliament for the Northwest Territories, demanded to know "why this report was not made available, who was responsible for holding it back and how will the situation be corrected."[11] Even more pointedly, a former Yellowknife alderman, Bill Walton, surmised, "the only reason for the report being held back was because it contained something bad." He went on to suggest that "the bureaucratic asses who decided in the first place to sit in judgement on whether or not the study ought to be released should be hung from the nearest tree."[12] Organized labour did not go so far as to call for vigilante action but still decried what it saw as the "cover-up" of the arsenic issue. The United Steelworkers of America (USWA) claimed that the de Villiers and Baker study had been undertaken at the behest of the union, but a

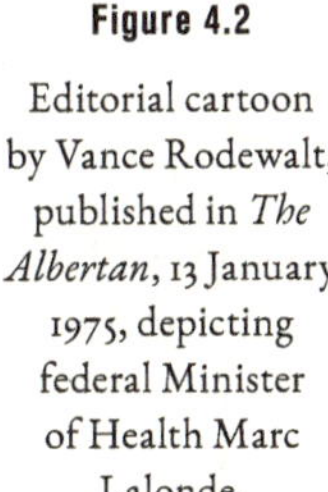

Figure 4.2

Editorial cartoon by Vance Rodewalt, published in *The Albertan*, 13 January 1975, depicting federal Minister of Health Marc Lalonde.

"conspiracy of silence" among local officials had resulted in the report being "squirreled away."[13] Unsurprisingly, the environmental activists at Ecology North adopted a similar position, lamenting the suppression of the report and calling for "some mechanism" whereby reports with a public health dimension would actually be made available to the public.[14]

The *As It Happens* episode inspired several concerned citizens from outside Yellowknife to write to the federal government. Carolyn and Brian Holstein from Erin, Ontario, echoed Kay's comments when they asked their local member of Parliament, "are these people being used as an experiment to study the progressions of diseases related to arsenic?"[15] Josie Toews from Winnipeg accused Health Minister Marc Lalonde of denying that there was any danger associated with arsenic, and asked rhetorically, "do you have arsenic with your coffee?" She went on to ask Lalonde, "how many people have to die before anything is done about this?"[16] Charles Wiese from Edmonton wrote to Prime Minister Pierre Trudeau, arguing that "to jeopardize the lives of citizens of this country without their consent or knowledge just to protect a mining company is *criminal*." In a separate letter to Lalonde, Wiese evoked the major political scandal of the era when he wrote, "we are Canadians and we will not tolerate any Watergate type of thinking in this country."[17] Clearly the arsenic problem at Yellowknife had touched a nerve with some members of the general public who were concerned about the issues of pollution and political scandal that were so salient in the first half of the 1970s.

Federal officials denied any cover-up, noting that the de Villiers and Baker report had been merely delayed between 1969 and 1971. As soon as the full report was ready, Health and Welfare distributed four copies to the commissioner of the Northwest Territories, who was then supposed to pass one on to the town of Yellowknife.[18] In May 1971, Gordon Butler, the chief medical officer in Yellowknife, had recommended that a summary of the report be made available to the public (or in his words, "to those who will request information on the report"), but there is no evidence this was ever done.[19] Indeed, a retrospective memo written in the wake of the *As It Happens* uproar suggested two things. First, the town of Yellowknife did not receive a copy of the report from the commissioner, and Health and Welfare did not furnish one until 1972. Second, the results of the study may not have been made public because of Chrétien's ban on public statements regarding arsenic in response to Butler's threats to go public over the issue of contaminated vegetables.[20]

So, even if the federal government did not completely "squirrel away" the de Villiers and Baker report, there was hardly a sense of urgency to distribute the results. Health and Welfare initially only shared five copies of the report to the two other levels of government concerned about the issue. As there was clearly no large print run of the report, copies were difficult to obtain. Administrative shuffling also made the few copies that were available difficult to track down. In November 1974, C.A. Lewis, a member of the Northwest Territories Water Board (a public service body with an obvious interest in the arsenic issue), had difficulty locating the report because Health and Welfare's Public Health and Engineering Section had been transferred to Environment Canada.[21] Tataryn and McLoughlin's experience suggests that the de Villiers and Baker report was effectively hidden from members of the general public. Indeed, the designation of the report as an "internal document" was emblematic of the government's largely secretive approach to the arsenic problem at Yellowknife. The CBC's exposé meant, however, that the mining companies and the federal government could no longer tightly control the arsenic narrative. The bureaucratic tendency to keep things quiet on the arsenic file had effectively backfired. After the *As It Happens* episode, a new era of public protest and public accountability over Yellowknife's arsenic problem had begun.

Yellowknife Exposed

Barely a week after the *As It Happens* broadcast, the intergovernmental committee on arsenic in Yellowknife waters, chaired by Dan Billing, the Northwest Territories' chief of environmental protection, met for the first time to review environmental sampling undertaken in the wake of the 1974 tailings spill (described in chapter 3). Noting the continued detection of arsenic in Back Bay, the committee issued further warnings on the use of ice, snow, and lake water for drinking. Responding to the unfolding public furor around arsenic, the committee also recommended a new, wide-ranging public health study by Health and Welfare Canada, with a special focus on long-time residents ("particularly those that are not using piped city water"), previously sampled residents, and mine and mill workers, as well as anyone else interested in participating.[22] Finally, the committee also recommended a series of studies on water and air pollution control and tailings containment, and recommended the determination of a "safe level" of arsenic in food and drinking water. Crucially, given the controversy around the unreleased de Villiers and Baker report, it suggested that "all data collected by government agencies be made available" to city and territorial governments, and the final reports be made public.[23] In response, federal and territorial agencies immediately launched the Yellowknife Environmental Survey (YES), a coordinated effort to document the extent of regional arsenic contamination and public health impacts. The scope of the YES mandate was considerable, ranging from water, snow, and air pollution characterization (including risks to humans and wildlife), to testing for occupational exposures, to addressing the question of underground arsenic storage.[24]

But if government officials believed that YES would help dissipate the public controversy around arsenic, they were sorely mistaken. Rather, the following two years of environmental and public health reports, along with related bursts of media coverage, kept the issue more or less constantly simmering. The initial health study launched in February 1975 sought hair samples from Yellowknife residents and mill workers for laboratory testing for arsenic content. The study's coordinator, Otto Schaefer of the federal Medical Services Branch, claimed that he particularly targeted Indigenous residents in the sample, given their concerns about exposure. Collection points were set up at both Dettah and Latham Island, and public health nurses visited homes in Ndilǫ. Even these early efforts generated criticism. Few Dene participated, and an article in the local *Native Press* claimed that, of four hundred residents sampled, fewer than fifty were Indigenous.[25] Somewhat more bizarrely, Schaefer's own colleague in the Northern Medical Research Branch, R.D.P. Eaton, went public with his view that the study itself was a waste of funds. Eaton's comments earned him a scathing editorial rebuttal in the *Yellowknifer*, which derided him (and the study) as "amateur" and suggested that he "acted like the typical southern government bureaucrat whose only concern is to save the North for the south at the expense of the north."[26]

In any case, the interim results of Schaefer's study no doubt soothed Eaton and his colleagues in the northern health service – at least initially. Released in late May, the study reported that 90 per cent of the residents tested had low levels (below five parts per million) of arsenic in their hair, but that some Giant mine and mill workers registered over five and even over ten parts per million. The study found little correlation between hair arsenic levels and drinking water sources, and concluded that "it is not likely that arsenic poses a health hazard for residents other than mine and mill workers."[27] Indeed, mill workers, particularly those working in the roaster complex, Cottrell plant, and baghouse, had the highest arsenic levels; these workers were immediately identified for follow-up sampling and health scans. The internal review of the study also noted "moderately raised levels" in both Indigenous and non-Indigenous children, which it attributed to exposure to arsenic in soils, rather than ingested arsenic. Eaton's own internal summary concluded that the results pointed to "an absence of general airborne or waterborne pollution" in Yellowknife and a very low health risk for the public. For its part, the Standing Committee on Arsenic also rushed to reassure Yellowknifers, noting that city water supplies remained "safe," as did fish caught for local consumption – although residents were still urged to wash locally gathered and grown berries and vegetables.[28]

Critics remained unconvinced. Reporting on the study, the *Globe and Mail* pointedly noted the lack of reference by the government to arsenic's carcinogenic properties and other risks of chronic exposure.[29] The interim results, and the survey itself, also came under immediate challenge both from the USWA and from the National Indian Brotherhood (NIB). Local Steelworkers leaders sent a strongly worded telex to the minister of Health and Welfare, noting their longstanding concerns around employee arsenic exposures and registering strong concern at the high arsenic levels noted among Giant workers. Union leaders criticized the lingering uncertainty around what constituted safe exposure levels for both workers and the public, and demanded answers to a series of questions about what these exposures meant for acute and long-term health.[30] United Steelworkers Area Council president Marsh Hawes complained publicly that the union was "always the last to know" about health issues and demanded immediate action to reduce occupational arsenic exposure.[31] Hawes also submitted a letter requesting $20,000 from the federal government to support the union's own study of health impacts on workers. In his responses, the minister assured the union of its commitment to follow-up studies of exposed workers and, citing these ongoing studies, denied the funding request.[32]

More explosively, a series of press releases from the NIB and Indian Brotherhood of the Northwest Territories almost immediately derailed federal efforts to allay public concerns around pollution and health in Yellowknife. As noted in chapter 3, these organizations had spoken out and supported Yellowknives Dene concerns in public forums such as Water Board hearings since their founding in the early 1970s. Their engagement reflected a growing radical political consciousness among Indigenous activists in the Northwest Territories that questioned government rhetoric around "inclusion" in the benefits of resource development and criticized weak development assessment and regulation. Their strategies included political organizing among Indigenous communities and (frequently successful) legal challenges asserting Dene claims to lands and resources in their traditional territories.[33] The national body supported these broader political objectives as well as engaging in specific local controversies like the one at Giant.

It is thus not surprising that the NIB rejected the YES studies as a "public relations survey," and was openly critical of Schaeffer's strategy of sampling hair from volunteers because it did not do enough to include results from at-risk groups.[34] In response, the NIB undertook its own small hair-sampling program, collecting samples from eighteen residents of Latham Island and Dettah for both mercury and arsenic. Although it is unclear how participants were chosen, arsenic values obtained from samples sent to the University of Toronto for testing showed a wide range, with higher values for Latham Island residents (who lived closer to Giant). Alarmingly, five of six children tested had values above the "arbitrary" level of concern of five parts per million. "Why weren't these children found by Ottawa?" the NIB demanded. "How many more children with high levels like this live in Yellowknife – particularly in Indian communities?"[35] Steelworkers spokesman Ed McCrae joined the NIB in calling for more widespread testing and monitoring in the wake of the Schaefer report and NIB results.[36] Defending their strategy, federal health officials pointed to their ongoing health and environmental studies, and invited the NIB to send names of people it sampled for inclusion in follow-up examinations.

Critics of Giant Mine's pollution record also used the Northwest Territories Water Board hearings held in April 1975 as an opportunity to challenge the company and the government. The hearings were a follow-up to those held in October 1974, at which the board had granted Giant Yellowknife Mines additional time to prepare detailed answers to technically complex questions. Although the hearings held the previous autumn had been contentious (see chapter 3), the acrimony at this follow-up hearing had reached new heights in the wake of the *As It Happens* episode and the tailings spill controversies of the previous year. One participant, Bernie Bintner, captured the mood of the room when he noted, "there is a lot of ill-feeling here tonight."[37] Another participant, Tapwe Chretien, offered the most pointed and lengthy challenge to Giant Mine. Originally from the Métis community of St Victor, Saskatchewan, Chretien had moved to the Northwest Territories in the 1960s and developed close ties with Dene and Métis communities in the region, travelling widely as a well-known fiddler on the northern music circuit. In his testimony, coming after a lengthy and somewhat dry presentation from the company, Chretien did not hold anything back, proclaiming, "You are killing my people with your industrialization and your high ways of thinking, with your technology, modern technology, that you say is supposed to be a benefit to man, yet is used to kill people." Chretien went on to argue that unless the mine could reach zero arsenic emissions in its wastewater and airborne emissions, it ought to close. He also claimed that many Indigenous people had avoided the hearings because of the overly technical language, an approach Chretien derided as using "ten-dollar words to try to express a five-cent idea."[38] Using similarly impassioned language, Gerry Sutton, a representative of the NIB, called the history of gold mining at Yellowknife "sordid" and argued, "the record of the mining industry in Yellowknife patently demonstrates that government responsibility has been lacking. The fact that deaths have occurred shows not merely irresponsibility, but frightening negligence on the part of the government." Sutton argued for a general cleanup of Yellowknife Bay and reinforced the concerns of the Yellowknives Dene about paying for water, criticizing "the humiliating means test" associated with a government program to provide free water to low-income people.[39]

Members of the settler population also offered few kind words for Giant Mine. The City of Yellowknife's representative, Collin Wynne, highlighted the impacts of water pollution in Back Bay on wildlife, fish, and vegetation, arguing that Giant should only get a water licence if it presented a viable plan to control waterborne emissions. Yellowknife resident Sandy Jacobsen raised concerns about pollution in Baker Creek, while Juliet Burnford asked how the public could be assured that the criticism aired at the hearing would be meaningfully incorporated into the board's decision on the licence. Bintner called the hearing a "charade" and asked the board to think deeply about the issues at stake. Varion Hason called for a stepped-up arsenic monitoring program, and Pat Anderson inquired whether the board had considered the impact of meltwater from contaminated snow on the waterbodies around Yellowknife.[40] Only one member of the public, Glenn Ball, spoke vaguely in favour of Giant Mine's licence application, fearing the possibility it might be rejected based on "secret information" passed on to the board.[41] The remaining hearing participants were critical of Giant's pollution record, with several supporting Chretien's proposal for a zero-discharge approach to managing arsenic at Giant Mine. The Water Board was not ready to adopt such a radical idea, however, and soon awarded Giant its first water licence, with board members likely won over by the company's promise at the hearings to spend $1.5 million to improve the dykes, dams, and other pollution control infrastructure at the mine.[42]

Through the remainder of 1975 and into the following year, government scientists worked to better understand the two main issues that had sparked the public uproar: environmental arsenic levels and occupational health issues. The major source of concern for Giant workers was elevated arsenic levels among those most exposed at work: those working in the roaster, the Cottrell plant and baghouse (where the dust was captured), and "operators involved in the transport, collection and handling of arsenic trioxide."[43] Characterizing these occupational hazards meant understanding the risks, but health officials also struggled to clarify exactly what constituted safe levels for arsenic exposures in the workplace. "This is complicated by a lot of recent work linking arsenic and carcinogenicity," admitted the Medical Services Branch's F.H. Hicks. "[T]he allowable threshold exposure levels are being questioned everywhere, and right now any figure we take would be an arbitrary one."[44] In the end, federal officials adopted the threshold-level values for arsenic trioxide exposures used by American industrial hygienists: for "safe" daily exposures, in-plant levels should be kept below fifty micrograms per cubic metre ($\mu g/m^3$) of air. Based on these levels, reports by the federal Occupational Health Unit in 1975 and 1976 concluded that Giant workers were largely safe, but recommended continued monitoring and beefed-up safety procedures, particularly in the areas of the Cottrell plant and baghouse.[45]

In late September 1976, the Standing Committee on Arsenic gathered for what was supposed to be a final meeting to discuss the YES results and recommend any follow-up actions. Rather than reviewing a single study, however, the committee ended up with two somewhat contradictory reports from the engineers charged with reviewing the evidence. The main YES report, presented by D.A. Gemmill of the federal Environmental Protection Service, reviewed data on Giant stack emissions; the environmental deposition of arsenic in snow, soil, and vegetation; and the human health studies noted above.[46] Results showed that emissions were higher than previously reported by the company, although much reduced from historical levels. Alarmingly, the report found "a high degree of contamination" in soils and vegetation of the Yellowknife area, including in garden soils and on locally grown vegetables. Yet it also noted that arsenic was not taken up from the soil by plants and, echoing past studies, concluded that "washing vegetables and fruit removes the bulk of the contamination." Drinking water in Yellowknife remained below Canadian standards for arsenic content, though snowmelt water (potentially used by some Yellowknives Dene) continued to register high levels. Overall, Gemmill concluded that there was "no evidence that the general public of Yellowknife is exposed to excessive or dangerously high levels of arsenic," nor evidence of general public health impacts. Nevertheless, noting the widespread presence of arsenic in the environment, he recommended a comprehensive program of environmental monitoring, further research into the toxicological hazard posed by arsenic exposure, and the improvement of safety procedures at the roaster complex.

A separate report, filed by Jack Grainge, still a public health engineer for the Department of National Health and Welfare, was even more dismissive of the arsenic threat.[47] As discussed in chapter 3, Grainge had a long acquaintance with the problems of arsenic at Giant, dating back to the 1950s. His report provided a comprehensive review of past studies leading up to the YES report and emphasized the significant reductions in arsenic emissions by Giant since 1949. Grainge cast doubt on the health impacts of low-dose exposures to arsenic, noting that several surveys had cleared long-time Yellowknife residents of adverse health effects and pointing to the lack of scientific consensus on the issue. Reflecting his sanitary engineering perspective, he also dismissed the environmental impacts from arsenic emissions, beyond certain "mixing zones" in the air and water around the mine. Baker Creek, he acknowledged, was devoid of life due to mine tailings discharge, but "the creek has little economic or social value as indicated by the lack of local interest with the tailings discharge arrangement in the first place." Similarly, while Back Bay was polluted, the bay acted as a sink for arsenic, and contamination did not extend into the much larger Yellowknife Bay. In other words, dilution provided the solution to Giant's pollution. In effect, Grainge blamed Latham Island residents themselves for using contaminated water in spite of public health warnings, rather than pay for trucked water. Based on these conclusions, he rejected additional incremental pollution controls as pointless economic burdens on the local mines.[48]

Whatever their differences, for the Standing Committee (which included Mayor Henne), the reports provided a clear indication that the public health hazard from arsenic in the city was minimal. As the committee readied to disband, it prepared a public statement intended for release at a public event later in fall 1976, aimed at reassuring the public that "experts may disagree on details but they all agree that the people of Yellowknife are not being harmed." Meanwhile, environmental monitoring should continue, and Giant encouraged to continue reducing workplace exposures. Although the statement only briefly noted the issue of underground storage of arsenic waste, the committee suggested that, when the mines eventually closed, the company would "seal off" residual arsenic underground and surface contamination would "slowly leach away."[49]

"Ottawa Hides the Poison"

Authorities may have hoped the arsenic issue would similarly dissipate, but public controversy could not be defused. First, an *Edmonton Journal* writer obtained leaked copies of the Gemmill and Grainge reports, publishing a story highlighting the "sharp clash of personalities and opinions in their research" that led to their "bickering" and filing separate documents.[50] Echoing the earlier accusations around the de Villiers and Baker report, Billing was forced to defend against hints of government "secrecy," while emphasizing the reports' shared basic message dismissing public health hazards. The engineers' debate spilled into the Yellowknife news: in interviews, Gemmill urged ongoing monitoring of workers and the environment, while Grainge commented that "as long as mines are important to Yellowknife's economy we will just have to put up with some damage to the environment."[51] Even the basic agreement of their conclusions, it seemed, could not avoid reinforcing public uncertainty around arsenic.

Behind the scenes, however, a greater threat to public confidence in government pollution studies loomed. Concerned by Schaefer's failure to include hair samples from Indigenous children in his 1975 arsenic survey, the NIB teamed up with the USWA to undertake a more complete survey of both Dene children and Giant smelter workers. Led by Tataryn, now working for the NIB, the two organizations collected hair samples from these groups, as well as from "control" groups of Indigenous children and Steelworkers members living in Whitehorse, then sent samples to a lab at the University of Toronto. There, chemical engineer Robert Jervis analyzed the samples using radiological testing techniques, with alarming results.[52]

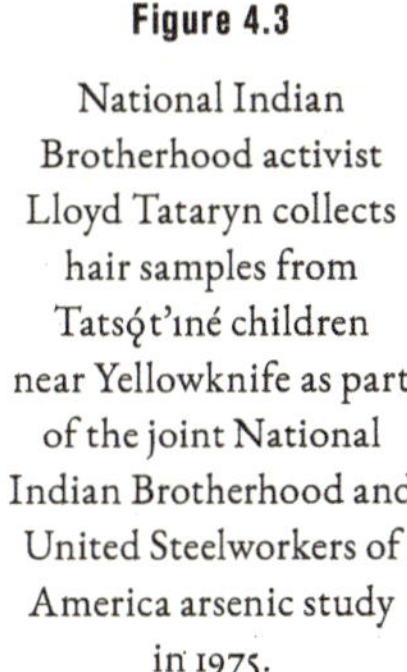

Figure 4.3

National Indian Brotherhood activist Lloyd Tataryn collects hair samples from Tatsǫt'ıné children near Yellowknife as part of the joint National Indian Brotherhood and United Steelworkers of America arsenic study in 1975.

The study detected arsenic levels up to 278 parts per million in hair samples from Giant workers, with a mean value for all samples of 25 parts per million. This contrasted with the Whitehorse control samples, which revealed a mean value of 0.4 parts per million and a maximum of 1 part per million. These results also diverged significantly from the Schaeffer study results, which had found some high values among smelter workers, but fewer than 10 per cent of Yellowknife residents overall with arsenic levels above 5 parts per million. Just as they had in 1975, the NIB and USWA released these results to the press on 15 January 1977, as well as a subsequent report reviewing the arsenic saga. Their statement emphasized the "independence" of Jervis's analysis and accused the federal government of downplaying the extent and impacts of arsenic contamination in its own studies to quell public concern.[53] Using Statistics Canada data, the NIB–USWA report also hinted darkly at rising cancer rates in Yellowknife, though admitted that the link to arsenic remained uncertain.[54] More bluntly, Ed McCrae, Steelworkers representative in Yellowknife, denounced the YES report as "a text book example of a cover-up."[55]

The sensational NIB–USWA study reignited the focus of national media on the Yellowknife arsenic issue. Front page stories reported the "horrendously high" levels of "cancer-causing arsenic," while celebrity scientist David Suzuki expressed his concern during an appearance on the CBC Television program *90 Minutes Live* with Peter Gzowski. Appearing alongside Suzuki, George Erasmus, president of the NIB's Northwest Territories chapter, accused the federal government of "systematically and deliberately [covering] up its own frightening findings up here" and decried "the old incestuous relationship between the mines and government."[56] Erasmus also outlined for the national TV audience the history of arsenic poisoning and territorial displacement faced by Yellowknives Dene and the lack of Indigenous community benefits from mining. The Government of the Northwest Territories' Dan Billing, who also appeared on the show, expressed frustration at the seeming contradictions and lack of clarity from previous studies, but suggested that the NIB study's statistics were also suspect.[57] A major story in the *Edmonton Journal* reviewed the controversial studies, quoting one Giant worker as saying he had not seen results from samples he gave to both the government and Steelworkers, and concluding, "nobody knows who to believe."[58] The company itself rushed to reassure workers and the public, citing its major reductions in arsenic emissions through the 1960s and the results of the YES studies, which showed that arsenic levels in most workers were "within acceptable limits."[59]

Facing mounting pressure from Indigenous organizations, opposition politicians, and the media, Marc Lalonde, federal minister of Health and Welfare, immediately announced the creation of an independent task force to study the arsenic issue.[60] The investigation came together remarkably quickly: even as Lalonde was defending previous studies in the House of Commons, criticizing the NIB study findings released earlier in the month, and deflecting scathing media critiques of the government's response, his ministry was drawing up a funding agreement and terms of reference for the non-governmental Canadian Public Health Association (CPHA) to lead the task force.[61] For the federal government, the appearance of independence, credibility, and scientific authority was key to the selection of the CPHA and task force members. "There is an obvious need for an unfettered relationship that will permit maximum freedom of action and choice of research or review methodology by members of the Task Force," wrote C.-E. Caron, assistant deputy minister of the federal Medical Services Branch in an internal memo.[62] A mere ten days after being announced, the CPHA confirmed the terms of reference and membership for the task force. The three-man review committee included two physicians and an engineer: C.J.G. Mackenzie, a public health doctor and head of the BC Pollution Control Board; R.B. Sutherland, an industrial hygiene specialist from Nova Scotia with experience related to smelter workers' health; and engineer E. Tupper, also from Nova Scotia, where he previously headed a task force investigating arsenic contamination of drinking water. The NIB and USWA requested that the task force be enlarged to include union and Indigenous representatives, but the government denied the request and the CPHA merely invited observers and submissions from interested groups.[63]

As with previous studies, the creation of the task force failed to allay the concerns around the NIB–USWA study – at least initially. A searing *Globe and Mail* editorial entitled "Ottawa Hides the Poison" declared the appointment of the task force a tacit admission of government "incompetence" and a play for credibility. The editorial highlighted discrepancies in previous reports and statements on arsenic, and, echoing the de Villiers and Baker report controversy, hinted at other suppressed information.[64] National political columnist Richard Gwyn similarly recounted the litany of studies and denials of risk, linking the government's failure to address arsenic concerns with similar occupational health scandals related to uranium in Elliot Lake, Ontario, asbestos in Quebec, and the fluorspar mines in St Lawrence, Newfoundland.[65] The *Edmonton Journal*'s Jon Ferry, who first reported on the leaked YES studies, was more sanguine, suggesting the NIB–USWA study was itself alarmist – though he also chastised the government response and endorsed "the need for unceasing vigilance" on arsenic.[66] Lalonde was forced to defend the federal arsenic response repeatedly in the House of Commons and in the media, touting the task force's independence and expertise while continuing to undermine the NIB study's findings.[67]

Amidst this uproar, the CPHA task force itself moved quickly. In addition to reviewing previous reports and other available information on arsenic contamination, the task force held two public hearings in March 1977, one each in Yellowknife and Ottawa. Briefs and testimonies at the Yellowknife hearing by both the USWA and the recently certified Canadian Association of Smelter and Allied Workers (CASAW, which had conducted a successful takeover campaign to replace the USWA local) launched strong critiques of both environmental and occupational exposure to arsenic at Giant. The USWA extensively recounted the history of arsenic production and pollution at the mine, noting that workers were offered premium pay for working in the baghouse – compensation for what was known as "arsenic time."[68] In a section of their hearing brief called "The Cover-Up," it accused the government of colluding with the company to downplay reports of occupational exposure to arsenic and suggested that recent studies were part of a longer pattern of government deceit and denial. The union brief also surveyed the history of environmental pollution and arsenic contamination of local drinking water, concluding that "the pollution of the environment in the form of stack emissions should be stopped as soon as possible."[69]

For its part, the NIB declined to participate in the Yellowknife hearing. Indigenous testimony was confined to a recorded interview with Yellowknives Dene Chief Joe Charlo, decrying the lack of response from the company to concerns over water and fish contamination. NIB President Noel Starblanket did, however, testify at the Ottawa hearing, asserting that if the company was unable to control arsenic emissions, then the mines should be shut down. Rejecting the notion of a "safe level" of arsenic exposure, the NIB brief also linked arsenic contamination with the broader impacts of mining:

> The Indians in the Northwest Territories have not been the primary beneficiaries of the arsenic-contaminating industries located in Yellowknife. We feel it is unjust that companies can make profits from jeopardizing the health of the people who have lived on the land since time immemorial.[70]

Gina Blondin of the Indian Brotherhood of the Northwest Territories also testified in Ottawa, suggesting that the widespread contamination of the Yellowknife region posed a threat to Indigenous health, and demanding compensation and greater Dene control over industrial development in their territories.[71]

Giant Mine's majority owner, Falconbridge, sent its director of environmental control to testify at the Yellowknife hearing on the company's pollution control efforts and occupational health at the mill and roaster. His terse answers focused on the history of improvements to arsenic reduction since 1951, and asserted that Giant met pollution control standards from BC and Ontario, "except in most severe weather conditions."[72] The company did admit, however, that there was no air quality monitoring done at the mill, nor was there a plant doctor to monitor employees (although roaster and baghouse operators did receive regular medical checkups, including X-rays). By contrast, at least two Giant employees contended that workers were exposed to arsenic owing to aging equipment and operational problems. One worker testified to dizziness and rashes from working in the baghouse. Another worker, echoing Starblanket and Tapwe Chretien, suggested, "if Giant can't make improvements they should be forced to shut down."[73] Workers also raised concerns that water at Giant used for drinking and showering was drawn not from the city's safer water supply, but from heavily polluted Back Bay.[74]

Government civil servants and scientists involved in the arsenic file approached the hearings with trepidation, given the intense media focus on their previous studies. In fact, federal and territorial officials attended, but initially did not testify at the Yellowknife hearing, even as they were raked over the coals and called liars by critics.[75] Schaefer, who led the YES health studies, and Grainge, who participated in the Ottawa hearing, did provide a vigorous defence of the government's arsenic studies. Schaefer triumphantly declared that his data refuted the NIB–USWA study results, and dismissed criticisms of the YES study design.[76] Grainge's experience was less comfortable. In his memoir, he recalled being "badgered" by questions from Tataryn and his own stumbling response.[77] For federal scientists and engineers, the scrutiny afforded by the public hearings created considerable anxiety and discomfort, and they were at pains to re-establish their authority over the question of arsenic and public health.

Reflecting the urgency of the task force's work, the CPHA issued an interim report in June 1977. At least initially, the report and its recommendations had the paradoxical effect of partially defusing the controversy while also deepening skepticism of the review process. Based on its investigations, the CPHA concluded that most Yellowknifers were not at risk from arsenic exposures, but did suggest further investigation of local Dene communities. It also concluded that, owing to potential risks for some workers at Giant, an occupational health unit should be formed in the territory to monitor workplace health risks. Relieved with these initial findings, Minister Lalonde and senior Health and Welfare officials quickly moved to create a Yellowknife-based intergovernmental committee, similar in composition to the previous Standing Committee on Arsenic.[78]

The NIB and USWA immediately called into question the interim report's conclusions, bolstered by their expert consultant, H.P. Blejer, a California-based occupational health specialist. Even before its release, Blejer issued a dissenting report on the task force's work, arguing that it was fundamentally flawed because of its focus on acute arsenic poisoning rather than the long-term effects of arsenic exposure. Reflecting wider toxicological debates around threshold values and body burdens for carcinogenic substances, Blejer disputed the finding that the population was not at risk: "Arsenic exposure can produce cancers. Citizens in Yellowknife are clearly exposed to arsenic in their environment. There is no scientific evidence that there is a 'no effect' level for carcinogens. The chances are therefore greater for contracting cancer in Yellowknife than in a community not exposed to carcinogens such as arsenic."[79] While endorsing the need for further epidemiological evidence for long-term impacts, Blejer was also critical of the of the task force's implicit tolerance of higher arsenic exposure for workers.

Blejer's critique did not reach the CPHA task force before it landed in the media in September, possibly leaked by the NIB and USWA. Blejer's criticisms, in which he called the interim report "sloppy," featured prominently in a report in the *Globe and Mail*, amplified by critical comments from the NIB's Starblanket and national USWA environmental representative Paul Falkowski.[80] Blejer contended he had been "sidelined" during the investigation and that it appeared that a lack of up-to-date knowledge and expertise on occupational and environmental health had been brought to bear on the arsenic question. In spite of the CPHA's claims that the task force had reached out to him, Blejer's comments only fuelled the long-standing suspicion of government smokescreens.

Notwithstanding ongoing condemnation from organized labour and Indigenous groups, the federal and territorial governments welcomed with relief the release of the final CPHA task force report in December 1977.

Crucially, the 144-page report reaffirmed the interim conclusions that there were no "immediate" health impacts on the wider Yellowknife population and that past studies indicated no "clear-cut evidence of acute or chronic arsenic poisoning" amongst Giant workers. Nevertheless, it did acknowledge arsenic exposures among workers, resulting in some incidence of skin rashes and respiratory irritation. The final report also attributed the overall high incidence of lung cancer in the Northwest Territories (and the Yukon) to higher disease prevalence amongst Indigenous people, but concluded that arsenic exposure was not to blame. The task force also asserted that, while minimizing exposure to carcinogens is desirable, "we feel that that balance of research to the present tends to favour the threshold concept."[81] In doing so, it rejected Blejer's and other experts' assertions of "no safe level" for arsenic exposure in favour of a "negligible risk" occupational level of 30 micrograms per cubic metre of airborne arsenic over an eight-hour period.

Beneath these assurances, the report's detailed findings and its forty-six recommendations reinforced the scale of the arsenic contamination in Yellowknife resulting from decades of emissions. Airborne arsenic levels exceeded national air quality objectives about 10 per cent of the time and were highest in the vicinity of the mill. These emissions produced "considerable contamination by arsenic compounds in the soil and vegetation of the area" – although similar to the YES study, the report concluded that there was little uptake of arsenic by plants and animals, and that local berries and vegetables were safe to eat, if washed. The use of snow for drinking water still posed a serious health hazard, especially in the vicinity of the roaster. The waters and sediments of Back Bay and Yellowknife Bay still showed a significant zone of influence from arsenic and heavy metals at sewage outfalls and at the mouth of Baker Creek. The report also noted the lack of secure water supply to Latham Island and Dettah, and suggested that Giant and Con should pay for water trucked to these unserviced communities.

Though dismissing concerns over widespread arsenic "poisoning" from environmental exposures, the task force report acknowledged the necessity of both workplace and public health monitoring. It outlined a detailed monitoring program to detect long-term, low-dose, and subacute effects of arsenic exposure in the wider Yellowknife population. It also recommended further studies of the most exposed groups: mill and smelter workers, and Indigenous children. Overall, the report asserted that it was vital that "everyone has an arsenic-free water supply" and that continually reducing arsenic emissions was crucial. In fact, it suggested that Giant adopt "best available control technology" for arsenic capture from the mill, arguing that emissions could be decreased from current levels as high as 500 pounds per day to twenty-five to thirty pounds per day within two years.[82]

"Most of YK Safe from Arsenic," *News of the North* proclaimed upon the public release of the CPHA report in January 1978 – a storyline both government and mine officials were quick to embrace.[83] Giant Mine manager W.A. Moore quickly affirmed the mine's agreement and compliance with the report's recommendations, in typically tetchy fashion: "Do you think we like to be needled by every outfit in the country?" he told the *Yellowknifer*.[84] The Northwest Territories Chamber of Mines also endorsed the report, although unsurprisingly balked at the recommendations to create a northern-based environmental health unit and an environmental review board, citing regulatory duplication.[85] Even interim report critic Blejer now agreed with the report's overall findings, having been consulted on the final version.[86] But for the major arsenic pollution critics, the USWA and NIB, the task force report offered cold comfort. The USWA endorsed most of the CPHA recommendations for improved monitoring and environmental controls, but argued that the suggested occupational exposure level still left workers unduly at risk.[87] For its part, the NIB blasted the report as ineffectual, saying in a press release, "in fact, the message of the task force's report is that only Indian people are in danger of arsenic poisoning, so there is not really any problem."[88]

In spite of these criticisms, the final task force report had the (doubtlessly intended) consequence of largely quieting the public controversy while charting a policy response by federal and territorial officials that did not disrupt production at Giant. In fact, the local response to the task force began in advance of the final report. In June 1977, the reformed intergovernmental Standing Committee on Arsenic reviewed the interim task force report, providing feedback and largely concurring with its findings. This committee, still chaired by Billing, was responsible for coordinating and reviewing governmental action in response to the report, including overseeing research, sampling, and monitoring activities, and industry compliance with pollution control recommendations. As with the report's previous iteration, federal officials suggested that the arsenic committee include

Figure 4.4

Winter view of Giant Mine, with Back Bay, Latham Island (Ndilǫ), and part of Yellowknife in the background, 31 January 1975. In spite of emissions reductions, arsenic pollution from Giant remained a source of ongoing controversy in the 1970s.

representation from the mine unions and the NIB – a suggestion initially resisted by the commissioner of the Northwest Territories, but which was eventually adopted.[89]

On the public health front, the federal Health Services Branch undertook follow-up studies on both Giant workers and the general population in Yellowknife, including Indigenous children. One study used electromyography, or nerve impulse testing, to detect subacute effects of arsenic poisoning, related the results to hair and urine samples, and compared the results with a control population in Hay River, Northwest Territories. This study documented "exceedingly high levels" of arsenic amongst some Giant workers, and higher levels among Indigenous residents in Yellowknife than in Hay River (though the latter were similar to the rest of the non-mining population in Yellowknife).[90] While these initial results raised alarms for participants (especially union members), R.D.P. Eaton from the northern health service assured union representatives that they did not indicate serious medical concerns for either individuals or the community as a whole.[91] The final health study concluded that high arsenic levels in hair resulted from "deposition," not ingestion, and electromyographic results demonstrated no significant difference between arsenic-exposed populations and unexposed populations.[92]

Although federal scientists largely refused to accept data indicating elevated cancer rates in Yellowknife, particularly among Indigenous people, they quietly continued to investigate the question. Schaefer reasserted his opinion that the cancer data were inconclusive, and any connection to arsenic doubtful.[93] In a subsequent review of Yellowknife cancer data, CPHA task force member R.B. Sutherland grappled with the challenge of reconstructing exposure histories for both Giant workers and Indigenous people, taking into account changing residency and varying exposure levels, as well as personal health factors such as smoking. He also noted that the Northwest Territories lacked a cancer registry, and even determining ethnicity from death certificates proved problematic, but he echoed the task force's recommendation of cohort studies of Giant and Con workers.[94]

Addressing the occupational health recommendations from the task force report proved more controversial. Giant Mine and the Northwest Territories Chamber of Mines argued that the task force's recommended mill arsenic level of thirty micrograms per cubic metre of air exceeded standards in some US jurisdictions. Giant Mine manager Moore pressed the inter-agency Standing Committee on Arsenic to adopt a much higher workplace arsenic air standard of fifty micrograms per cubic metre.[95] By contrast, union representatives challenged the proposed standard of thirty micrograms per cubic metre, arguing that the government should adopt the even stricter level recommended by the American National Institute for Occupational Safety and Health (NIOSH) of two micrograms per cubic metre – a standard that mine and government officials regarded as technically unachievable.[96] Nevertheless, correspondence and research by Medical Services Branch personnel and consultants reveals an awareness of the mounting scientific evidence that there was "no safe level" of exposure to trivalent arsenic, and that proposed US federal occupational standard of ten micrograms per cubic metre reflected an achievable level, rather than full protection from carcinogenic effects.[97] In the end, task force chair

C.J.G. Mackenzie cited the uncertainty around threshold level values and cancer risk to conclude that the thirty micrograms per cubic metre standard "has the advantage of being attainable in the immediate future."[98] In terms of worker health monitoring, Giant and Con both adopted pre-placement and annual medicals for employees who could be exposed to arsenic, but the overall establishment of a coordinated occupational health response remained mired for years in jurisdictional conflict and overlap between the federal Medical Services Branch, the regional Occupational Health Unit, and the Government of the Northwest Territories.[99]

A final high-profile health-related report recommendation – and one of grave concern for local Dene communities – was the provision of a safe water supply for Ndilǫ and Dettah. As noted previously, trucked water for these communities (and some other informal settlements) had been provided at cost since 1969, but it became clear during the task force's investigations that not all households had purchased or used the water (which was supposed to be paid for out of assistance cheques for utilities).[100] Unsurprisingly, the mines strongly opposed the task force recommendation that Giant and Con take financial responsibility for providing public water supplies to communities. Perhaps more surprisingly, the re-formed Standing Committee on Arsenic agreed, suggesting that this service was a municipal responsibility. Trucked drinking water continued to be supplied to these communities with a charge, yet years later it remained unclear, even to Medical Services Branch personnel, whether a cost-sharing agreement had been reached between the mining companies and the government.[101]

Wasting Time

Although the focus of the task force was (not unreasonably) on questions of public health and occupational exposures, it also explored ongoing concerns around tailings disposal and the underground storage of arsenic waste at Giant. As noted in chapter 3, the question of tailings management at both Giant and Con had reached both the Northwest Territories Water Board and the Standing Committee on Arsenic by 1975, thanks in part to the prosecution of Giant for tailings spills earlier that year.[102] A 1977 internal report on tailings pollution confirmed the acute toxicity of Giant tailings effluent, with its high values of heavy metals and arsenic, flowing into Baker Creek. However, the author dismissed the impact on aquatic life in Yellowknife Bay beyond the small "zone of influence" in Back Bay and claimed, perhaps wishfully, that "fish are repelled and swim away from water containing toxic substances."[103]

Reviewing the evidence from studies of tailings effluent from both Giant and Con, the CPHA report noted that the mines discharged very high levels of arsenic into the local environment. At Giant, tailings effluent polluted lake water and sediments in Yellowknife Bay, and "seepage" events (spills) introduced arsenic, cyanide, and copper into Baker Creek. Similarly, seepages continued to occur from the Con tailings impoundment, contaminating Kam Lake. The report emphasized the need to curtail these contamination events, to shore up tailings storage, and to reduce contaminant levels in tailings overflow discharges at both sites through effluent treatment.[104] It also noted the need to control wind-dispersed tailings – a particularly important issue for residents of Latham Island across Back Bay from Giant Mine.

More dramatically, the unfurling controversy of the mid-1970s also brought additional scrutiny of the mounting underground arsenic problem at Giant Mine. As noted in chapter 3, warnings issued by a mining inspector in 1973 and a government biologist in 1974 had previously brought the issue to government attention, to little effect. Underground arsenic storage barely merited mention in the YES studies, although Grainge's report included data tables showing that, by 1973, nearly 156,000 tons of arsenic had already been buried at Giant.[105] However, after the earlier warning memos were leaked by the 1977 NIB–USWA study, media outlets already covering the arsenic controversy jumped on the issue, prompting stories about the alarming underground accumulation of enough arsenic trioxide "to eradicate the world population."[106] An *Edmonton Journal* report suggested that "experts appear divided about the urgency" of the problem, though they were united about the need to avoid flooding the mine (a common post-closure practice) before determining the extent of permafrost. Federal mining engineer Mel Brown suggested that a permanent solution to the problem could perhaps await closure, pointing out that the concrete bulkheads securing the waste underground were visibly frozen. Environment Canada scientists were less sanguine, calling for a detailed study of permafrost conditions around the arsenic-filled stopes.[107] To assuage concern in Yellowknife, Giant arranged for local media to tour the mine to view the storage chambers, while emphatically claiming that "arsenic will never escape" the mine.[108]

Federal bureaucrats struggled to come to grips with the problem. Because the underground arsenic was not an active pollutant, just a potential one, the issue fell between the cracks of Environment Canada, Indian and Northern Affairs, and the Northwest Territories Water Board. Health and Welfare officials also got involved, referring the question to the CPHA task force, "because of the possibility of hazard to human health."[109] In its report, the task force reviewed the design criteria for the arsenic storage areas and concluded that underground storage represented "the safest and most acceptable approach to the problem." The report noted the potential longer-term concern of mine flooding post-closure, and recommended that the federal Mining Inspection Branch be charged with monitoring the site.[110]

Indigenous and union critics remained unconvinced. At the CPHA inquiry hearings, USWA and NIB intervenors condemned the accumulation of toxic waste below Giant Mine, and the long-term threat it posed to the community. "We would like to know who is going to be responsible for monitoring these wastes forever," demanded Gina Blondin at the Ottawa hearing. She went on to ask, "When Giant Mines has removed the last easily recoverable gold from the land, made its last profits and gone home, who will pay for the storage shaft to be pumped forever?"[111] In its response to task force's endorsement of underground storage, the Steelworkers union presciently cited climate change as a potential threat to the "perma" of permafrost and urged additional design safeguards and further study of the storage plan.[112] In the end, government officials remained content to allow for the accumulation of massive volumes of toxic waste in the rock below the mine and failed to demand any kind of clear closure and reclamation plan for Giant Mine, implicitly accepting potential responsibility for perpetual monitoring of the site.

Conclusion

In 1978, the NIB released a summary report on the Yellowknife situation, called "Arsenic and Red Tape." Authored by Tataryn, it reviewed the decades-long saga of arsenic contamination, repeated public studies, and recent rolling controversies over pollution in Yellowknife, chronicling what he and the NIB alleged was a pattern of bureaucratic obfuscation and information suppression. "The government's manoeuvres to minimize the arsenic difficulties at Yellowknife produced distrust among the gold mine workers," he suggested. "It also heightened the native peoples' suspicions that government officials had little concern for their well-being."[113] Tataryn also celebrated the alliance between mine workers and northern Indigenous Peoples that challenged government and industry claims around the safety of the living and working environment in Yellowknife. This alliance was embodied on the union side by Paul Falkowski, the USWA's national environmental and occupational health and safety representative, who was active in arsenic advocacy and addressed the NIB's national assembly in September 1977. "Today, many of our members continue to work in polluted environments," Falkowski declared, "and many of your people, through no fault of their own, are forced to live on contaminated lands." These shared risks made unions and Indigenous organizations natural allies against what he called "insensitive industries and foot-dragging governments."[114]

Through the arsenic controversies of the 1970s, the remarkable collaboration between these groups included not only political and media advocacy, but also citizen science initiatives aimed at countering what they saw as government control over information. This heady activism combined the spirit of Earth Day, Indigenous rights, and union activism around occupational health, with more than a dose of Watergate-era suspicion of government cupidity and cover-ups. In so doing, the USWA and NIB, along with journalists and other Yellowknife citizens, launched the issue of pollution in this remote northern mining town onto the national political agenda, and forced a new era of responsiveness – if not exactly transparency or accountability – from federal and territorial officials. What their advocacy did not do, however, was dispel or diminish the looming environmental disaster posed by the continuing accumulation of arsenic trioxide underground at Giant, a threat that remained obscured by the turmoil that gripped the community in the last two decades of the mine's operation.

5

Regulation and Resistance

"The pattern in Yellowknife," wrote the CPHA Task Force on Arsenic, "has been to have a survey and a review of the [arsenic] situation every ten to fifteen years." In response to these studies, "industrial practices have been modified and improved but the provision of public health and industrial medical monitoring and practice have lagged."[1] In other words, government and industry had adopted a piecemeal rather than a comprehensive response to arsenic pollution in the wake of previous crises. Ironically, the main conclusions of the task force ensured that its report would meet much the same fate. The authors' bold announcement that only a small portion of the Yellowknife population – workers and Indigenous youth – faced any danger from arsenic provided very effective protective cover for government and industry (even if the health of workers and children should have been a cause for concern). The end of Yellowknife's "health scare" pushed the arsenic issue off the national political stage, out of the national and local media, and seemingly off the priority list of local activists (who likely did not have the resources to run a sustained campaign against the mine). All of this, in turn, diminished any imperative to impose further regulations on Yellowknife's gold industry. Dan Billing, chief environmental officer for the Northwest Territories, summed up the prevailing attitude at a meeting of a national Gold Roasting Industry Task Force on Arsenic Emissions in May 1978, when he "questioned whether there is a mandate for the development of gold roasting arsenic regulations since the CPHA report on Yellowknife had determined that there was no risk."[2]

As if to underscore this idea, the federal and territorial governments continued to emphasize a voluntary, technology-driven approach to arsenic control rather than air quality standards or strict end-of-pipe caps on water pollution. So long as the mines developed improved methods to capture arsenic, they were still permitted to pollute the work environment of the mine and the air and water near Yellowknife, without having to seriously account for the long-term risks of arsenic exposure for workers, the general public, and non-human life. While activists from various constituencies had challenged Giant Mine's pollution record beginning in the mid-1970s, by the end of the decade Giant Yellowknife Mines had begun to fight in earnest against government regulation, always dangling the possibility of a shutdown of the mine as a way to keep pollution targets within the range the company considered feasible. This pattern continued over the subsequent two decades, as Giant's changing ownership faced down calls for regulation with job blackmail threats, and the territorial and federal governments treated the mine with kid gloves. The rise of a new era of local activism in the 1990s, sparked by air pollution concerns, came too late to provoke meaningful environmental regulation before the mine itself entered its death throes at the turn of the millennium.

Persistent Problems

Almost immediately after the task force had declared an effective end to the arsenic emergency, ongoing monitoring reports indicated that arsenic pollution at Giant Mine still posed many problems. In 1978, the federal Environmental Protection Service highlighted the fact that mine effluent deposited in Baker Creek was so contaminated that it still had markedly reduced the density of aquatic life in a zone stretching three kilometres into Back Bay. Sediments deposited from the creek contained high levels of various heavy metals, and the water in Yellowknife Bay still contained arsenic at levels well above the recommended amount for drinking water (often as high as 0.74 parts per million, when the drinking water limit was 0.05 parts per million). The Environmental Protection Service report predicted that the ongoing dumping of "lethal waste" into Yellowknife Bay would further expand the contaminated zone of influence, further destroying aquatic life and increasing arsenic levels in the bay.[3] The local CBC News obtained a copy of the study and reported that the lower part of Baker Creek was "dead" and Back Bay largely devoid of aquatic life. The story also challenged the prevailing idea that pollution from Giant Mine did not threaten the health of local residents, suggesting that people on Latham Island still used contaminated drinking water from the bay. Giant Yellowknife Mines pushed back on the main conclusions of the Environmental Protection Service report, arguing that many of the projections of future impacts were "conjecture" or "unscientific." W.A. Moore, the mine's irascible manager, wrote that "one gets the opinion that the authors are very biased against industry."[4] Regardless of how one felt about industry, there was no denying that water pollution problems at Giant Mine persisted. In fact, the company consistently exceeded water quality limits that the Northwest Territories Water Board had imposed for arsenic, cyanide, and various heavy metals through a water licence granted in 1981. In January of that year, the company reported that the six million litres of groundwater pumped from the mine annually and then dumped in Baker Creek measured above the licence limit for arsenic in effluent (five parts per million) 61 per cent of the time.[5]

It must have come as a relief to many in Yellowknife when the company completed construction of a new water treatment plant in 1981. It took two additional years to iron out various technical problems and reduce water contaminants (cyanide, arsenic, copper, nickel, zinc, and lead – all except ammonia) below the limits of the water licence. When this work was completed, the company was able to point to the treatment plant as evidence of its new attentiveness to environmental responsibility.[6] In 1982, the company touted the fact that its "most significant expenditures [in 1981] were for environmental purposes." These included $342,000 spent on a new tailings dam and $169,000 spent on the new, state-of-the-art alkaline-chlorination-arsenic-precipitation plant to treat effluent pumped from the mine and tailings ponds.[7] The new dam, along with improved techniques such as piling tailings material with low permeability at the base of all dams, further contained the flow of water pollution, thereby diminishing seepage from the tailings ponds to "negligible levels."[8] At the Northwest Territories Water Board hearings for Giant Mine's 1985 licence renewal, Ken Blower, the mine's new general manager, boasted that "Giant has made dramatic progress in its water treatment activities. In the past two years, we've become an industry showcase. Our effluent treatment plant has been the subject of numerous technical papers and we have conducted technical tours for visitors from around the globe."[9] From the company's perspective, Giant Mine had shed its former image as an environmental and public health laggard, and become a shining example of the mining industry's ability to clean up its own backyard.

And yet, the mine's improved control systems still did not eliminate water pollution problems. The company reported spills of solid waste (tailings or arsenic trioxide) and/or effluent on at least fourteen occasions between 1981 and 1988.[10] In 1985, the company petitioned the Water Board to end its closed-loop system for water treatment and resume the practice of dumping treatment plant effluent directly into Baker Creek. Since the treatment plant had become operational, the company had pumped mine water into the tailings ponds, where it inevitably absorbed additional contaminants, thus requiring another round of treatment at the plant and greatly increasing the cost of the overall system. In July 1985, the board approved the plan to use Baker Creek for the deposit of treated mine water, so long as the effluent met pollution limits as set out in the current licence. Between August and October 1985, however, the effluent released into Baker Creek contained arsenic at levels above the licence limits on seventeen occasions, while ammonia levels consistently exceeded the allowable limits. The latter contaminant was a by-product of sewage and dynamite made of ammonium nitrate and fuel oil (colloquially named "ANFO," in accordance with its acronym), and the treatment plant was not capable of removing it from wastewater. The presence of ammonia in effluent pumped into Baker Creek once again raised the specter of a "dead zone" in Back Bay because the chemical is acutely toxic to aquatic life.[11]

At Giant's water licence hearings in 1985, Environment Canada's Scott Howarth and David Sutherland reported that, during testing, effluent samples from Giant Mine had killed more than 50 per cent of trout and daphnia. Howarth and Sutherland also pointed to ongoing problems with arsenic-laden sediments in Back Bay, particularly the fact that arsenic continued to seep out to the wider Yellowknife Bay. They were confident, however, that the latter problem would resolve itself over time as the cleaner sediments flowing out of Baker Creek after the construction of the treatment plant eventually covered the more contaminated material from previous decades. Somewhat surprisingly, Howarth and Sutherland supported Giant's petition to keep ammonia levels unregulated, estimating that the pollutant's zone of influence on aquatic life extended only 100 metres from the outlet of Baker Creek. In contrast, Lloyd Norn, representing the Dene Nation, suspected that there were broader impacts of mine water on fish, reporting that many Tatsǫ̨t'ıné had complained about poor fish quality, especially soft and strange tasting flesh, since the mine began operations. Although Water Board chair Glenn Warner responded enthusiastically to Norn's call for a fish sampling program, he was more inclined to celebrate Giant Yellowknife Mines' progress on pollution control, congratulating the company on "your state of the art and your exemplary record. It's not often that the Environment Canada people hand out these bouquets, believe me. So I daresay they are well earned. And congratulations, we look forward to the long and fruitful life of your mine."[12] If the company had improved on previous practices, especially when it abandoned the pumping of untreated effluent into fish-bearing waterways, Warner's praise ignored the fact that the company had, in some ways, taken a step backwards when it resumed the dumping of partially polluted water into Baker Creek.

Such a mixture of progress and regression was also a feature of the company's efforts to address workplace exposure to arsenic trioxide dust. Despite the company's adoption of the task force's relatively liberal indoor airborne arsenic standard of thirty micrograms per cubic metre, and its efforts to install new air filters capable of extracting fine dust and exchanging the air in a room four times every hour, it still had trouble meeting workplace air quality guidelines. In June 1979, Joe Donnelly, CASAW president, complained to Moore about indoor air test samples that were "substantially higher in arsenic than the recommended level of 30 micrograms per cubic metre."[13] A year later, not much had improved: inspectors from the federal government's Occupational Health Unit found that air samples exceeded the thirty micrograms per cubic metre limit for arsenic dust in twelve of forty-six samples in the roaster, eleven of forty-four samples in the Cottrell electrostatic precipitator facility, and nine of twenty-six samples in the baghouse. On 29 June, one sample revealed arsenic air levels at

7,800 micrograms per cubic metre, the result of a ruptured bearing that caused the pumping system to release a large cloud of arsenic trioxide dust in the baghouse. The cleanup crews responding to the incident wore only standard overalls, gloves, boots, head gear, and 3M paper masks. The inspectors recommended adequate clothing and safety gear for cleanup crews, ongoing monitoring and vigilance to keep arsenic below the air quality limit, and the deployment of a truck-mounted vacuum system in the event of further spills. Ultimately, however, the inspectors found the results of their survey to be "adequate," even though they demonstrated that the company was out of compliance with the CPHA's air quality limit roughly 25 per cent of the time.[14] Once again, as long as Giant Yellowknife Mines made some kind of effort to control pollution, federal regulators tended to downplay repeated failures by the company to meet targets.

Even with such flexible enforcement measures, the company still vigorously opposed any attempt to impose strict regulatory limits on pollution. One particularly contentious arena for debate was the federal government's proposals to impose a strict cap on emissions from the roaster facility. Much discussion of this proposal took place at the hearings of the Gold Processing Industry Task Force on Arsenic Emissions, a joint industry and government task force on gold roasting. The federal government convened this committee in 1977 to respond to a Department of National Health and Welfare report pointing to uncontrolled emissions from the four mines that practised gold roasting in Canada as a significant threat to human health.[15] When the task force members from Environment Canada proposed a strict emissions limit of seven milligrams per standard cubic metre (mg/Sm^3) under the Clean Air Act, which would have required a reduction from 250 pounds to 14 pounds of arsenic stack emissions per day at Giant Mine, the company fought back. L.S. Price, the company's manager of environmental controls, pressed the issue with Earl Gagan at Environment Canada, arguing that it was not feasible to bring about such a drastic reduction in arsenic output because workers would be forced to inspect every inch of every bag in the baghouse, fearful that a loose stitch or weak point might result in a violation. On a more political note, Price suggested that the regulator seemed to think "it would be very convenient if this segment of the gold industry could be encouraged to quietly disappear," and reminded Gagan of the consequences of such a collapse in terms of lost jobs and wealth destruction in the millions of dollars.[16] Moore echoed these points when he circulated an internal company memo saying that "this will effectively close down the plant and put 353 employees out of work, adding to the unemployment rolls." As for the proposal to charge and fine the company $200,000 per day for non-compliance, Moore bluntly stated, "They can forget that. There is no way I would agree to continue to operate under that threat."[17]

In May 1978, Environment Canada proposed to the arsenic task force a higher stack emission limit of seventeen milligrams per standard cubic metre, along with a declaration that the department was not inclined to charge companies for only minor violations.[18] Although the limit was never implemented, the company managed major improvements to their arsenic collections system through the installation of new and improved Porritts & Spencer bags in the baghouse, resulting in a reduction of roaster stack arsenic emissions from 250 pounds per day in 1977 to 20 to 29 pounds per day in 1979. Such dramatic improvement to the bag filtration system reduced particulate emission levels at the end of the roaster stack from an average of 76.6 milligrams per standard cubic metre in 1975 to 14.07 milligrams per standard cubic metre in 1981 – not as low as Environment Canada's initial proposal, but slightly below the second suggested limit.[19]

As one might expect, much less arsenic trioxide dust billowing out of the roaster stack meant that there was less accumulating in the local environment, with monitoring results showing an 80 per cent decline in arsenic trioxide concentration in snow cores near Yellowknife.[20] By 1989 the yearly average ambient air levels for arsenic in Yellowknife had, at 0.013 micrograms per cubic metre, fallen below all provincial guidelines, though this amount was still thirteen times higher than the levels in other Canadian cities with monitoring stations.[21] Despite the improvements to stack emissions, corporate resistance to regulation had won the day. Environment Canada failed to establish a cap on arsenic emissions from Giant Mine's roaster stack and an ambient air quality limit for arsenic trioxide. Any air pollution control that occurred remained strictly voluntary on the part of the company.

One key point often lost in the debate about Giant Mine's emission levels was whether even the markedly reduced amounts of arsenic pollution in the Yellowknife environment were safe for the local population. As we have discussed in previous chapters, for much of the twentieth century, the fields of environmental toxicology and industrial hygiene had been shaped by the idea that a "safe" threshold level of exposure existed for every substance. Nothing was inherently harmful on its own, according to the dominant view, but it was the dose that made the poison. By the end of the 1970s, however, the fields of occupational health and toxicology were at the early stages of a paradigm shift in which practitioners increasingly recognized that some substances could harm living organisms through long-term exposure at infinitesimally small amounts.[22] Arsenic was one of them. In 1978 the US Occupational Safety and Health Administration (OSHA) concluded that arsenic, particularly in its trivalent form, could cause cancer at very low dose exposures over long periods of time, possibly more than three decades from the time of first exposure. The organization cited studies (at Dow Chemical, Kennecott Copper, and at the ASARCO smelter in Tacoma, Washington) showing high lung and lymphatic cancer rates among workers exposed to arsenic trioxide over several decades. In the Dow study, 32.9 per cent of exposed workers compared to 20.7 per cent of non-exposed people had developed lung cancer, and across all the studies, mortality rates among those exposed to arsenic trioxide were four to eight times what would be expected in a non-exposed population. OSHA concluded that arsenic trioxide should be regulated as a non-threshold carcinogen for which no safe level of exposure existed.[23]

Federal and territorial officials on the Giant file were well aware of OSHA's basic findings. Not only was a copy of the OSHA report in the files of the inter-agency Gold Processing Industry Task Force on Arsenic, several of the group's meeting minutes and reports make reference to the new knowledge emanating from the United States about arsenic as a non-threshold carcinogen, including a report in January 1978 from the Science Advisory Board of the Northwest Territories critical of the CPHA task force's reliance on the threshold concept, and calling for more investigation of the risks from long-term, low-dose exposure to arsenic trioxide.[24] Behind the scenes, D.A. Gemmill worked diligently from his office in the Environmental Protection Service in Calgary to collect as many scientific papers on arsenic as he could, forwarding dozens to Billing, who dutifully placed them in the files of Yellowknife's Standing Committee on Arsenic for consideration.[25] In April 1978, a report from the Department of National Health and Welfare cited a broad literature review, including a computer search of the

Figure 5.1
Giant Mine roaster and smokestack in 1980.

National Science Library of the US Environmental Protection Agency, as the basis for concluding that "arsenic emissions could constitute a significant danger to the health of persons."[26] And yet, the federal government never seriously deviated from the threshold-limit approach to arsenic throughout the 1980s. The Health and Welfare report called for the creation of a national standard for arsenic trioxide emissions at gold roasting facilities (in other words, a safe limit), but as shown above, Giant Mine pushed back hard against this approach. Fearful of jeopardizing the company's survival, federal (and eventually territorial) regulators had to remain content with the mine's best efforts to control arsenic emissions in spite of the long-term threat of low-level exposure to workers, Indigenous communities, and the general population in Yellowknife.

Ironically, the efforts of the company and government to control airborne arsenic exacerbated another long-term threat: the arsenic trioxide dust stored underground, which grew markedly with every passing year. By 1985, the company had pumped 208,613 tons of arsenic trioxide into underground chambers. Still, nobody had addressed the persistent, difficult questions about what would happen to all of this toxic material after the mine closed.[27] In 1985, the Northwest Territories Water Board demanded that the company produce its first abandonment and restoration plan as a condition of its water licence. In it, the company hatched a scheme to empty the mine of arsenic trioxide and then seal it from residual arsenic outflow using fans to blow cold winter air into the upper levels and re-establish permafrost. At the lower levels, the company planned to allow groundwater to flood the mine (a process projected to take 145 years), and still somehow prevent the outflow of any contaminated groundwater.

The removal plan represented a "win-win" for the company because the recovered arsenic could be sold as a commodity, with the added bonus that any remaining gold in the arsenic trioxide dust could also be processed and sold. The company's timing for such a scheme was not ideal, however, as the use of arsenic to manufacture pesticides in the United States had declined markedly in the 1980s in advance of a ban set to take effect in 1988. For the time being, a market still existed for chromated copper arsenate to protect lumber from insects and microbes, and the company managed to sell approximately 3,500 short tons of arsenic per year between 1981 and 1986 to the Koppers Corporation in Georgia. Koppers ultimately found Giant's arsenic unsuitable for their plant, however. The failure of the Koppers arrangement, the collapsing price, and local opposition to Giant's plans to build a white arsenic trioxide (WAROX) transfer facility in Enterprise, Northwest Territories (to transform the toxic dust from the mine to a granular form more suitable for industrial applications), signalled the death knell for a market-based solution to the arsenic storage problem. Perhaps anticipating the diminishing market value of arsenic, the company's abandonment and restoration plan for 1985 argued that, if the sales plan went awry, the toxic dust stored underground was generally dry and could be contained safely in place far into the distant future.[28]

The relative stability that the company ascribed to the underground arsenic might have served as an apt metaphor for its evolving relationship to government and the public in the 1980s. After the public relations disasters of the 1970s, Giant Yellowknife Mines largely managed to keep national news stories about its operations buried in the business section. Having rehabilitated Giant Mine as an apparent model of green corporate citizenship, the company also managed to fight off the federal government's efforts to impose further regulations, especially end-of-the-pipe emissions caps or a serious plan to address the looming liabilities associated with the underground storage of arsenic. Indeed, archival records from this period suggest that controlling pollution at Giant Mine had become a routine administrative matter rather than one of political urgency. In the 1980s, there were no figures such as Kingsley Kay or Gordon Butler taking activist stances from within government. Nor were there many instances of local residents or environmental groups challenging the company (the defeat of the WAROX plant being one exception). The new union at Giant Mine, the Canadian Association of Smelter and Allied Workers (CASAW), continued to challenge management on pollution issues, but focused less on public policy–driven campaigns for lower stack emissions or strict air quality standards, and more on incremental improvements to specific work process issues such as arsenic testing protocols for workers (especially the frequency of tests and distribution of results), improving dust monitoring in the mine, implementing dust suppression on roads, upgrading ventilation in the mine, and better handling of arsenic dust when emptying the roaster flue.[29] In a somewhat similar way, the Yellowknives Dene continued to question Giant Mine's environmental record at official forums such at the Northwest Territories Water Board, but even here the concerns were very specific (as with the apprehension over fish quality), rather than the sweeping anti-colonial and proto–environmental justice arguments that had infused the debates of the 1970s. It took a new owner, accompanied by a deteriorating environmental record, volatile labour relations, and unresolved issues associated with the closure of the mine, to place Giant Mine at the centre of Yellowknife's contested politics once again.

The Battle for Giant Mine

In 1980, CASAW led its first strike, a four-month-long legal walkout beginning in July after a brief wildcat strike in April. As mentioned in the previous chapter, CASAW was an upstart union that had successfully displaced the USWA at Giant Mine as part of a broader campaign to Canadianize union representation in smelter and mining towns. When contract negotiations loomed in 1980, no doubt many factors, including the six-fold increase in gold prices between 1976 and 1980, the high inflationary environment of the late 1970s, and the corresponding increase in profit at Giant Mine from just over $5.9 million in 1978 to $13.1 million in 1979, prompted CASAW's bargaining team to push for a 57 per cent wage increase over three years. Journalists Lee Selleck and Francis Thompson have written that most Giant Mine employees have good memories of the ensuing strike, with many recalling that the picket lines were "fun," featuring relatively good-natured jeering of managers who crossed the line and minimal vandalism (though the company noted increasing incidents of the latter near the end of the strike). The end result was good for the workers: a 50 per cent wage increase over the life of the contract, not far off the amount CASAW had demanded at the bargaining table. According to Selleck and Thompson, the wage increase meant that Yellowknife was no longer seen as a transient place where one came to make a quick buck, but a town where a miner could stay, raise a family, and put down roots.[30]

The price of gold began to fall off the market cliff almost immediately after the strike. It lost half its value by 1982, briefly rallied in 1983, and then dipped to a low of US$298.32 per ounce in 1985, less than half the peaks of five years earlier. As a consequence, Giant posted a tiny profit of $450,382 in 1981, and generated only small profits (at least compared to 1979) of $2.1 million in 1985 and $3.7 million in 1986.[31] At the mine site, the problem of poor market conditions was compounded by the fact that most of the buildings had aged and fallen into disrepair (with many containing asbestos, making maintenance work risky and expensive). Beneath the surface, most of the higher-grade ore had been mined out. Majority owner Falconbridge almost closed Giant outright in the 1980/1981, but decided to attempt a modernization program, building some new facilities, refurbishing others, and cutting wider openings at the surface so that vehicles could more easily enter the mine.[32]

Figure 5.2

Graffiti message to W.A. Moore, Giant Mine manager, during the strike of 1980. A series of labour disputes at Giant culminated in the brutal and tragic lockout of 1992, which ended in the deaths of nine replacement workers.

By 1986, however, Falconbridge (Giant's majority owner) decided that it was finished with gold mining in Yellowknife. It sold its stake in Giant Yellowknife Mines to Pamour, which controlled a large historical gold mine in Timmins, Ontario (the Pamour Mine). Pamour subsequently underwent its own dizzying array of ownership changes (mostly involving Australian mining and investment firms) before it, too, walked away from Giant in 1990. At this point Giant Mine was hanging by a thread, a victim of the global downturn in the commodity super cycle that hit the mining industry hard throughout the 1980s (in part owing to the brutal recession in the early years of the decade). As many older legacy mines closed in Canada, investors began to question whether gold mining was a sunset industry.[33]

Into this bleak situation stepped a metallurgical engineer from Nevada named Peggy Witte, whose shell company, Royal Oak Mines, had never actually operated a mine. Determined to become a major player in the industry, Witte's strategy was to buy up failing gold mining operations and make them profitable through rapid cost cutting. Her first acquisitions were Giant Mine and Pamour, which Royal Oak bought in 1990 for the bargain-basement price of, collectively, $35.6 million (Pamour had paid $200 million to acquire Giant Mine four years earlier). Witte and new mine manager Mike Werner then quickly turned the operation of Giant Mine upside down, moving the head office from Toronto to Vancouver and laying off most of the staff while also letting go several administrators in Yellowknife. The new bosses imposed their power over the unionized workforce in the form of a step system for disciplinary infractions (with four steps in a single category, or seven in total leading to termination). For the first time, the company penalized workers with steps for safety lapses, concerned that the cost of lost-time injuries was a major impediment to profitability. The company's demand for the union to drop all grievances (many of these directed at managers who had been laid off), and deteriorating personal relationships between Werner and several miners, added to a growing atmosphere of toxic labour relations. The cost cutting nevertheless earned Witte an honour as first female recipient of the *Northern Miner* newspaper's "Mining Man of the Year" in 1991, even though year-to-date operating profits at the Giant Mine division declined from $2.8 million to $1.9 million between December 1990 and December 1991.[34]

Amid such acrimony, it is remarkable that CASAW's and Royal Oak's bargaining teams reached a tentative contract agreement during their first set of negotiations in April 1992. The union, facing an aggressive employer and stubbornly low gold prices, did not have much leverage at the bargaining table. It agreed to a weak contract that featured a wage freeze, shift premium rollbacks, and a reduction in safety inspections. CASAW's membership voted to reject the tentative contract but Royal Oak would not move from its bargaining position. On 22 May, the company announced a lockout of CASAW members (a day before they were in a legal strike position) after the union rejected its demand for a second vote on the tentative contract. Security guards shouted at CASAW members while they evicted them from the property, drawing battle lines for the conflict to come.[35]

Most Canadians who recall anything about Giant Mine remember the events associated with the lockout (more often referred to as a strike). It was a top national news story for many years, impossible to ignore even with the most cursory attention paid to print, radio, and television news. In the decades since, two books, magazine features, a television movie, and, recently, a six-part CBC podcast have all documented the strike in painstaking detail (more than this broader history of the mine can hope to do).[36] All of this attention is warranted by the fact that the strike was easily the most violent in Canada since the Second World War. Although the heightened tension stemmed partly from the generally poor relationship between labour and management, Witte's highly provocative decision to operate the mine with replacement workers, something that had not been done in a Canadian mining strike since Kirkland Lake in 1941 to 1942, added fuel to the idea that the company was out to break the union. Striking workers watched helplessly as the company transported "scabs" to the mine site, severely diminishing the bargaining power of those on the picket lines.[37]

Tensions reached a boiling point as picketers blocked vehicles for long periods, threw rocks, and vandalized buses carrying replacement workers. In response, Royal Oak's lawyers obtained a court injunction limiting the number of picketers to five per gate, all of whom had to be CASAW members. The company further inflamed the situation a few days into the strike by hiring Pinkerton, a notorious private security firm with a long history of using intimidation tactics to bust unions (and which CASAW members quickly accused of throwing rocks and following strikers around town). The territorial government requested and received help from the RCMP in the form of a tactical squad (more colloquially known as riot police), which Witte publicly pressured to enforce the court injunction despite the reluctance of the police to appear as an adjunct to the mine's security force.

On 14 June, CASAW organized a rally at Giant Mine's front gate that attracted over two hundred union members and supporters, a clear challenge to the injunction. Despite an initial festive and family atmosphere, an argument between a group of strikers and Pinkerton guards escalated, a section of fence came down, and a full-scale riot ensued. The RCMP reacted quickly with riot gear and tear gas, driving strikers off the property and charging twenty-nine people with various offences. The intensity of the conflict eased somewhat during the summer, but there was no resolution to the dispute, even through mediation, as Witte continued to insist on a concessionary contract and the firing of all workers charged with offences during the strike.[38]

The labour dispute took a dark turn on 18 September as an explosion tore through a tunnel at the 750-foot level of the mine. Its strength and location suggested it was not part of the routine blasting of tunnel faces to dislodge ore. The first Giant employees to arrive at the scene found that the worst had happened: the explosion had destroyed a man-car, killing all nine men aboard. As word of the explosion leaked out, CASAW members thought it was another example of Royal Oak's lax approach to safety, reasoning that inexperienced replacement workers had probably transported dynamite in the man-car. An RCMP investigation, however, revealed that the blast was no accident: a trip wire and a detonator at the site indicated that the deceased miners – Vern Fullowka, Norman Hourie, Chris Neill, Joseph Pandev, Shane Riggs, Robert Rowsell, Arnold Russell, Malcolm Sawler, and David Vodnoski – had been murdered. Some of the more radical CASAW members had previously used dynamite to commit acts of vandalism on the surface, but a mass murder was unprecedented.[39] Barbara Hoddinott, a local nurse, recalled that Yellowknife became a "living hell" in the aftermath of the murders; anger, violence, marriage breakdown, and alcohol abuse all increased as the stress of the police investigation, the ongoing strike, and the national media glare took a toll on city residents. In October 1993, more than a year after the murders, the RCMP arrested one of Giant Mine's most experienced miners, Roger Warren, after he confessed to the crime during a police interview. Warren later recanted his confession, but a jury convicted him of nine counts of second-degree murder and he was sentenced to life in prison in 1995. Warren once again confessed that he was responsible for the killings in 2003.[40]

Amid Warren's high-profile arrest, it seemed unlikely that CASAW and the company would find a resolution at the bargaining table anytime soon. The breakthrough came through a different pathway in November 1993, when the Canadian Labour Relations Board (CLRB) ruled in favour of CASAW's bad-faith bargaining complaint. The ruling highlighted three key issues: Royal Oak's illegal demand for the mass dismissal of workers suspected of picket line vandalism as a condition for further bargaining, the company's refusal to bargain while awaiting the result of an attempt to organize a rival union among a small group of workers who had turned on CASAW, and management's insistence that all striking workers be put on probation for one year following a return to work (a demand that was illegal because it denied workers their right to arbitration and discriminated between striking and non-striking union members). Skeptical that an agreement could ever be reached between the two sides, the CLRB ordered that the original tentative agreement serve as the basis for a new contract, with negotiations to proceed on wages, benefits, and the issue of safety inspections. Royal Oak still demanded concessions on these issues, and the union insisted that the company was refusing to bargain, so they left the final decision on outstanding issues to mediators. CASAW members finally returned to the mine in December 1993. The union won a major victory in April 1994 when an arbitration board reinstated all but two of the workers that Witte wanted fired. For its part, Royal Oak (at Witte's behest) challenged the CLRB's bad-faith decision in court, finally losing on appeal at the Supreme Court of Canada in 1996.[41] Despite the hard-fought nature of the battle, neither side really gained much from the labour dispute, and soon they faced new challenges as the end of Giant Mine's operational life drew near.

Pollution: The Third Act

With the strike occupying so much attention in Yellowknife, one could fairly assume that environmental issues at the mine had been forgotten. Throughout the 1990s, however, CASAW continued to press management on arsenic-related issues, including long-standing disputes over dust sampling protocols and access to workers' test results, newer concerns such as the occasional rashes that affected workers who had been exposed to highly contaminated mine water, and the frequency and accuracy of smokestack sampling results.[42] Among the general public, a third upsurge in public concern over arsenic and other types of pollution happened simultaneously with the strike. Why this occurred is not exactly clear; there was no obvious catalyst such as the tragic death of a child, as in the early 1950s, or the high-profile *As It Happens* episode that sparked the anti-pollution movement during the early 1970s. Certainly the late 1980s and early 1990s were another period of high salience for environmental issues in Canada. Protests against clear-cut logging of old growth forests in places such as Temagami, Ontario, and Clayoquot Sound, British Columbia, reached the national media almost daily. In the policy arena, the federal Progressive Conservative government under Brian Mulroney was extremely active on the environment portfolio, passing the Canadian Environmental Protection Act (CEPA) in 1988 (legislation meant to consolidate existing regulations to protect human health and the environment from pollution), developing Canada's comprehensive Green Plan in 1990, and signing the Canada–United States Air Quality Agreement in 1991 to address acid rain.[43] In Yellowknife, local activists and Indigenous communities seized on the environmental zeitgeist, hoping to use the new "green" federal policy instruments, particularly CEPA, to impose stricter regulations on Giant Mine. The arrival of Royal Oak also likely played a role: local activists were more than likely inspired, some might say provoked, by a company that was equally aggressive on environmental issues as it was with its workers.

One of the pollution issues that gained a public profile during this period – a sudden spike in ammonia emissions from the mine – was directly connected to the strike. The company thought it had solved the ammonia issue in the mid-1980s through changes to the chemical processes in the treatment plant. In June 1993, however, the problem had returned, with the company storing highly contaminated water in its tailings ponds. Larry Connell, the company's manager of environmental and metallurgical services, requested the outright removal of the ammonia limit of two parts per million from the mine's water licence, threatening to shut down within two and a half months if the mine could not discharge the contaminated effluent from the tailings ponds (which would reach capacity by that point). Connell admitted that the spike in Giant Mine's ammonia emissions resulted from inexperienced replacement workers mishandling ANFO explosives, and also likely the increased sewage (which can produce ammonia when it degrades in water) dumped into the Northwest Tailings Pond because the mine was housing large numbers of replacement workers behind the picket lines.[44] Northwest Territories Water Board Chair Dave Nickerson quickly responded to the request, raising the limit to fifteen parts per million. Water testing through early summer revealed that the amount of ammonia in the tailings ponds had increased to between sixteen parts per million and twenty-two parts per million, despite an education campaign promoting improved handling of ANFO underground. Connell asked again for the removal of any regulations, but Nickerson suggested it would be "inappropriate" to approve a second amendment to the water licence without first holding public hearings. In the meantime, Nickerson asked the mine to do its "level best" to meet the fifteen-parts-per-million limit for ammonia.[45]

Concerns about Royal Oak's understanding of "level best," and the Northwest Territories Water Board's handling of the issue, quickly surfaced in the public realm. Among many media reports, the Canadian Press headlined an article on ammonia with the somewhat damning general assertion "Gold-Mine Owners Seek Laxer Environmental Laws." Even the normally pro-mining *Yellowknifer* ran a cartoon that depicted a mine worker dumping ammonia into Baker Creek and declaring that the fish were "jumping for joy," while in reality they were coughing and gasping for breath. Weeks later, an editorial in the *Yellowknifer* called for the water board to invoke the "precautionary principle" and establish a reasonable ammonia limit.[46] Local citizens also made their concerns known through Water Board hearings. Peter Atamanenko, a local environmentalist, claimed that the ammonia issue demonstrated a "credibility problem with your Board's license enforcement process," while Clark Marcino blamed the ammonia problem on Royal Oak's aggressive approach to labour relations, urging the board to "hold them accountable for the damage, both to the environment and the community, their decision has resulted in."[47] Darrell Beaulieu, Chief in Ndilǫ, reminded the board that the Yellowknives Dene were generally the group most heavily impacted by Giant Mine's effluent, and called for public hearings specific to his community, a request that was not granted.[48]

At the general public hearings held on 3 November 1993, Chris O'Brien, a Yellowknife environmental activist, called for strict restrictions on the use of ammonia underground until a viable technological solution could be found. Royal Oak countered the criticisms with three claims: Giant Mine did not emit more ammonia than the average municipal sewage facility, the ionized form of ammonia being released was less toxic to aquatic life, and there was no viable, cost-effective treatment technology that could be quickly installed at the mine. The generally pro-development Department of Indian and Northern Affairs backed Royal Oak's position at the hearings, but dissent came even from within the federal government. Both the Department of Fisheries and Oceans and Environment Canada opposed unregulated ammonia emissions into the aquatic environment, noting that under certain conditions, there was still potential for the release of the highly toxic, un-ionized form of ammonia, which would severely impact aquatic life in Baker Creek and Back Bay.[49] Five months later, the board finally ruled that it would continue to place a limit on Giant's ammonia emissions, but only at a level that Royal Oak could realistically hope to achieve. The Water Board eventually raised the mine's ammonia limit to a generous 19.5 parts per million with no thorough assessment of the impact on aquatic life. Royal Oak managed to lower emissions to 12.2 parts per million in 1996, but the ammonia issue was never effectively resolved. In 1998 Environment Canada remained concerned that the mine's release of "substantial amounts" of ammonia still represented a threat to aquatic life in Back Bay.[50]

During this same period, environmentalists in Yellowknife also began to challenge Royal Oak's record on air pollution. In April 1991, O'Brien and Kevin O'Reilly, an activist who had moved to Yellowknife in 1985 (and whose advocacy on Giant Mine issues has spanned more than three decades), requested an investigation of the health and environmental impacts of arsenic and sulphur dioxide under the Northwest Territories Environmental Rights Act, passed just a year earlier. Sulphur dioxide is far from an unknown contaminant in Canada; it has a notorious history in pulp mill and smelter towns (Sudbury, Ontario; Rouyn-Noranda, Quebec; Trail, British Columbia) because of its deleterious effects on vegetation (including farm crops) and its impact on respiratory health (particularly among vulnerable groups such as those with asthma). A less immediately obvious impact was sulphur dioxide's primary role in the creation of acid rain.[51]

It is surprising, then, that the issue of sulphur dioxide only arose in Yellowknife at this time. Residents of smelter towns are typically reminded of the gas (produced when sulphur in ore is converted to gas through roasting) on a daily basis, owing to its distinctive rotten egg smell. Certainly this was the case in Yellowknife. O'Reilly told the media that "even on the [Yellowknife] river you can smell the emissions sometimes. Anyone who drives by can smell the emissions."[52] Another local resident, Arlene Bell, wrote to the *Yellowknifer* about a hike through a "treeless swath of rocky land" near Giant Mine, where a "burning" and "clutching" sensation afflicted her and a friend, all because of air that was "like breathing in bug dope or vaporized metal."[53] Despite the smell and harrowing stories such as Bell's, the issue of sulphur dioxide emissions never gained traction with the public or government officials in the same way as arsenic pollution, likely because the threat was to the environment and vulnerable people, rather than to public health more generally. It is also possible that Giant Mine was viewed as only a minor producer of sulphur dioxide. The emission rate of fifty to sixty-five tonnes per day on average was roughly one-fifth of what the biggest polluters such as the Inco roasting operation at Sudbury produced at the time.[54] O'Brien and O'Reilly nevertheless cited a report suggesting that sulphur dioxide emissions from the mine had produced "disturbing phenomena observed during the summers of 1989 and 1990 – the premature yellowing and falling of leaves in a number of species of trees within 5 km of the Giant stack." They called for an investigation into the environmental and human health impacts of sulphur dioxide and arsenic in the Yellowknife area, a request Titus Allooloo, the territorial minister of renewable resources, granted two months later.[55]

The territorial government was, in fact, aware of the sulphur dioxide issue prior to the activists' request. In October 1990, a committee met to discuss the same report cited by O'Brien and O'Reilly, as well as air sampling data indicating that sulphur dioxide levels in the Yellowknife area had exceeded the Alberta guidelines ten times between 20 September and 18 October 1990.[56] The territorial government was hardly quick to act, however, only beginning to monitor sulphur dioxide levels in downtown Yellowknife (where, obviously, the highest density of people lived) in 1992, and taking a full two years to produce a report on air emissions. That report, when it appeared in June 1993, confirmed the tree damage and identified Giant Mine as a major emitter of sulphur dioxide. It also noted that sulphur dioxide levels downtown periodically rose above national air quality guidelines, especially when the wind blew roaster fumes southward from the mine. On the issue of airborne arsenic, the report argued that levels had only exceeded the Ontario limit of 0.3 micrograms per cubic metre (Ontario being the only province with a legally enforceable limit) on two occasions since 1978, and had declined to a yearly average of 0.01 micrograms per cubic metre since 1988. It contained no answers to questions O'Reilly and O'Brien had asked about further mitigating the impact of air pollution, presumably because the authors of the report did not think that there was a problem.[57]

The territorial government's report received negative reactions from all sides of the issue. O'Reilly noted, "All they've done is measure what comes out of the stack ... I guess we're disappointed there were no regulations in the report. We wanted to know what measures need to be taken to eliminate these impacts on the environment."[58] An editorial in the *Yellowknifer* suggested that the report was incomprehensible to the layperson, arguing, "If we are to have a truly responsive piece of law, the government will have to give more information than dry numbers."[59] A second editorial several days later asked whether Mr Wizard – the host of a popular science TV show for kids – might be able to help interpret the report.[60] Three striking workers who had staffed Giant's arsenic collection facility, Don McNealy, Norm Plante, and Dale Johnston, claimed in the *Northern Star* that the report's stack testing results for arsenic were likely severe underestimates (possibly by a factor of ten) because the company slowed down the roaster feed rate, turned down the stack fan, and isolated faulty compartments in the baghouse on the days on which inspectors were on site. They also argued that the problems with sulphur dioxide and dead vegetation had greatly worsened eight years previously when the company removed the deteriorating top portion of the roaster stack, limiting dispersal of the noxious gas.[61] Another *Northern Star* editorial noted that the report had only confirmed "the fairly obvious," but with no regulatory limits on arsenic or sulphur dioxide in the Northwest Territories, all the government could do was "ask, nicely, if Giant wouldn't mind please adding a scrubber or other pollution control device."[62] Richard Nuttall, a territorial medical health officer, echoed this sentiment when he lamented that the territorial government could only encourage Royal Oak to reduce emissions as "good corporate citizens." He also told the media that, while there was no "imminent health hazard" owing to air pollution, the emissions "were not doing anyone any good," especially those with respiratory conditions.[63] Royal Oak did not show much willingness to play the part of the good corporate citizen, accusing the government of overestimating sulphur dioxide emissions and claiming that existing processes for extracting arsenic prevented the use of cost-effective technology (such as scrubbers) to reduce the sulphur dioxide. And, as the company hinted in a press release, there was really no reason to further reduce contaminants from its stack because there was no legislated air quality standard for arsenic or sulphur dioxide in the Northwest Territories.[64]

Royal Oak's intransigence only seemed to embolden its critics. In July 1995, O'Reilly wrote a guest column for the *Yellowknifer* in which he reminded readers that arsenic trioxide was a known carcinogen, calling into question assurances from the federal and territorial governments that there was no "imminent health hazard" from Giant's stack emissions. He acknowledged that the territorial government's new air quality guidelines for sulphur dioxide (adopted June 1994) represented a positive step forward, but as non-enforceable suggestions they lacked any teeth. O'Reilly then challenged the threshold-limit approach to regulating pollution, arguing that, for a non-threshold carcinogen such as arsenic, "a clear principle – zero discharge – must be pulled out of the policy fog."[65] On 28 August, the City of Yellowknife followed suit and passed a motion calling for the complete elimination of arsenic and sulphur dioxide emissions at Giant Mine. Royal Oak responded with a bitter letter to Mayor Dave Lovell, suggesting that the city "no longer considers the presence of the Giant Mine to be an economic asset to the community of Yellowknife," and once again threatened to shut down the mine.[66]

Still the criticisms kept coming, especially as Yellowknives Dene leaders became more active on the pollution issue. In May 1995, CBC Yellowknife radio reported that the Yellowknives Dene were "stepping up their campaign for regulations against arsenic and sulphur dioxide emissions" in the Northwest Territories.[67] To that end, several Yellowknives Dene members offered passionate testimony at public hearings on pollution prevention that were held locally by the federal Standing Committee on Environment and Sustainable Development. While they were clear that tougher federal pollution limits should replace weak to non-existent territorial regulations, Tatsǫ̨t'ıné also linked the contemporary debate to their communities' nearly half-century encounter with pollution from Giant Mine. Elder Michel Paper spoke of the issues that the communities had been raising for decades:

> Back then, the water was fresh. We lived at the mine site and used the water from the shore for drinking and to make tea. Today, we are restricted from using the water for a radius of 15 miles or more because the water is contaminated. Many people, including children, have died from drinking the water. The emission of smoke from Giant Mines has killed many people. Today, the people have to pay for safe drinking water. In all fairness, Giant Mines should be paying for our water bills.[68]

Elder Isadore Tsetta similarly noted that air pollution from Giant Mine "causes me to easily get a cold and sore throat," and stated that "our land is becoming more contaminated now, and we feel they should somehow give us compensation for something – maybe some help for the water that we have to pay for." Fred Sangris, a member of the Yellowknives Dene First Nation Land and Environment Committee, also spoke of the ongoing impacts of contaminated air and water on the subsistence economy of the Tatsǫ̀t'ıné:

> Since the mine has been here in our traditional territory, we have tried to live side by side and coexist with the mining industry and the industry that inhabits our homeland. The people who live in this area have to live and use the water and the land that are around here. The harvesting has stopped over the last five years because of more dangers and warnings from the people and their leadership. We continue to tell our people not to use anything within this area, because over the years we've found that the arsenic and sulphur dioxide have done a lot of damage to our people and their health.[69]

As a follow-up to the committee hearings, Yellowknives Dene Chiefs Jonas Sangris and Darrell Beaulieu, along with Dene National Chief Bill Erasmus, wrote to the federal environment minister, Sheila Copps, to request federal regulations for arsenic (in air and water) and sulphur dioxide under CEPA. The Chiefs noted that the territorial government had refused to do so because it believed that the matter fell under Ottawa's jurisdiction.[70]

As public concern mounted, the federal and territorial governments continued to display little appetite for decisive action. At the territorial level, Renewable Resources Minister Stephen Kakfwi introduced regulations in May 1996 that would have required a 90 per cent reduction in sulphur dioxide within ten years, but his government never passed the regulations prior to Giant Mine shutting down the roaster stack in 1999. Members of the Northwest Territories Legislative Assembly may have felt some pressure owing to Royal Oak's renewed threat to close the mine.[71] As one astute letter writer to the *Yellowknifer* observed, "Royal Oak is to be given ten years to meet what are probably the most lenient sulfur dioxide emission standards on the continent and they respond by threatening to shut down rather than comply. It seems to me, Royal Oak trots out this handy-dandy threat with alarming frequency."[72] Alarming or not, the threat was certainly effective, as Royal Oak continued to pour sulphur dioxide into the Yellowknife atmosphere with impunity. In 1998, sulphur dioxide emissions in Yellowknife exceeded hourly air quality guidelines on forty-five occasions, and the yearly average was on the rise from the previous three years, hardly an indicator of progress on the issue.[73]

On the arsenic file, Minister Copps promised the Yellowknives Dene Chiefs federal action on airborne arsenic regulations in September 1995. No doubt the issue was important to Copps because Environment Canada had added arsenic to the list of priority toxic substances (highlighting its links to cancer) under CEPA in the previous year, which meant the department was required to develop an action plan to reduce exposure risks.[74] By 1997, however, any momentum for quick and decisive action had clearly been lost. Copps's department had weighed the costs and benefits of reducing arsenic emissions in Yellowknife to one kilogram per day, and concluded that the financial burden would exceed the value of the health benefits. Environment Canada was also aware of Royal Oak's threats, noting that the mine had "stated publicly several times that a requirement to spend the capital costs estimated in the report for alternate processing technologies would probably result in the closure of Giant Mine." The department had come to a different conclusion, arguing that closure was not likely because the installation and operational costs of equipment to reduce arsenic emissions by 90 to 95 per cent would have amounted to $550,000 to $707,000 annually, or just 2 per cent of the annual operating cost of the mine.[75] Another consultant's report confirmed the company's ability to handle the extra burden of pollution control: "it appears unlikely that financial considerations alone would cause Royal Oak to close the Giant Mine if required to control airborne arsenic emissions." Any additional regulations on sulphur dioxide emissions or liquid effluent "could create more serious financial challenges," the report noted; "however, cumulatively, these added costs should not significantly affect the economic viability of Giant Mine."[76] Nonetheless, Environment Canada seems to have bowed to the company's job blackmail, ultimately failing to establish an air quality standard for arsenic. Despite all the activist energy poured into the issue, Royal Oak's intransigence, and government's unwillingness to take on one of Yellowknife's biggest employers, prevented any meaningful progress on air pollution.[77]

It is difficult to assess the health impacts of largely unregulated (albeit much-reduced) pollution at Giant Mine in the 1980s and 1990s. Information about the impacts of sulphur dioxide is limited to anecdotes about tight chests and burning sensations in the lungs. Few people regarded the concerns of these few vulnerable people as worthy of a human health assessment. On the arsenic front, the territorial and federal government did make some attempts to analyze health impacts in Yellowknife in the late 1990s, but these studies relied on reductive mathematical models rather than a comprehensive epidemiological assessment of the local population. One multi-agency report produced in 1997 used a simplistic exposure/potency index to determine that current levels of drinking water contamination in Yellowknife (0.0003 parts per million of arsenic) would only result in 0.26 to 0.27 additional cases of skin cancer over a seventy-year period. A second report used occupational exposure data to estimate 0.14 to 0.86 additional deaths from lung cancer over seventy years due to airborne arsenic.[78] It is likely that the image of mere fractions of an individual dying every seven decades did little to provoke alarm among government officials, reinforcing the general apathy that characterized the regulatory response to pollution from Giant Mine.

There was still, however, no shortage of reasons to be concerned. Both of the reports that forecasted low mortality from arsenic admitted that the mathematical models did not account for the cumulative effects of multiple pathways of exposure (especially occupational exposure for many in Yellowknife), the impact of historical exposures, or the ongoing uncertainties about the health impacts of low-dose exposure to arsenic trioxide. One of the reports also highlighted the lived experience of the Tatsǫ̨t'ıné, foregrounding their concerns about long-term and combined exposures to arsenic via country food, air pollution, and water taken directly from the lake or snowmelt:

> They believe that their water is unsafe to drink, that their food (in particular the fish from Yellowknife Bay and Back Bay) is unsafe to eat, and that the air is unsafe to breathe. They base their concerns on the historical observations of the elders, and on the fact that the

> incidence of cancer appears to be rising in recent years. In particular, they noted that over the last winter, two elders who had continued to fish in Yellowknife Bay died of cancer. The community attributes these deaths to exposure to chemical contaminants from fish, and see this as further evidence of a significant health risk.[79]

Fred Sangris made similar claims about the health impacts of Giant Mine's pollution in his comments before the Standing Committee on Environment and Sustainable Development: "Over recent years a lot of our elders have been getting leukemia, cancer. We didn't really understand it until more started to get it. As we looked into it more, we realized this had something to do with the mine. No amount of money will compensate for or replace the lives that have been lost."[80]

One might look to jobs or money as some form of compensation for what the Tatsǫt'ıné had lost, but there were never many jobs or revenues to be had from the mining companies. In 1996, not a single member of the Yellowknives Dene First Nation was working at Giant Mine.[81]

Conclusion

Ultimately, Yellowknives Dene criticisms failed to resonate much with Giant Mine's owners or within the halls of government. The basic approach of government and industry, far from adopting the precautionary principle, was to limit pollution as much as the company deemed feasible and hope for the best in terms of long-term health impacts. The emphasis was on what pollution limits were achievable for Giant Mine, and not on what was actually safe for people and protective of the environment. The company's managers largely did what they pleased, because neither the territorial nor federal government imposed meaningful, enforceable air pollution limits or air quality standards in the mine's working environment or in the adjacent communities. The federal government's water licensing system did provide for some measure of regulatory control over water pollution, but Royal Oak easily obtained exceptions and variances to the rules by threatening to shut down an older mine that might not easily attract a new buyer. As a result, pollution at Giant Mine remained, for the most part, poorly regulated, and control efforts voluntary, subject to the ever-changing whims of the company. The environmentalists and Indigenous leaders who challenged Giant Mine's pollution record failed to make much of a dent in this permissive regulatory regime, even if the resurgent activism of the 1990s played an important role in raising public awareness of key health and environmental issues.

Although Royal Oak's obstinacy deserves a large share of the blame for the lack of headway on pollution control, it is also likely that activists simply ran out of time to make any meaningful progress. By the end of the 1990s, Royal Oak started to flounder financially and the end of Giant Mine became a real possibility rather than a strategic threat on the part of the company. As the company staggered towards closure, bankruptcy, and scandal, local activists, Indigenous leaders, and governments abruptly turned their attention from the problems of the present day toward the overwhelming environmental legacies that would afflict Giant Mine long after it ceased to be an operating mine.

6

The Death and Afterlife of Giant Mine

Miners and mining communities live under the omnipresent threat of industrial collapse. The whirlwind of exploration and development that accompanies the advent of a mine may just as suddenly go into reverse, with jobs, capital, wealth, and even physical infrastructure departing a mining community with little notice or time for adjustment. What mine operators leave behind in the wake of such disinvestment depends on local economic and environmental circumstances. Inevitably, however, mine abandonment results in a diminished economy for its host community (if the community survives at all), and very often an environmental mess – problems such as acid rock drainage, soil contamination, and toxic tailings ponds. Companies may clean up a shuttered mine where laws require it, though historically the public and local communities have often been saddled with environmental problems that are complex and sometimes intractable. People cope in a variety of ways: some move on to other mines or try to find work in new areas such as tourism, while others become active on environmental issues or find paid work on remediation projects. Many, however, face the twin shocks of community displacement and unemployment, unable to adjust to the collapse of everything that had sustained them. The key issues and challenges vary, but all mine workers and communities live with the dull fear that everything they have built might one day grind to a halt, leaving behind only economic deprivation and environmental threats.

By 1997, there was a growing consensus that Giant Mine and its owner, Royal Oak, were both on their last legs. Giant was only two years out from its fiftieth anniversary, a comparatively long life for a Canadian gold mine. But much of the mine's equipment and facilities had started to show their age, ore grades kept declining, environmental liabilities continued to pile up (literally, in the case of the underground arsenic), and the balance sheet of Royal Oak – widely regarded in business circles as a miracle company that turned mines nobody wanted into money makers – was stretched thin. Of course, Yellowknife in the 1990s was hardly the single-industry mining camp it had started out as in the 1930s. While mining had made up the lion's share of formal employment in Yellowknife's early days, this had fallen to 6 per cent by the end of the 1990s as jobs in government, the resource services sector, education, and health care sustained a population of over 17,000 people.[1] With almost exquisite timing, the next mining boom arrived in Yellowknife in 1998, when the Ekati Diamond Mine opened on the tundra 310 kilometres to the northeast, providing opportunities for the city's miners and service contractors. Still, Giant Mine employed roughly 300 people in 1997; the potential impact of closure on individual workers and the local economy was significant.[2]

Even more alarming was the possibility that Royal Oak might abandon Giant without addressing the mine's extraordinary environmental problems. If the company was to walk away, it would leave behind a site that was saturated with arsenic on the surface (in tailings, soil, and water), and which stored 237,000 tonnes of arsenic trioxide in five mined-out stopes and eleven purpose-built chambers (many the size of a small, multi-storey building) at depths ranging from 100 to only 10 metres below the surface.[3] As Giant's closure loomed, environmentalists, government officials, and Yellowknife community members quickly shifted from air and water pollution issues to the question of who was responsible for the mine's abandonment and restoration, expressing a growing sense of urgency as the magnitude of the post-abandonment issues became clear.

The story of Giant Mine's final collapse is a cautionary tale about how quickly and easily a mine that generated immense private wealth for some became an environmental liability for all. In many ways, Royal Oak Mines (along with the mine's previous owners) hoodwinked all of us – government regulators, Yellowknifers, and the Canadian public – running from problems that were plain to see, but which the company had neglected for decades. The scale of these environmental liabilities meant that the final closure of the Giant Mine in 2004 was not the end of the story, but the beginning of a new "afterlife" – a remediation project of such complexity that it will continue for decades, at minimum. As previous chapters have shown, environmental groups, Indigenous communities, and the Canadian public fought the mine owners' neglect of the environment and public health for decades, often pointing to the weak regulatory system that allowed arsenic trioxide pollution to proceed without caps or limits. Now, facing a massive and complex remediation project, the Yellowknife community articulated its concerns about the plans to clean up and secure what had become a toxic disaster site, working in solidarity to establish community oversight over the remediation plan and address the intergenerational "deep time" questions associated with freezing the arsenic underground for all eternity.

The Fall of Giant Mine

In November 1997, Royal Oak announced a layoff of twenty-six people at Giant Mine. Although a relatively small percentage of the total workforce of 320 people, the layoff was a sign of turbulent waters ahead.[4] The previous year, Royal Oak had managed to turn a profit of over $15 million across all its mines, but in September 1997 the company reported a loss of over $62 million for the nine months prior. This stunning reversal of fortune was the result of a declining average gold price over the period (from US$472 to $410 per ounce), combined with increasing production costs (from US$337 to $344 per ounce). The situation quickly worsened, with gold prices bottoming out at US$285 per ounce in December 1997. Amid this precarious global price environment, Royal Oak's recent growth plans started to look like a case of misplaced optimism. The company had recently invested heavily in its brand new Kemess gold and copper project in northern British Columbia, a development that severely restricted cash flow because Royal Oak was on the hook for $30 million to $50 million in essential capital costs. To tighten its belt, Royal Oak announced the imminent closures of the Colomac gold mine, located about 200 kilometres north of Yellowknife, and the Hope Brook gold mine in Newfoundland.[5] In Yellowknife, the question on everyone's mind was whether Giant Mine would be next.

Government, organized labour, and the Yellowknife business community predicted disaster if Giant Mine closed. The Northwest Territories Government Finance Department, the City of Yellowknife, the Northwest Territories Chamber of Commerce, and the Canadian Auto Workers union (whom CASAW had merged with shortly after the strike) produced a multi-stakeholder analysis that estimated 256 direct job losses, a further loss of 125 indirect jobs, and a net outmigration of 750 people (from a territory with only 41,105 people) if Giant Mine were to go under. The same study pegged revenue losses at approximately $4.2 million annually for the federal government and over $12 million for the territorial coffers (although, given the emerging diamond boom, the report's assumption that no displaced employees would find alternate jobs seemed unrealistic).[6] A second study by the Canadian Auto Workers union also highlighted the $14.6 million dollars that Giant Mine spent on labour, the $699,905 in city property taxes that would be forfeited, the probable loss of eleven teachers and three support staff in the school system owing to declining enrolment, and the potential reduction in health and social services because of the declining tax base.[7] For all that the Yellowknife economy had diversified, a shutdown at Giant Mine still promised major impacts on public services and the local workforce.

One can therefore understand why the territorial government wanted to squeeze every last drop of life out of the mine. In the first two months of 1998, the Government of the Northwest Territories organized several meetings between Giant's managers and government officials to develop an assistance plan for both Giant and Con. The meetings produced a laundry list of proposals that included property tax relief, hydro rate relief, reductions in the financial security paid toward remediation costs, an extension to timelines for underground arsenic cleanup, and direct financial assistance for exploration and development. The Government of the Northwest Territories decided on the latter option, offering a $5,000 subsidy per employee for exploration work, capped at $1.5 million per year (with the City of Yellowknife providing $150,000 of the total).[8] The government promoted the subsidies as "forward looking," suggesting (against all hope) that the money might help extend the life of Giant Mine, rather than simply help the company liquidate existing reserves.[9] At the same time, the Government of the Northwest Territories was well aware of the poor optics: a briefing document on strategic communications noted that "providing financial assistance to a gold mine which has a questionable corporate and environmental track record, despite its economic importance, presents a number of communication challenges. It is vital to distance this financial assistance agreement from Royal Oak's corporate perception and the environmental practices at Giant Mine and instead focus attention on the importance of the operation to the northern economy."[10]

If the Government of the Northwest Territories still saw a future for Giant Mine, the Northwest Territories Water Board was starting to focus on the enormous problems that closure might bring. Royal Oak had done little to inspire the board's confidence with its inconsistent approach to underground arsenic storage over the previous five years. At the public hearings for its 1993 water licence, Royal Oak was still advancing the idea that the company could just walk away from the underground arsenic. Larry Connell, the company's manager of environmental and metallurgical services, claimed that Royal Oak had purposefully built new storage chambers within known permafrost zones, and was actively pumping cold winter air into the mine to re-establish the permafrost as a barrier to arsenic leakage. The Water Board wanted to see evidence that permafrost would actually form a permanent barrier around the chambers, and thus required Royal Oak to study the issue (along with surface contamination, acid rock drainage, tailings stabilization, and erosion control in Trapper Creek) as a key component of an updated abandonment and restoration plan.[11] But by the time the preparatory phase for a new licence had arrived in 1997, Royal Oak still had not completed the study.[12] Gordon Wray, chair of the Northwest Territories Water Board, warned that "the unresolved matter of arsenic storage will come under intense public scrutiny during the renewal process and it is advisable that you can state, with certainty, the final disposition of this material."[13]

At this point Royal Oak decided on a complete shift in direction. In August 1997 the company informed the Water Board that any plan to leave the arsenic underground "would not receive widespread acceptance from government or public sources without some degree of perpetual maintenance and environmental monitoring."[14] Clearly rattled by the possibility of having to maintain the arsenic chambers forever, the company quickly organized a large workshop of consultants and government representatives (without any public or First Nations representation) to examine technical options for removing the arsenic from the chambers.[15] By the time hearings for the new water licence commenced in January 1998, Rick Allan, a Giant Mine engineer, confirmed that arsenic removal had become official company policy. He testified that the company could not just walk away from the underground arsenic in its present state because no permafrost currently surrounded the chambers and there was no evidence that there ever had been (suggesting that Connell's previous testimony about pumping cold air and careful placement of chambers in permafrost zones was a fiction). Royal Oak could freeze the chambers using thermosyphon technology (i.e., passive heat exchange tubes used frequently in the mining industry to create freeze walls as a barrier to flooding), but Allan reiterated that any requirement to pump water from the mine in perpetuity was a "large commitment" that the company did not feel was "a good permanent solution."[16] Much more palatable, from Royal Oak's perspective, was a revival of the plan to recover the arsenic and sell it on the open market along with whatever residual gold might remain in the deposits. Allan acknowledged several challenges with the approach: arsenic removal presented risks to the surrounding communities, the market for the material might be "sensitive" to the large amount of arsenic Royal Oak had on hand, techniques for "washing" residual arsenic from the storage chambers had yet to be developed, and finding a safe and suitable method for storing and processing the arsenic aboveground represented a significant challenge. Nonetheless, he anticipated that the project would be ready for environmental screening and approval in just eighteen months.[17]

Royal Oak's delays and waffling on the issue of arsenic removal prompted Indigenous representatives to take a hard line at water licence hearings held in January 1998. Fred Sangris, the Yellowknives Dene First Nation Chief in Ndilǫ, and Bill Erasmus, Dene Nation Chief, pleaded with the board not to approve Royal Oak's water licence application until the company produced a reclamation plan and an arsenic management plan that included the traditional knowledge of Elders from the community. They also recommended that the board increase the current financial security deposit for reclamation – then set at the laughably tiny amount of $400,000 – to $10 million.

Sangris reminded the board yet again of the severe impacts that the mine had brought to his community: sickness, death, and lost access to water, berries, and fish. He stated, "The Yellowknives Dene do not want a repeat of their past experience. They do not want the Mine to close and leave the arsenic where it can contaminate our water supply again. We are asking that the Water Board exercise its authority to safeguard our people, my people, and the people of Yellowknife and the Northwest Territories."[18] Bob Turner of the North Slave Métis Alliance, a group formed in 1996 to represent a cultural group often forgotten in Yellowknife, recommended a $9 million security deposit and suggested a more ambitious remediation plan: "our definition of 'restoration' would be when we see these experts out on that site drinking the water from the creeks or eating the fish from the rivers."[19]

The settler community in Yellowknife honed in on many of the same issues. Kevin O'Reilly reminded the board that the $400,000 security deposit would not cover the estimated $7 million to $9 million cost of surface cleanup, and was not even intended to fund the unknown cost of addressing the underground arsenic.[20] Chris O'Brien, representing Ecology North, recommended financial penalties for Royal Oak if the company failed to produce an abandonment and restoration plan with a proposal for managing the underground arsenic.[21] In a written submission, Northwest Territories EnviroWatch noted the risks associated with the mobilization and transport of arsenic trioxide and the moral questions raised by exporting the toxic waste elsewhere. The organization called for a thorough review of options to deal with the underground arsenic and an unspecified "maximization" of the security deposit.[22] Criticism came also from outside the local environmental community. Dave Talbot, a prominent local businessperson and self-described supporter of the mining industry, presciently argued that "putting the mine's detailed proposal [on the underground arsenic] off until May 2000 is, in my opinion, clearly a stalling tactic, designed to keep the mine in production until the owners walk away and the proven reserves are gone." Talbot warned that if Royal Oak walked away from the thousands of tons of underground arsenic and it subsequently leaked into the environment, the board could face charges of criminal negligence.[23] Although concerns continued to be raised about arsenic surface contamination and ammonia pollution, most viewed the problems with abandonment planning and underground arsenic management as so acute that they recommended that Royal Oak not receive a new water licence until the conditions of the previous one had been fulfilled. Because of these concerns, the Water Board decided to adjourn the hearings without a decision, citing a need for more time and possibly more hearings to deal with complex issues such as the security deposit and the length of the licence. The board also demanded that Royal Oak provide a complete arsenic management, and abandonment and reclamation plans by 31 March 1998 to fulfill the conditions of the previous licence.[24]

Royal Oak managed to meet this deadline, producing a report that essentially reiterated the idea of arsenic removal as the option with "the least long-term risk," even as the company admitted that it had no answers about how to mitigate the long-term impacts of residual arsenic in the chambers.[25] However, the company begged for leniency and obtained an extension of the deadline for the more comprehensive abandonment and reclamation plan to November 1998. In April, the *Yellowknifer* reported that Wray was satisfied with Royal Oak's responses to the Water Board's concerns and no longer saw the need for further public hearings.[26] The board issued a new licence to Royal Oak on 23 November 1998, one that required a security deposit of $7 million and further plans for tailings, hazardous waste, and arsenic trioxide management.[27] An abandonment and reclamation plan finally arrived in December 1998, but when the federal Department of Indian Affairs and Northern Development (DIAND) sent it to M.J. Brodie (an engineering consultant) for review, the feedback was not encouraging. Not enough had been done, according to Brodie, to ensure that the bulkheads blocking openings to the arsenic chambers would withstand the pressure of flooding (most were concrete, but a few were made from wood), or to ensure that contaminated mine water (some samples of which contained 3,600 parts per million of arsenic) would not escape the mine via fractured bedrock. Brodie also suggested that Royal Oak's plans to cap the older tailings areas were likely to fail, and the company had likely lowballed costs for soil remediation and the disposal of hazardous material. In general, the abandonment and restoration plan for Giant Mine still had "many deficiencies," according to Brodie, "and it presents some concepts with low potential for success."[28] As the mine neared the end of its life, the company had still not developed a viable and responsible plan to shut down. Recognizing this fact, Chief Erasmus implored the federal government not to bail

Figure 6.1

Concrete bulkhead for an arsenic storage chamber, 2012. The potential failure of these storage chambers spurred the proposal to freeze the arsenic underground as part of remediation.

out Royal Oak as its financial position became even more tenuous in February 1999, at least not until the company could "develop a comprehensive cleanup plan that meets the satisfaction of the Dene."[29]

Just two months later, Royal Oak imploded amid the twin pressures of debt and cash flow problems. The proximate cause was the $480 million that the company had spent to build Kemess, a mine that was its "crown jewel" but which performed well below expectations, producing only 38,789 ounces of gold, nearly 200,000 ounces short of what had been forecast.[30] Royal Oak also owed over $40.5 million to 1,400 creditors spread across Canada, ninety-six of these in Yellowknife. The size and nature of the local debts varied, everything from large amounts – $1.1 million owed to the Government of the Northwest Territories Department of Finance, another $1.1 million to the Yellowknife city government for property taxes and other bills, and $1.5 million to the Northwest Territories Power Corporation – to smaller bills for photocopying ($1,441.30), office supplies ($941.77), taxis ($49.75), and flowers ($225.50), and even a bill for $14.95 owed to Bruno's Deli and Pizza, presumably for an unpaid meal.[31] As a result, on 16 April 1999 an Ontario court placed Royal Oak into receivership and appointed PricewaterhouseCoopers (PwC) to control the company's operation and assets. Peggy Witte and the entire Royal Oak board of directors immediately jumped off the sinking ship, resigning the same day. Witte attributed Royal Oak's insolvency to misfortune rather than poor management: "It seems like every morning we would get up and wonder whether we would have some good luck this day." No matter, Witte was "ready to put the past behind me so that I can go out and be an entrepreneur again."[32]

For people in Yellowknife (and Canadians in general), putting the past behind them might not be so easy. The media had recently reported on figures from DIAND suggesting that the costs to address the underground arsenic issue would be between $50 million and $250 million – possibly running as high as $1 billion.[33] Add in a new estimate of $16 million for surface cleanup at Giant Mine, $6 million to $7.5 million to clean up Royal Oak's Colomac Mine north of Yellowknife (where a tailings pond polluted with cyanide was threatening to overflow), and $10 million to do the same at the Hope Brook mine in Newfoundland (where cyanide and waste rock piles threatened the local environment), and it was clear that the taxpaying public was potentially on the hook for massive environmental liabilities.[34] Just weeks before Royal Oak went into receivership, Andrew Spaulding, a director at Ecology North, argued, "There is no doubt that it is going to be really costly to taxpayers. If you look at the life of the mine and the benefits the mine has given to the North, I think the cost of cleaning it up is going to wipe out any benefits."[35] Patrick Howe, a Royal Oak spokesperson, responded with a statement about the company taking its environmental commitments seriously, but the poor financial situation had hobbled the company's ability to act. "It's not Royal Oak's decision to not do what is environmentally responsible," Howe stated; "it is more the position it found itself in because of circumstances beyond its control."[36] According to the company's official line, it need not take responsibility for anything – not its unpaid bills or the environmental problems at its mines – because it all could be explained away as pure hard luck.[37]

Others were less sanguine about Royal Oak effectively walking away from a looming environmental disaster. Roy Erasmus, a member of the Northwest Territories Legislative Assembly and the Yellowknives Dene First Nation, argued that the Yellowknives Dene wanted immediate action on the Giant Mine cleanup, especially to prevent arsenic trioxide from leaching into Great Slave Lake. Erasmus warned, "Environmentalists say there is enough arsenic there to kill every last human being on this planet," and accused the federal government of avoiding its responsibilities for the site.[38] Yellowknife Mayor Dave Lovell similarly called for immediate action: "We're not going to let someone study the problem for a decade. We have to have an action plan that has a definitive time frame outlined for full reclamation."[39] The Northwest Territories Federation of Labour criticized DIAND's lack of contingency planning, argued that the environmental liabilities at the mine would make it impossible to find a buyer, and asked, "Why did [the] Water Board continually renew [the] license to Royal Oak with a minimal security bond for environmental clean-up, knowing full well what the potential for arsenic contamination at the mine site involved?"[40] An editorial in the *Yellowknifer* echoed these themes, acknowledging that "the people of Canada should not have to pay for Royal Oak's crimes against nature," but unless the federal government was willing to take on the environmental liabilities at the mine, the receiver would never find a buyer and the mine would close.[41]

For its part, DIAND informed the receiver PwC in June that it might be "willing to bend" on the issue of who was responsible for cleanup at Giant Mine.[42] By the end of summer, the situation had become desperate, as PwC had failed to find a buyer and planned to shut down the mine on 27 September.[43] Earlier, the Canadian Auto Workers had hatched a scheme to buy the mine and save the jobs on site, but concluded that its proposal was not economically viable.[44] As a result, PwC practically gave away the mine to a cross-town neighbour, Miramar Mining Corporation, the current operator of Con Mine, selling for a nominal fee of ten dollars in December 1999. As part of the deal, the new owner assumed none of Giant Mine's existing environmental liabilities, but was required to contribute $425,000 towards reclaiming the site and $500,000 for further exploration on the Giant and Con properties (an amount to be matched through a shared subsidy from DIAND, the Government of the Northwest Territories, and the City of

Yellowknife). Miramar also agreed to assume the cost of ongoing environmental maintenance at the site, especially work necessary to meet water licensing requirements. In turn, the territorial government provided a generous $750,000 subsidy to Miramar to offset the cost of property taxes at Giant Mine (the company received the same amount for Con Mine).[45] For all this, Miramar planned a modest operation, digging up small amounts of ore with a skeletal staff of about fifty people and transporting it to Con for processing at facilities that included an autoclave to transform arsenic trioxide to a less toxic state.[46] As part of the agreement, PwC agreed to terminate all Giant Mine workers, allowing Miramar to avoid any severance or pension liabilities and then "cherry pick" the few employees needed to run what amounted to a salvage operation. The new owner did not need Giant's workers and did not want its crumbling infrastructure; the once mighty Giant Mine would operate as a shadow of its former self.[47]

On 12 November 1999, Giant Mine ceased to operate as a full-scale mining operation as PwC issued the final layoff notices and shut the gates in preparation for Miramar's transformation of the site into a minor satellite of Con Mine. PwC had already laid off much of the former workforce throughout the fall, whittling the staffing numbers down to the planned complement of fifty by the middle of November. One worker who was handed a pink slip said he had been employed "eighteen years at that mine, and I got one hour's notice before the end of my shift. I didn't even have time to move my tool box."[48] Some of the laid-off miners headed south for training on mine reclamation at a college in Alberta, hoping to obtain work on the Giant Mine Remediation Project. Others hoped to fill vacancies at the Lupin gold mine in the newly created territory of Nunavut.[49] Some stayed in town, frequently visiting the Canadian Auto Workers union hall in Yellowknife to get help with job applications and advice on education and training programs.[50]

On Giant Mine's last day, several members of the territorial New Democratic Party and the media came to talk with the remaining miners, and security told them to leave. Wayne Campbell, president of the Northwest Territories Federation of Labour, told the CBC it was "the typical Royal Oak scenario right to the bitter end ... I am really kind of glad they showed their true colours here on the final day for the cameras and this is just typical attitudes we have had to put up with since Royal Oak took over

Figure 6.2

The iconic Robertson headframe at the Con Mine site in Yellowknife, now demolished. Con Mine operator Miramar processed gold ore from the Giant site between 2000 and 2004, when it, too, closed.

the place in 1990." An unidentified worker expressed a kind of solemn relief as he left: "I am just glad it is over. I have been waiting so long. I have been waiting months and months, rumour after rumour. We are going to hit the bar and celebrate for a few hours."[51] In June of 2000, Giant's workers also likely celebrated the fact that the Canadian Auto Workers had managed to protect enough of their pension fund during the receivership process that retirees would now receive 82 per cent of what they would have, had

Royal Oak remained solvent.[52] But this was only one small, partial win in a series of setbacks that had hurled the mine's workers toward a very uncertain future.

Despite the pretense of abandonment and reclamation planning, Royal Oak ultimately walked away from the environmental problems at the mine. While the underground arsenic loomed as the largest and most complex issue on the site, there were many others. Giant Yellowknife Mines had dumped arsenic-laden mine tailings on the shores of Great Slave Lake between 1948 and 1950 (the so-called Beach Tailings area, created prior to the development of contained tailings ponds). In 1999 these tailings continued to erode into Great Slave Lake, while the tailings impoundment needed some kind of cap to prevent the leaching of arsenic and other heavy metals and the spread of contaminants through wind erosion. The mine complex also contained a vast collection of contaminated buildings, industrial chemicals, and other dangerous material: thirty-nine tanks containing 5.6 million litres of fuel and lubricants, 3,500 drums of waste petroleum stored at four sites, mill reagents and assay chemicals (sodium cyanide, copper sulphate, hydrogen peroxide, fire suppressants, etc.) stored in five major use areas, and ANFO explosives left underground. Waste material such as scrap metal, old tires, used vehicles, broken machinery, waste oil, old batteries, and drums containing arsenic trioxide, cyanide, and asbestos had been dumped into tailings ponds, old pits, and a landfill. Of the 100 buildings on the site, many were contaminated with asbestos (possibly 2,000 cubic metres of the deadly material), and the old roaster complex was infused with arsenic contamination. Dangerous polychlorinated biphenyls (PCBs) were present in heavy electrical equipment. At many places on the site, contaminants (PCBs, arsenic, and hydrocarbons) had leaked into the underlying soils. Baker Creek constantly flowed through the site, carrying contaminated runoff from the tailings and surface area to Great Slave Lake.[53] Amid all of these problems, there was one environmental benefit associated with the shutdown: Yellowknife's air quality improved almost immediately after the gold roaster permanently ceased operations, with some residents reporting an end to their asthma symptoms.[54] Most environmental problems at Giant Mine did not disappear so easily, however, and would instead require a massive (and massively expensive) cleanup operation.

Taming a Monster

Giant Mine's owners, past and present, were off the hook for the existing environmental mess, but the question of who was responsible for cleanup remained unresolved for months amid intergovernmental negotiations. The Government of the Northwest Territories had sought legal advice and initially adopted the position that, as the historical regulator of mines in the territory, the federal government, specifically DIAND, was responsible for all the mine's environmental liabilities. Complicating this analysis, however, was the fact that the lands leased to Giant had been transferred to the Government of the Northwest Territories in 1970. As a result, the two levels of government reached a compromise to share the costs of surface cleanup, albeit with the federal government assuming just over 70 per cent of the annual budget. The responsibility for the underground arsenic was more clear cut: the federal government had sole jurisdiction over subsurface mineral rights and therefore had no choice but to assume the massive bill and the technical challenges that would accompany any solution to the problem of underground arsenic.[55] DIAND also assumed from Miramar all of the costs (approximately $3 million) of ongoing environmental compliance at the mine, an incentive to keep the company from pulling out after the initial agreement on operating Giant Mine expired in December 2002.[56]

Amid all of this wrangling, the Yellowknives Dene communities lobbied for some measure of input on, and benefits from, remediation activities. By this point, the Yellowknives Dene First Nation owned an environmental cleanup firm, Det'on Cho Corporation, and company president Darrell Beaulieu and Ndilǫ Chief Fred Sangris argued that Indigenous Northerners should be the ones guiding and completing the remediation. Det'on Cho Corporation did conduct the initial surface assessment that produced a cost estimate of $16 million (and obtained a great deal of subsequent contract work on the remediation project), but DIAND was far from willing to share decision-making power over the remediation project with First Nations or the general public in Yellowknife.[57] Indeed, the department's remediation team equated its assumption of responsibility with near-total control over the remediation effort, a stance the Yellowknives Dene, the City of Yellowknife, and general citizens would challenge as the project moved forward.

DIAND's preferred approach to the arsenic issue was diametrically opposed to Royal Oak's. Rather than remove the underground arsenic, DIAND officials reprised the idea of entombing, for all time, the arsenic chambers in ice. But instead of waiting in vain for permafrost to return, project engineers would create their own artificial ice by encircling each of the fifteen arsenic chambers with thermosyphons – passive heat exchange tubes that would protrude from the ground as if each cluster were a grove of branchless white trees. The resulting landscape promised to evoke something straight out of science fiction (with the thermosyphons even bearing some resemblance to the white moisture vaporators of the *Star Wars* desert planet Tatooine). While such a technological intervention might inspire some confidence in the project manager's ability to control a dangerous environment, the new "freeze it and leave it" approach also presented some long-term problems. To be sure, the frozen chambers would contain the arsenic in the short term and avoid the very real risks associated with mobilizing such a massive amount of toxic material. Nonetheless, Giant Mine's new stewards would still have to pump groundwater for treatment, and to ensure that the water table would not rise above the level of the chambers. Project managers would have to replace the thermosyphons every twenty to thirty years, owing to wear and tear and to ensure, in the absence of a return to "natural" permafrost conditions, that the chambers remained frozen. Any breakdown and abandonment of the system would result in rising groundwater, the melting of the chambers (within a couple of decades), and the potential dissolution of 237,000 tons of arsenic trioxide into surrounding rivers and lakes.[58] DIAND's so-called "frozen block" method thus carried with it an obligation for perpetual care of the mine, a project timeline that stretched into the unimaginable future. Under the frozen block plan, the arsenic would present a deep time problem akin to that of nuclear waste, raising profound questions about how to communicate the underground arsenic threat across vast spans of time.[59]

DIAND's formal adoption of the frozen block method came very quickly after it assumed control over Giant Mine. In June 1999, the department assembled a group of scientific experts in Yellowknife to consider options for remediating the underground arsenic. While this group came up with a range of approaches (i.e., hot water leaching, processing to a less toxic form in an autoclave, removal via sublimation, bioleaching, treating the arsenic with microwaves to transform it into glass or non-toxic metal), the freezing option featured prominently in a public information bulletin and the delegates expressed strong support for some kind of stabilization-in-place approach.[60] Another technical workshop in June 2001 – one that included some members of the public and First Nations – examined several options for removing the arsenic, but Daryl Hockley, the senior project lead with SRK Consulting, made it clear that the government preferred the freeze-in-place option because it "poses lower risks than any of the other alternatives and is the lowest cost alternative." Indeed, as Hockley argued, "the maximum cost(s) for this alternative is significantly below the minimum net costs for the others."[61] By December 2002, DIAND had whittled the options down to just two: freeze the arsenic in place or remove it and encapsulate it in concrete or bitumen. A report on the remaining arsenic management alternatives tilted heavily in favour of the frozen block method, suggesting that it was low risk and had a price tag of only $90 million to $120 million, as opposed to the high risk and much higher cost ($230 million to $280 million) for the removal and encapsulation option.[62] After two more multi-stakeholder workshops (in January and May 2003), eighteen public meetings, a review by an independent peer-review panel, and reports from a technical advisory committee, DIAND concluded that "the freezing option is the most widely preferred in-situ management alternative," and thus adopted this approach as the centrepiece of the Giant Mine Remediation Project.[63]

While DIAND's attempts at public consultation have appeared to be laudable, the department's claims of social consensus for the freeze option were more manufactured than real. Certainly, there was some support for the freeze option, most notably from four territorial members of the Legislative Assembly who endorsed the approach publicly.[64] People who lived in and near Yellowknife were aware of the risks associated with the mobilization and removal of the arsenic, not least because they were the ones who would face the consequences of a spill or release of arsenic into the air. Yet many who spoke at the public consultation expressed concerns about the long-term consequences of the "freeze it and leave it" approach. At the June 2001 workshop, some participants argued that removing the arsenic was too risky, while others "expressed the concern that this generation received the benefits of the gold extraction and that it would be irresponsible to not address the arsenic problem."[65] A summary of the workshop's breakout group discussions and subsequent focus group research revealed other concerns. How would the federal government ensure funding for perpetual care of the arsenic chambers over very long periods of time? Would there be funding for ongoing research into management alternatives? Had the project proponents considered the threat of a seismic event? How could freezing and leaving the arsenic be reconciled with ethical obligations to future generations? What would happen if the power went out and stopped the pump? Could the arsenic then leak into the lake?[66]

Consultations in Ndilǫ and Dettah in January 2003 brought even more pointed criticism of the proposal. Reanna Erasmus raised the possibility that an earthquake or climate change might represent a threat to future generations, noting that "when they started putting arsenic trioxide into the chambers fifty years ago, they didn't realize what the problems would be. We don't know what problems there will be fifty years from now."[67] Sangris argued that, even with the arsenic contained underground, "our people will continue to be afraid and to live in fear. The proposals are band-aid solutions and you are going to walk away. At the end of the day, you people are going to decide to leave it there, leave the time-bomb there but who will be responsible?"[68] The Yellowknives Dene also reiterated their concerns about arsenic contamination at the surface and argued that remediation ought to include restorative compensation for the historical health and environmental impacts of arsenic trioxide in their communities. Chief Darrell Beaulieu stated that "we don't agree with just focusing on the 237,000 tonnes of arsenic. People see the whole mine, not just certain parts of it. People aren't blind – arsenic isn't just in those chambers. Everyone who grew up here, the elders, they know that it is everywhere on top. There are lots of very strong feelings about the mine and the things that have happened over the years."[69] Rachel Crapeau emphasized that the issue of compensation for these past injustices was a "huge issue," noting that people in the communities were still paying for water delivery. Alfred Baillargeon similarly argued that his people would never give up on asking for compensation because the mine had compromised their ability to live off the land: "The water is ruined in Back Bay area for future generations. What will future generations use to survive? They won't be able to eat fish at all. There is no place for future generations to turn to for their survival."[70] Chief Beaulieu further emphasized this point, contending that any remediation program must consider the broad impacts of Giant Mine on the Yellowknives Dene: "We don't want a band-aid solution but a long-term solution that respects the health and safety of the people. The issues are still the same. Nothing has changed. The issues for the Yellowknives are longstanding and will take a lot of work to resolve."[71] For the Yellowknives Dene, the frozen block solution seemed to almost underscore the historical indifference of government and industry to the health of their land and people; any attempt to remediate the mine without addressing broader issues of environmental health, financial compensation, and the condition of the land in relation to subsistence harvesting was clearly insufficient.

In February 2004, DIAND's Giant Mine remediation team announced the adoption of the frozen block method without really addressing these concerns. The territorial government formally agreed to the freezing option through a cooperation agreement signed in 2005.[72] The Government of the Northwest Territories likely found the agreement attractive because it limited its liability for Giant Mine to $23 million. It also declared that the site would be remediated to an industrial land use standard, much to the chagrin of the City of Yellowknife, which had hoped to develop recreational amenities, especially a marina, at the mine's abandoned housing complex. Three years later, the full "Giant Mine Remediation Plan" outlined in detail the plan to freeze the arsenic chambers, using "active" refrigeration pipes (similar to what is used for indoor skating rinks) to establish the initial subterranean frost, and then replacing them with "passive" thermosyphon tubes capable of maintaining the freeze wall without any energy inputs, even in the most extreme climate change scenarios. The plan also contained detailed proposals for surface cleanup – capping the tailings ponds, backfilling the open pits with waste rock, stabilizing the tailings deposits on the shore of Back Bay, rerouting Baker Creek (so that there was no risk of flooding one of the open pits), removing soils contaminated with arsenic and hydrocarbons (to be deposited in one of the open pits in a section that sits on top of two of the frozen chambers), demolishing most buildings, and treating both surface and underground water to minimize arsenic discharges into Yellowknife Bay.[73]

Remarkably, however, the plan did not contain any detailed analysis of the challenges of trying to contain such a large amount of toxic material

Figure 6.3
Thermosyphon test plot at Giant Mine, 2011. This air exchange technology is designed to keep the ground, including arsenic chambers, permanently frozen.

Figure 6.4
Underground test freezing, 2011. This "active" freezing uses refrigeration to restore or mimic permafrost surrounding the underground arsenic chambers.

through the vast gulf of deep time. After so many public consultation sessions in which people had raised fears about the "forever" nature of the project and ethical obligations to future generations, the remediation plan remained resolutely silent on the issue of perpetual care. And for those who had advocated for a more permanent solution to the underground arsenic problem, the remediation plan failed by not defining the frozen block method as a provisional containment strategy – one that could buy time until a more permanent solution could be developed, as the City of Yellowknife had proposed in its recommended principles for the remediation of Giant Mine.[74] For DIAND, the freeze method *was the only permanent solution*, even if the project would have to be managed for all eternity.

Despite the obvious controversy, DIAND was loath to surrender its authority over the remediation project to any form of public oversight or local control. While DIAND officials might have argued that, as a government department, they represented the broad public interest, their role also raised the confounding problem of the department serving as both the proponent and regulator of the project, a conflict of interest that seemed to cry out for external oversight. Nonetheless, in its remediation plan, DIAND committed to only the most cursory forms of public involvement: more public information sessions and opportunities for the public to ask questions, but no public oversight or power sharing with local authorities. Indeed, the cooperation agreement had already excluded the City of Yellowknife from decision-making processes, committing the federal department only to discussing issues that affected municipal services and city-leased land. DIAND's refusal to share power seemed particularly glaring with respect to the First Nations who had been so negatively impacted by the mines. The authors of the remediation plan had boldly proclaimed that they had incorporated traditional knowledge into their work, but did not mention even one specific example where this had been done.[75] In general, as Kevin O'Reilly recalled, local exasperation with the superficial nature of public consultations on the remediation plan had been building steadily since 1999:

> There was a series of successive workshops run as consultation sessions where the federal government and its consultants presented findings and options but with very little public input in-between and

> little or no involvement in the development of evaluation criteria and selection of preferred alternatives. Materials were often not provided ahead of time, no participant funding was provided to help parties obtain independent technical advice, and there was very little flexibility shown by the government in fully assessing new or preferred alternatives as expressed by workshop participants. In no way could this process be compared to principles of free, prior and informed consent or consultation and accommodation in terms of the federal government's fiduciary obligation to Aboriginal people.[76]

Mounting frustration and apprehension prompted a remarkable convergence of interests and resistance among the City of Yellowknife and the Yellowknives Dene First Nation, governments that had not often worked toward common cause in the past. At the urging of the Yellowknives Dene First Nation, local member of the legislative assembly Bob Bromley, and former city councillor O'Reilly, the Yellowknife city council decided in March 2008 to refer the Giant Mine Remediation Project's water licence application to a mandatory environmental assessment by the Mackenzie Valley Environmental Impact Review Board (MVEIRB). While the board had resisted an environmental assessment, claiming it would be a costly delay to a project that had been "studied to death," Mayor Gordon Van Tighem noted that Giant Mine was located on municipal lands and that the project "may have significant adverse effects on the environment in the city." Thus the Mackenzie Valley Resource Management Act granted the municipal government the power to mandate an environmental assessment.[77] Yellowknives Dene representatives argued that the environmental assessment would "provide the City and the YKDFN [Yellowknives Dene First Nation] with an open and independent process," one that could address ongoing apprehension about "issues of plan design, implementation, and oversight all being within the same department; the sheer magnitude and complexity of the project; the potential impacts should the remediation plan not work as expected; determining whether the targeted remediation levels are appropriate; and lastly, the long-term issues associated with what the YKDFN feels what is at best, a temporary solution to a long lasting problem."[78] At a special meeting of the city council to discuss the issue, O'Reilly raised similar concerns about the temporary nature of the frozen block method:

> The most important thing to me in cleaning up or managing the Giant mine is to minimize perpetual care requirements so that fifty, 500, or 5,000 years in the future, someone does not need to know how to replace thermosyphons or activate a freezing system. The plan does not do that but sets up a perpetual care situation with no commitment to on-going research and development, or for independent oversight. This is not the kind of future I want to leave for generations to come in Yellowknife.[79]

Clearly, DIAND's promotion of the frozen block method as a permanent solution had failed to persuade local governments and the activist community in Yellowknife. Now the proponents would have to defend their plan before an environmental assessment, a process that would include extensive public input through written submissions and open hearings.

The environmental assessment process also enabled local groups to make creative use of intervenor funding (even if such funding was sometimes difficult to obtain) to produce alternative perspectives on the remediation project. In many ways, the research initiatives of civil society and Indigenous governments were attempts to answer tough questions that had been omitted from the official remediation planning process. Particularly active in these efforts was Alternatives North, an environmental and social justice group (with whom O'Reilly was a founding member),[80] and the Yellowknives Dene First Nation. In 2011, Alternatives North published two commissioned research reports on the theory and practice of perpetual care at a selection of contaminated sites (Love Canal, the Hanford Nuclear Reservation, the Zortman and Landusky mines, and Port Radium) and at deep geological nuclear waste repositories such as the Waste Isolation Pilot Plant in Carlsbad, New Mexico. These reports asked the basic question that previous remediation plans for Giant had largely ignored: How will future generations know about, and know how to maintain (or avoid), perpetually contaminated sites?[81] In September 2011, Alternatives North and the Yellowknives Dene First Nation hosted a community workshop on perpetual care that identified the challenges of maintaining a site such as Giant Mine over the long term, including communicating the arsenic hazard to future generations, whether through stories, signs, symbols, or archives.[82] Alternatives North also commissioned a report on various financial mechanisms to ensure long-term funding for perpetual care (with trust funds and endowments being the most stable arrangements), and another report that argued that independent oversight was critical to maintaining public trust in the project.[83] Perhaps most importantly, the Yellowknives Dene First Nation produced a traditional knowledge report that recorded community members' observations of the social and environmental impacts that a half-century of mining had brought to their traditional territories – insights they felt had been excluded from the remediation planning process.[84]

Still, DIAND showed little willingness to incorporate public input or consider new approaches to the remediation project. In October 2010, the department submitted its voluminous *Developer's Assessment Report* (DAR), a required element of the environmental assessment process in which the project proponent essentially summarizes potential environmental impacts and the plans to address them. Despite the apprehension in Yellowknife, Ndilǫ, and Dettah about the long-term risks of freezing the arsenic, the DAR adopted a very short-term, twenty-five-year time span for the project (fifteen years to implement the freeze plan and then only ten years for monitoring). The plan ignored any perpetual care issues that might arise after that period, saying they would be "considered in the future by the relevant regulatory authorities."[85] The DAR also dismissed concerns about the potential long-term failure of the thermosyphons, claiming that once frozen, the chambers could withstand flood, earthquake, and climate change. The only conceivable way the system could fail, according to DIAND, would be via a "complete breakdown of civil order," a circumstance that "would presumably entail more immediate risks to both the environment and human health."[86] The DAR acknowledged the economic and environmental impacts of Giant Mine on the Yellowknives Dene, but declared the historical "legacy issues" as being outside the scope of the environmental assessment.[87] DIAND was also largely unwilling to budge on governance; the DAR merely restated that a federal–territorial committee of government officials would maintain oversight over the project, and Indigenous traditional knowledge would be incorporated for some monitoring and restoration activities (such as revegetating Baker Creek).[88] While DIAND's refusal to engage with public anxieties about the project did little to build public support, trust was also at a low ebb by the end of the environmental assessment process because of DIAND's less than transparent practices: hiving off smaller parts of the project (such as the site stabilization plan) to avoid the scrutiny of the environmental assessment, stonewalling the environmental assessment process (including thirteen occasions when the federal and territorial governments had requested delays or extensions), and a tendency to conceal information, such as the revelation in March 2012 that the project proponents had kept secret a revised cost estimate that doubled the price tag for the project from $449 million to $903 million.[89] As the environmental assessment process drew to a close, the remediation project seemed to be repeating an old pattern: barrelling ahead with a development project while paying little heed to the people who lived nearby.

If DIAND (by now renamed the Department of Aboriginal Affairs and Northern Development, or AANDC) still maintained doubts about the depth of public anger and skepticism over its approach, public environmental assessment hearings held over five days in September 2012 should have finally dispelled them. On the first day of hearings, O'Reilly expressed frustration that, after more than four years of engagement with the environmental assessment, "there's been little progress made on the issue of trust." Speaking on behalf of Alternatives North, he claimed that too many of AANDC's public workshops on the remediation project had been devoted to the dissemination of information rather than the gathering of public input.[90] Sangris similarly wondered aloud why the Yellowknives Dene First Nation's requests for health studies and a more permanent solution for the arsenic problem had been ignored. "We made a lot of good recommendations," Sangris testified, "but sometimes we're ignored. It's as if this isn't our homeland any more. It's as if we don't exist."[91] Sangris, and many other Yellowknives Dene First Nation Elders, reminded government officials at the hearings of the dire historical impacts of arsenic on the Yellowknives Dene, and repeated the longstanding call for financial compensation and free water to be provided to the residents of Dettah and Ndilǫ.[92] AANDC continued to insist that such legacy issues were outside the scope of the remediation project (which, technically, they were, according to the Review Board mandate), even if the testimony of the Tatsǫ́t'ıné provided a vital explanation for their mistrust of government activities at Giant Mine.

Most Yellowknives Dene First Nation members and Yellowknife residents who testified at the hearings remained doubtful of AANDC's assurances that the project would have no adverse environmental impacts. They wanted more studies to allay their fears about the impact of dumping contaminated effluent (containing up to 0.1 parts per million of arsenic) directly into Back Bay, and the effect on winter ice safety of an underwater diffuser meant to dilute the effluent (resulting in the generation of turbulence and heat). Critics also highlighted the risks associated with tearing down contaminated buildings, as well as ongoing human health risks associated with arsenic. Hearing participants repeatedly called for independent oversight of the remediation project, coupled with a binding agreement between AANDC and local governments outlining clear commitments to mitigating environmental impacts. The vast majority of the public presenters at the hearings also disputed the idea that the frozen block method represented a permanent solution to the underground arsenic problem. They implored AANDC to produce a perpetual care plan, combined with a strategy for communicating the plan to future generations, if no permanent solution could be found in the foreseeable future.[93] Mary Rose Sundberg, a band councillor from Dettah, emphasized this point when she spoke "on behalf of my future generations that are not yet born," raising fears about the prospect of living with a "forever" project and the need to pass on knowledge of the underground arsenic "monster" through stories and other messages etched into the landscape.[94] In general, the fractious nature of the hearings largely confirmed O'Reilly's assertion that the project had no support from the Yellowknives Dene First Nation or the City of Yellowknife, and "we [Alternatives North] don't think there is actually a social license to carry it out."[95]

AANDC officials often tried to side-step these public concerns. On the first day of the hearings, Adrian Paradis, one of the project managers, claimed that the remediation plan already included a perpetual care plan (because, he reasoned, the frozen blocks would last a long time) and a plan for community oversight, even though critics had clearly pointed out that these were insufficient. Later that same day, the chair of the MVEIRB had to remind AANDC officials to provide clear answers to questions from the public.[96] On the second day, faced with criticisms from Alternatives North about the plans for effluent dumping and the diffuser in Back Bay, Paradis said, "I understand the cause for concerns, but a lot of it comes from a lack of understanding."[97] Such comments must have been a difficult pill to swallow for community activists who had expended so much volunteer time and energy educating themselves about the project and researching best practices for complex mine remediation projects.

For AANDC, the local resistance, coupled with the MVEIRB's powers to impose binding measures on the remediation project, carried significant potential to derail the project timeline. Unlike in decades past, when the settler community dominated regulatory bodies such as the Northwest Territories Water Board, most of the MVEIRB members (six out of seven) were Indigenous Northerners; two of these, Rachel Crapeau and Richard Edjericon, had played leadership roles within the Yellowknives Dene First Nation and had previously been critical of Giant Mine and AANDC.[98] Accordingly, AANDC's final comments to the MVEIRB tried to hit all the right notes in response to community concerns, including promises to develop a perpetual care plan, consider the question of communicating with future generations, and create an independent environmental monitoring committee (albeit one that would only be advisory in nature). However, AANDC's cursory discussion of these issues provided little detail on what these activities might look like and left the distinct impression that they were last-minute efforts to placate critics of the remediation plan. Indeed, AANDC maintained that existing bodies within government – the Federal Treasury Board, the Auditor General, and the MVEIRB – provided enough formal oversight for the project, implicitly rejecting the idea of a local oversight board with the authority to enforce environmental standards. On the key issue of the frozen block method, the remediation team somewhat bizarrely claimed "there was wide support for the ground freezing approach as the best option available at this time," even if most of the public participants in the hearings raised fears about a catastrophic failure of the freeze blocks at some point in the distant future.[99] Despite AANDC's last-ditch effort to persuade the MVEIRB that it had adequately addressed local concerns about the project, if anything the department's final submission underscored the disconnect between the department's priorities and those of the Yellowknife-area communities, and the fact that the project had been guided by engineering and technical priorities, rather than social considerations.

The MVEIRB's release of its final report on the environmental assessment in June 2013 marked a clear victory for the critics of the remediation project. Contrary to AANDC's claim that the project was environmentally benign, the report concluded "that the proposed Giant Mine Remediation

Project is likely to cause significant adverse impacts on the environment, including cumulative impacts raising from the potential effects of the Project in combination with the effects of past activities. The Review Board also finds that significant public concern related to these impacts exists."[100] Accordingly, the board imposed twenty-six binding measures on the remediation project and sixteen additional suggestions. Probably the most important of these was the recasting of the frozen block method as an interim measure limited to a timeline of 100 years. In addition, the board required the project team to commission an independent review of the project every twenty years to assess progress toward a permanent solution. The board also mandated that a risk assessment be conducted "to properly predict and prepare for risks within the 100 year timeframe."[101] There were other important wins for community activists, including the requirement for an environmental agreement between the project proponents and local groups (similar to agreements already in place at Northwest Territories diamond mines), the development of an independent oversight board to enforce the provisions of that environmental agreement, a requirement for ongoing research and development into more permanent solutions than the frozen block method, and the creation of a plan for sustainable project financing. The board also ordered a human health survey to assess any possible impacts owing to project activities, and the treatment of effluent released into Back Bay so it would contain 0.01 parts per million of arsenic (instead of the previously mentioned plan to release water with ten times the amount of arsenic and to dilute it with a diffuser). Finally, the board mandated the diversion of Baker Creek away from the project area to reduce risks from flooding.[102] After more than a year of further deliberation and negotiations over the modification of the MVEIRB's proposed measures, Bernard Valcourt, the minister of AANDC, accepted all twenty-six of the binding measures with only minor modifications. In June 2015 the federal and territorial governments signed an environmental agreement with the Yellowknives Dene First Nation, the City of Yellowknife, Alternatives North, and the North Slave Métis Alliance that set out standards for independent oversight of the project through the newly created Giant Mine Oversight Board.[103] Over fifteen years after the collapse of Royal Oak, it appeared that a comprehensive effort to address Giant Mine's toxic legacies might finally begin.

Conclusion

The environmental assessment of the Giant Mine Remediation Project represented a dramatic shift away from prevailing top-down approaches to managing the site. For the first time, communities in the Yellowknife area had a formal agreement setting environmental standards for the cleanup, and an oversight role to ensure compliance with that agreement. The environmental assessment also broke new ground by imposing an unusually long time frame on the project, and by recognizing that a mere containment and abandonment strategy for large amounts of toxic material does not constitute a viable remediation strategy over the long term. If one was looking for hope amid the bleak history of Giant Mine, the final result of the environmental assessment process is probably the best place to find it. In an age of populist disdain for government, social media–fuelled political polarization, and skepticism around regulatory review processes, the Giant Mine environmental assessment is an important reminder of what can be achieved when informed citizens meet face-to-face, air their concerns thoughtfully, focus on factual information, and push for change.[104] If the process was, at times, painstakingly slow, the end result was a victory for local democracy in Yellowknife, a remarkable instance in which citizens effectively forced a historically aloof federal government to rewrite its plans.

The victory was a testament to the unwavering determination of Indigenous, environmental, and social justice advocates in Yellowknife. As with the arsenic controversy of the 1970s and the air pollution activism of the 1980s and 1990s, the grassroots coalition that fought the original design of the Giant Mine Remediation Project represented what historian Robert Gottlieb has identified as "alternative environmentalists": local activists who focus on "people and place," and who "accomplish change by being ornery, argumentative, mistrustful, and by mobilizing their base, often against one or another dimension of ... [the] environmental policy system."[105] Yellowknife was not a homogenous community with singular interests; the historical division between the settler and Indigenous communities, or newcomers and old-timers, has always loomed large. But the grassroots campaign for more local control over the remediation project featured another remarkable alliance between Yellowknife residents and Indigenous communities. Both groups rejected the remediation project precisely because it carried dark echoes of the history of the top-down decision making and colonial dispossession that had featured so prominently in the fraught history of Giant Mine. While the remediation team preferred to think of their work as a technical exercise, local activists thought it should also repair broken social and ecological relationships – between people and the land, between Indigenous and settler communities, between industry and community, and between present and future generations. Crucially, the opponents of the original remediation plan did not reject science and expertise (in fact they used both quite effectively), but they understood that the key issues at Giant Mine revolved around moral and political questions that ought to be resolved through a public, participatory process. They also advocated for the inclusion of local and Indigenous knowledge and expertise in all facets of the project, from the selection of remediation approaches to the challenges of perpetual care. Faced with what is likely Canada's worst contaminated site, Yellowknife's activists approached the mine remediation project as a means to reconcile with past injustices and to reckon with Giant Mine's uncertain future.

Conclusion

> People love the land, but mining has changed the land and made it dangerous.
>
> – ELDER MICHEL PAPER[1]

It is unusual to reach the final pages of a historical book, only to be told that the authors don't know how the story ends. As we write these final pages, the Giant Mine Remediation Project is well underway, having spent $710 million (including $331 million to Indigenous contractors) as of November 2022, mostly to complete important surface cleanup activities such as soil remediation, capping tailings ponds, filling the mine pits, and demolishing most buildings. But the work at Giant Mine is far from finished; the new end date for active remediation is pegged at 2038, and cost projections, as mentioned previously, have more than quadrupled from $1 billion to $4.38 billion.[2] Long-term uncertainty about the ultimate fate of the underground arsenic could remain for decades, centuries, or even millennia. Only one of the arsenic chambers has been frozen (the original test plot). At the time of writing, no official strategy has been developed to communicate this toxic hazard to future generations and ensure long-term transmission of the knowledge base that may be necessary for the site's perpetual care. Even if a plan to remove the arsenic can be developed, ensuring continuity in the site's management over the "best case" scenario of a century will be a tremendous challenge.

Important questions also remain about the risks and challenges of "off-site" pollution from the estimated 20 million kilograms of arsenic released over Giant's operational life. Numerous studies over the past twenty years have documented the accumulation of arsenic in soils in the Yellowknife vicinity. As geochemist Heather Jamieson noted, "Most of the arsenic trioxide in the soils is more than 50 years old, persisting from early stack emissions despite its high solubility and the expectation that arsenic trioxide would have dissolved after years of soil exposure."[3] Similarly, studies of local waterways, including Yellowknife Bay, highlight the long-term threat posed by potential remobilization of arsenic from sediments.[4] Arsenic and heavy metal contamination has had, and continues to exhibit, "multi-trophic" ecological impacts in some local lakes, from which biological assemblages have never recovered.[5] Little wonder, then, that Tatsǫ̀t'ıné land users continue to express concerns about hunting, gathering, and using water from the land up to twenty kilometres or farther from the former mine site. Testimony from land users indicates that they still see danger from the pollution of plants, animals, and waters, a continuing sense of unease, even alienation from their traditional lands that has forced some to travel further afield to engage in harvesting activities.[6]

In response to these concerns, the Giant Mine Remediation Project funded a Human Health and Ecological Risk Assessment in 2018. The study, which included participation by the Yellowknives Dene First Nation and the North Slave Métis Alliance, concluded that the risk to human health from typical arsenic exposure pathways (including the consumption of country foods) remained negligible, despite elevated arsenic levels in some soils, plants, and surface waters. It also confirmed Ndilǫ on Latham Island as the most contaminated area of the region, and suggested potential soil remediation for the community. Finally, the report noted that the remediation work at the former mine would have little impact on environmental arsenic levels beyond the mine site itself.[7]

Yellowknives Dene critics noted that the health assessment provided little insight into the effects of past exposures on local communities. Echoing Kingsley Kay's comments from decades earlier, the study's lead researcher, Dr Laurie Chan, agreed, telling the media that "we should have started the study way back in the '50s, or in the '70s, when the mine was in full operation."[8] Chan also noted that it was no longer possible to trace the historical medical impacts of arsenic trioxide pollution because arsenic does not stay in the body very long, making it impossible to identify even those who ingested large amounts or suffered from chronic exposure over decades. Tracking any elevated cancer rates is also difficult in a place such as Yellowknife, where so many miners moved away from the community, and many Elders who lived through the periods of the most intense arsenic exposure in the 1950s have passed on. Even if we had good records of cancer rates and deaths among those who lived in Yellowknife during the gold roasting era, it would be difficult to know which individual cases could be attributed to arsenic exposure.

Even so, Tatsǫ̨t'ıné have no doubt that cancer rates rose markedly in their communities after the advent of gold roasting. A consultants' report on a community workshop in 2001, for example, noted the need for "a broader perspective of health effects going back to the early years of the operation," and that "some elders expressed concern over sickness and death of some individuals living in the area during the 1940s to 1970s."[9] Fred Sangris has testified that "by the 1970s, cancer cases in the community became very high. Sometimes five to eight had cancer in the whole year. It was not normal."[10] As historian Linda Nash has noted, such local knowledge of toxicity and disease has generally been dismissed by public health officials who believed that the causes of illness could not be detected outside of a laboratory.[11] Even as the episodes of acute sickness and death among Tatsǫ̨t'ıné in the early 1950s have been more widely accepted as factual in recent years, Yellowknives Dene First Nation claims of more widespread cancer in their communities linked to five decades of arsenic exposure have largely been ignored.

Another toxic legacy of Giant Mine will continue to haunt the Yellowknife region for a long time to come: the underground arsenic. Around the time of the Giant Mine environmental assessment, the idea of the buried arsenic as an underground "monster" began to spread in Dettah, and Ndilǫ, and also somewhat in the city of Yellowknife. In public hearing testimony, media reports, and workshops, the image of arsenic trioxide as a malevolent beast that must be contained underground became a powerful metaphor not only for the toxic threat of its release, but also, as Caitlynn Beckett has noted, as the "material embodiment of a history of environmental destruction and the colonial, racialized violence of extractive geographies enacted across Canada and Yellowknives Dene First Nation territory specifically."[12] The Giant Mine monster narrative, as articulated by the Yellowknives Dene, illuminates not only the "pernicious woes" generated by mining, but also the urgency for and necessity of stories in both addressing (through remediation) and redressing (through reconciliation and compensation) the toxic legacies that remain on and under the land. Invoking the monster is at once a reckoning with the past, a call for justice, and a warning to the future.

Figure 7.1

A student-built conceptual model for how to communicate Giant Mine's underground arsenic hazard to future generations, built as part of a youth workshop held by the authors in Ndilǫ, 2015.

This book is a further attempt to grapple with the history of Giant Mine, addressing basic questions about the causes and consequences of the toxic disaster at the site, and placing the story in a wider context. If much of Giant Mine's story is about local environmental problems in a small, faraway place, such histories matter because, in the aggregate, they highlight the hidden costs of extractive economies that arise when developers pay little heed to the environment or to the health of local people. Giant, and places like it, illustrate in vivid detail a widespread pattern whereby governments (ideally, guardians of the public good) have permitted private mining companies to operate with little environmental regulation, voluntary pollution controls, no requirement to seek approval from Indigenous people who have inhabited their lands for generations, and no obligation to clean up and remediate environmental damage before moving on. Whatever wealth it generated, Giant Mine demonstrates in an egregious way how extractive development has often led to colonial displacement, negative health impacts, environmental destruction, and industrial ruin.

Obviously, Giant Mine is far from the only site where extractive development has carried harmful consequences. From the vantage point of the early twenty-first century, one can partly measure the staggering cost of the previous century's "great acceleration" through the innumerable abandoned mines that feature toxic tailings ponds, contaminated soils, acid-generating waste rock, or radioactive material.[13] Orphaned and abandoned mines constitute some of Canada's most toxic sites, major public liabilities that (like Giant) will cost taxpayers billions to remediate.[14] The most comparable example is also in the Canadian North: the former Cyprus Anvil (Faro) Mine in the Yukon, where thirty years of lead-zinc mining left behind 54 million tonnes of tailings and 260 million tonnes of waste rock, much of which is potentially acid generating. The cost for Faro's remediation is now estimated at nearly $800 million, a figure likely to rise.[15] Like Giant, Faro was staked and developed without consultation from or compensation for the Indigenous Kaska Dena people, for whom the mine is associated with colonial displacement and environmental degradation.[16] While it is difficult, and perhaps pointless, to measure which of these sites is the most polluted, or the biggest environmental disaster, Giant Mine nevertheless stands out because of the sheer volume of potent poison at the site – enough, as has been said many times, to fatally poison every human being on the planet four times. As at many contaminated sites, nobody currently knows what to do with the arsenic trioxide. So, for now, the remediation project will contain it, and hope to develop a better approach by the early decades of the twenty-second century.

Those who work in mining today might say that Giant Mine is an example from the "bad old days" of unregulated development. There is some truth to this claim. Mining companies operating in Canada today are generally subject to environmental assessments, stricter pollution regulations, and remediation requirements (in the form of mandated closure planning and "up front" financial obligations). Whether this regulatory regime is sufficient is a question beyond the scope of this book, but still today, if mines (and oil companies) go into receivership or bankruptcy while they are still operating, they will likely escape their environmental obligations. This exact scenario arose in central Yukon in June 2024 when the heap-leaching facility at the Eagle Gold Mine collapsed, causing a landslide and a massive spill of cyanide into the surrounding watershed. Fed up with the mine's operator (Victoria Gold), the Yukon government obtained a court order placing the company in receivership, a move that saddled the public with the estimated $150 million cost to clean up the site.[17] In the Northwest Territories, a recent report from the Legislative Assembly's Standing Committee on Economic Development and Environment noted that there had been several cases since 2014 in which resource companies had gone into receivership and burdened the public with significant financial and environmental liabilities.[18] Currently in Alberta, the provincial energy regulator has collected only $1.71 billion in financial security to cover future abandoned coal and oil sands mine cleanup costs, estimated to be $57.3 billion. Much of this liability comes from the oil sands, but the companies operating these mines have contributed only one dollar in financial security since 2010 because of a regulation requiring no reclamation security payments until oil reserves have less than fifteen years of operational life remaining.[19] Even amid such lax regulatory requirements, some mining companies and politicians, eager to take advantage of the global demand for critical minerals, have complained about "red tape" – the environmental assessments, remediation planning, and negotiations with Indigenous communities that slow the process of getting a mine into production. If there is one lasting lesson to come from Giant Mine, it is a reminder of why all that "red tape" was created in the first place.

Indeed, Giant Mine is a testament to the complicated and persistent environmental problems that can emerge when the pursuit of extractive wealth takes priority over foresight and planning. As noted, the current strategy of freezing arsenic wastes underground at Giant raises profound questions about how to manage, mitigate, and communicate to future generations about these perpetually toxic wastes. Who will ensure the ongoing care, maintenance, and monitoring at the site? Will future governments, assuming they exist, continue to fund this maintenance, as well as research into more permanent solutions? Who bears the risks and the responsibilities for ensuring the continuity of knowledge and care, especially as the site (and society) changes in the future? And what happens if this obligation breaks down? Local people raised these questions (and many others) forcefully during the environmental assessment. They remain effectively unanswered, but the creation of the Giant Mine Oversight Board, an independent voice in the debates over the remediation project, has offered hope in the form of publicly accessible research on more permanent solutions to the seemingly intractable problem of the underground arsenic.[20] Certainly, the knowledge, experience, and wisdom of Tatsǫ̀t'ıné, as past and future stewards of these lands, should feature centrally in developing strategies to address this complex challenge.

Ultimately, the multi-billion-dollar remediation of Giant Mine presents an important opportunity, not only to clean up an environmental disaster, but for all Canadians to contend with a difficult and troubling history – one that is all too present in the everyday lives of Yellowknifers. For decades, the highway east from Yellowknife towards Dettah, the Yellowknives Dene community on the east side of Yellowknife Bay, passed right beside the Giant Mine townsite and mine complex. Dettah also sits immediately across the bay from the former Con Mine; the mine headframes and buildings at both sites long provided a constant reminder of the transformative effects of mineral development. Even as the physical reminders of this history are dismantled as part of the remediation, it remains important to recognize, confront, and redress the social scars of these developments. The Yellowknives Dene and the federal government took a step toward reconciliation in 2021 with an agreement to work collaboratively on a process to create an apology and compensation framework for the historical damage caused by Giant Mine. The two parties also signed separate agreements pledging to work cooperatively "to address the environmental, economic and social priorities stemming from the legacy impacts of mining," and to ensure that the Yellowknives Dene receive economic benefits from remediation activities.[21] These were positive steps, but much difficult work lies ahead to attain justice for the Yellowknives Dene and develop a lasting solution to environmental threats at Giant Mine.

Are there reasons to be optimistic about Giant Mine's future? Here the Pandora metaphor might prove useful one last time. Some versions of the story suggest that the last thing that remained in the jar after its evils had been set loose was hope. The collective action of Yellowknives Dene and other Yellowknifers in the face of so much environmental damage has embodied such hope, a model of civic activism and local democracy that carries important lessons for the governance of large-scale resource projects adjacent to small communities. We may never be able to put all the evils unleashed by Giant Mine back into Pandora's jar (or even freeze them underground). But the mine's remediation may yet encourage Canadians to confront the legacies of contamination and colonialism, to come together to repair the land that was damaged, to support efforts to make certain that the site is cared for in perpetuity, and to ensure that no disaster on the scale of Giant Mine ever happens again.

Notes

Introduction

1 Hesiod, *Hesiod's Works and Days.*

2 Ureta and Flores, *Worlds of Gray and Green*; Bridge, "Contested Terrain," 205–59; Mudd, "Global Trends in Gold Mining," 42–56.

3 Refractory gold ores (like arsenopyrite) are characterized by the distribution of very fine gold particles throughout the mineral matrix, requiring additional thermal, chemical, or mechanical processes to break down the ore.

4 For more on arsenic pollution from mine smelters in the US, see LeCain, "The Limits of 'Eco-Efficiency,'" 336–51; Katherine G. Aiken has provided an excellent overview of technologies used to mitigate pollution from arsenic and other smelter emissions. See Aiken, "'The Environmental Consequences ... Were Calamitous,'" 132–64. See also Quivik, "Butte and Anaconda, Montana," 6–28. For smelter conflicts involving other pollutants (mainly sulfur dioxide), including some early case law on conflicts between mining companies and agriculturalists, see Kuhlberg and Miller, "'Protection to the Sulphur-Smoke Tort-Feasors,'" 225–57; Munton and Temby, "Smelter Fumes, Local Interests, and Political Contestation in Sudbury," 24–36; John D. Wirth, *Smelter Smoke in North America*.

5 We were not able to locate a complete inventory of gold roasting operations in Canada, but a national report on arsenic emissions published in 1979 noted that roasting occurred at three other mines besides Giant: Dickinson Mines, Campbell Red Lake Mines, and Kerr-Addison Mines. The report noted that Dickinson produced arsenic trioxide of such quality that it could be sold, so there was no underground storage. No mention is made about the fate of the arsenic dust produced at Kerr-Addison. See Gagan, *Arsenic Emissions and Control Technology*. The description of the post-closure arsenic challenges at Campbell Red Lake came from Dillon Consulting, *Giant Mine Arsenic Trioxide Technical Workshop*. The older Deloro Mine in Hastings County, Ontario, roasted gold ore from roughly 1896 to 1961, burying and scattering the arsenic that could not be sold around the site. Arsenic in the soil polluted local waterways for decades, until the Ontario government initiated a clean-up plan in the 2010s that included the construction of an arsenic treatment plant. See Ontario Ministry of Environment and Energy, Deloro Site Cleanup Project, https://www.ontario.ca/page/deloro-site-cleanup-project (accessed 24 September 2024).

6 The latest cleanup cost estimates come from Sandy Cohen, "Cost of Cleaning Up Yellowknife's Giant Mine Now Pegged at $4.38B, Up from $1B," CBC News, 10 November 2022, accessed 23 July 2023, https://www.cbc.ca/news/canada/north/giant-mine-remediation-cost-4-billion-1.6647952. For an overview of the long-term liabilities and challenges of communicating with future generations, see O'Reilly, "Liability, Legacy, and Perpetual Care," 341–76; and Sandlos, Keeling, Beckett, and Nicol, "There Is a Monster Under the Ground," 1–55.

7 One could create a very long list of works on these themes. The following list contains works that have influenced us (without being cited elsewhere in this introduction). For general surveys, see Berger and Alexander, *Making Sense of Mining History*; Lynch, *Mining in World History*; Smith, *Mining America*; Curtis, *Gambling on Ore*. For the work environment of a mine and occupational health issues, see Andrews, *Killing for Coal*. For the imperial reach of US mining around the globe, see Black, *The Global Interior*. For histories of open pit mines and the displacement of communities, see Leech, *The City That Ate Itself*; and Storm, *Post-Industrial Landscape Scars*. For more on the consequences of mine pollution, see Manuel, *Taconite Dreams*; Isenberg, *Mining California*; and Walker, *Toxic Archipelago*. While it is beyond the scope of this book, it is important to note that the negative environmental and social consequences of mining are not unique to capitalism, but common across modern industrial economies. For a discussion of the Soviet Union, for instance, see Bruno, *The Nature of Soviet Power*; Josephson, "Industrial Deserts," 294–321; and Josephson, "Technology and the Conquest of the Soviet Arctic," 419–39.

8 Keeling and Sandlos, *Mining and Communities in Northern Canada*; Sandlos and Keeling, *Mining Country*; McNeill and Vrtis, eds., *Mining North America*.

9 Barnes, "Borderline Communities," 109–22; Keeling, "'Born in an Atomic Test Tube,'" 228–52.

10 LeCain, *Mass Destruction*. LeCain's book focuses on open-cast mining but his general model of mining for low-grade ore, a process demanding more mechanized mining methods and more energy inputs, and which produces more waste, holds true for underground mines as well.

11 Normally provincial governments have jurisdiction over natural resources but the federal government retained control over the resource sector in territorial jurisdictions until devolution slowly unfolded starting in the 1970s, a process that was not completed until 2014. For an overview of governance in the Northwest Territories, see Dickerson, *Whose North*; and Hamilton, *Arctic Revolution*. For a classic formation of the argument that the state is the "client" of resource industries in Canada, see Nelles, *The Politics of Development*. For more recent case study work, see Longley, "Conflicting Interests," 97–125; and Mellor, "A Comparative Case Study of Uranium Mine and Mill Tailings Regulation in Canada and the United States," 256–79.

12 Zaslow, *The Opening of the Canadian North*.

13 Abel, *Drum Songs*; Fumoleau, *As Long as This Land Shall*. Importantly, as with Treaty 8, Indigenous signatories to these treaties did not understand them to be surrenders of land and territorial rights, a position vindicated in subsequent court decisions.
14 Piper and Sandlos, "A Broken Frontier," 759–95; Stuhl, *Unfreezing the Arctic*.
15 Stewart and Yakeleya, eds., *We Remember the Coming of the White Man*.
16 For a summary of all these events, see Sandlos, *Hunters at the Margin*, 17–18; 167. This period is also covered in Zaslow, *The Northward Expansion of Canada*. For the branch's resource boosterism, see Kitto, *The North West Territories, 1930*, 75.
17 For the report on Yellowknife gold from 1898, see Hoffman, "Report of the Section on Chemistry and Mineralogy," 33.
18 In reality, the alluvial gold rushes were far from environmentally benign, and often featured highly capitalized, mechanical approaches such as river dredging and hydraulic mining. See Tuffnell and Mountford, eds., *A Global History of Gold Rushes*. For the Yukon Gold Rush, see Green, "The Tr'ondëk Hwëch'in and the Great Upheaval." The gold mining operations that immediately followed the Klondike were worlds apart from the alluvial mines. The first gold mining operations to penetrate the near-northern shield region of Ontario, such as the Porcupine (Timmins) in 1910 and Kirkland Lake in 1911, marked a transition to heavily capitalized, corporate entities, dependent on heavy drilling equipment, vehicles, and processing facilities; significant energy inputs; and a formal wage-labour force. See Jorgenson, *The Weight of Gold*; and Mouat, *Roaring Days*. For a study focused on labour and political economy, see Clement, *Hard-Rock Mining*.
19 For the origins of radium mining at Great Bear Lake, see Bothwell, *Eldorado*. The price of gold was propped up by more than just nervous investors. As the economic sickness deepened, the United States government sought to increase cash liquidity in the broader economy, ending the gold standard in 1933, forbidding the conversion of cash to gold, and then nationalizing private gold holdings and allowing the price to increase $20.67 to $35 per ounce. For the end of the gold standard and subsequent legislation to prevent gold hoarding, see Elwell, "Brief History of the Gold Standard in the United States."
20 Piper, *The Industrial Transformation of Subarctic Canada*. For other studies of the expansion of exploration in the Canadian North during the interwar years, see Cronin, "Northern Visions," 303–30; Stuhl, *Unfreezing the Arctic*; and Adcock, "Many Tiny Traces," 131–77. The trajectory of Northern Canadian mining history is also discussed in the introduction to Keeling and Sandlos, eds., *Mining and Communities in Northern Canada*.
21 In contrast to Yellowknife, the war revitalized the moribund mines at Port Radium, which re-opened to mine uranium in support of atomic weapons research.
22 Data on the production and economic value of Giant Mine was taken from Bullen and Robb, "Social-Economic Impacts of Gold Mining in the Yellowknife

Mining District." Inflation calculations were made using the Bank of Canada online calculator.

23 Leddy, *Serpent River Resurgence*, 3–8. See also Scottie, Bernauer, and Hicks, *I Will Live for Both of Us*; and Keeling and Sandlos, "Environmental Justice Goes Underground?" 117–25. Of course, this process has been repeated throughout the globe. See, for example, Voyles, *Wastelanding*; and Kirsch, "Lost Worlds," 167–98. In an argument related to the material on extractive industries and colonialism, Michif scholar Max Liboiron has argued that the pollution is a form of colonialism because it so often renders Indigenous lands as an expendable sink for contaminated material. See Liboiron, *Pollution Is Colonialism*. For an example about dams rather than mining, but which covers many of the same themes of colonialism and resistance, see Luby, *Dammed*.

24 Johanne Black, quoted in "Distant Future Warnings: The Challenges of Communicating with Eternity," CBC *Ideas* episode, produced by Garth Mullins, Lisa Hale, and Dave Redel, first aired 17 June 2017, accessed 31 October 2023, https://www.cbc.ca/radio/ideas/distant-future-warnings-the-challenges-of-communicating-with-eternity-1.4158805.

25 Tuck, "Suspending Damage," 409–27.

26 For an excellent overview and case studies on this issue, see Clapperton and Piper, eds., *Environmental Activism on the Ground*. For a classic study of local environmentalism from the US, see Gottlieb, *Forcing the Spring*. For examples of community resistance to industrial pollution, see also Markowitz and Rosner, *Deceit and Denial*.

27 Historical work on the links between labour and environmental activism in Canada is sparse, but for an overview see MacPhee, "Canadian Working-Class Environmentalism," 123–49. For excellent case study work, see MacDowell, "The Elliot Lake Uranium Miners' Battle to Gain Occupational Health and Safety Improvements," 91–118 (which also features the United Steelworkers of America in a leading role); and Rennie, *The Dirt*. For a gendered analysis of workers' struggles with silicosis in the Canadian mining industry, see Forestell, "'And I Feel Like I'm Dying from Mining for Gold,'" 77–93. Historians in the United States have developed far more works on the occupational health movement. The general consensus is that the movement emerged with a flush of activist energy in the early years of the twentieth century (one of the earliest expressions of environmentalism, some have argued), but the radical politics of the movement became subsumed by the industrial hygiene movement, which relied on corporate science and company-led initiatives. The worker activism associated with the occupational health movement never disappeared, and emerged with renewed energy in the early 1970s as part of the broader anti-pollution struggles of that era. For overviews, see McEvoy, "Working Environments," 59–89; Derickson, "From Company Doctors to Union Hospitals," 325–42; Montrie, *A People's History of Environmentalism in the United States*; Montrie, *The Myth of Silent Spring*; Sellers, "Factory as Environment," 55–83; Sellers, *Hazards of the Job*; and Rosner and Markowitz, *Deadly Dust*. Van

Horssen's book, *A Town Called Asbestos*, provides an important Canadian example of occupational health activism among unionized workers, but complicates the story by presenting evidence mine workers in Asbestos, Quebec eventually aligned with management interests, defending their deadly product as national and international bans on asbestos threatened to shutter the industry.

28 For a seminal discussion of Dene struggles against capitalist forms of development, especially in the 1970s, see the work of Tatsǫt'ınę́ scholar Coulthard, *Red Skin, White Masks*, especially chapter 2. See also Page, *Northern Development*; Sabin, "Voices from the Hydrocarbon Frontier," 17–48; and Abel, *Drum Songs*, chap. 10.

29 Much of this work was funded by a Social Sciences and Humanities Research Council of Canada Partnership Development Grant that included the collaborators noted. For detailed project research activities and results, see www.toxiclegacies.com.

30 Sandlos, Keeling, and O'Reilly, *Communicating Danger*; Sandlos, *Communicating with Future Generations*; Sandlos, *Communicating with Future Generations at Giant Mine*. See also Sandlos et al., "There Is a Monster Under the Ground."

31 John Sandlos and Arn Keeling, "Giant Coverup," *Edge YK Magazine* 16 (November 2014), https://web.archive.org/web/20141011004247/http://edgeyk.com:80/article/giant-coverup; Sandlos and Keeling, *Giant Mine*.

32 Benoit, *The Guardians of Eternity*.

33 See Yellowknives Dene First Nation, *The Giant Gold Mine: Our Story*; Yellowknives Dene First Nation Elders Advisory Council, *Weledeh Yellowknives Dene*; Evans et al., *Summary of Research on the Establishment, Administration and Oversight of the Giant Mine*. For an excellent reflection of the issue of "insider" and "outsider" status when doing research in Indigenous communities, see Leddy, "Interviewing Nookomis and Other Reflections," 1–18.

34 Francaviglia, *Hard Places*; Robertson, *Hard as the Rock Itself*; Quivik, "The Historical Significance of Tailings and Slag," 35–52; Kojola, "Divergent Memories and Visions of the Future in Conflicts over Mining Development," 898–916; Rhatigan, "Mining Meaning: Telling Spatial Histories of the Britannia Mine," 36–47; Skeard, "Come Hell or High Water," 90–109.

35 Jackson, ed., *Yellowknife, NWT*; Foster and Heming, eds., *Yellowknife Tales*.

36 This discussion about the relative uselessness of gold was heavily influenced by Pollon, *Pitfall*. Similar comments about gold's lack of utility have been made in Demuth, *Floating Coast*, 199–200; and Morse, *The Nature of Gold*, especially chapter 1.

37 Data on the production and economic value of Giant Mine was taken from Bullen and Robb, "Social-Economic Impacts of Gold Mining in the Yellowknife Mining District," 3.

38 Sacco, *Paying the Land*, 249.

Chapter One

1 Nagle and Zinovich, *The Prospector*, 189–92.
2 Helm, *The People of Denendeh*, chap. 9; Yellowknives Dene First Nation, Trailmark Systems, and DownNorth Consulting, *Yellowknives Dene First Nation Knowledge and History of the Giant Mine*, 22–5; Piper, *When Disease Came to This Country*, chap. 7.
3 Yellowknives Dene First Nation, *The Giant Gold Mine: Our Story*, 11, 13. Some stories identify the chief as Joseph, or date the encounter later, coincident with the later prospecting that located Burwash and Giant mines.
4 Nagle and Zinovich, *The Prospector*, 205; Jackson, ed., *Yellowknife NWT*, 11.
5 A "greenhorn" prospector in the North; this term was popularized during the Klondike Gold Rush.
6 Abel, *Drum Songs*, 188.
7 Yellowknives Dene First Nation Elders Advisory Council, *Weledeh Yellowknives Dene*, 10. Our discussions of Tatsǫ̀t'ıné/Yellowknives Dene traditional territories draws from Yellowknives Dene First Nation, *The Giant Gold Mine: Our Story*, and Yellowknives Dene First Nation, Trailmark Systems, and DownNorth Consulting, *Yellowknives Dene First Nation Knowledge and History of the Giant Mine*. We have also used interviews we conducted with community members in Dettah and Ndilǫ in 2011.
8 Yellowknives Dene First Nation, Trailmark Systems, and DownNorth Consulting, *Yellowknives Dene First Nation Knowledge and History of the Giant Mine*, 17.
9 Since the 1970s, extensive interviews and mapping projects have documented this historical and continued land use. See especially the maps in Yellowknives Dene First Nation, Trailmark Systems, and DownNorth Consulting, *Yellowknives Dene First Nation Knowledge and History of the Giant Mine*.
10 The designations of Dene communities, names, and territories have changed historically. The five principal Dene Nation territorial and linguistic groups currently include Gwich'in, Sahtu, Deh Cho, Tłı̨chǫ, and Akaitcho (the latter of which includes the Tatsǫ̀t'ıné). See https://denenation.com. For an ethnohistorical overview of Dene language and territorial groups, see Abel, *Drum Songs*, chap. 1.
11 Yellowknives Dene First Nation Elders Advisory Council, *Weledeh Yellowknives Dene: A History*, 11. The specific land-based activities and resources supporting Dene lifeways varied by region, and are richly described in oral histories, cultural mapping projects, and other sources. Some examples include Blondin, *When the World Was New*; Stewart and Yakeleya, eds., *We Remember the Coming of the White Man*; Athabasca Chipewyan First Nation with Trimble and Fortna, *Remembering Our Relations*. See also the discussion of Dene land relations and identity in Coulthard, *Red Skin, White Masks*, 60–3.
12 Usher, *Fur Trade Posts of the NWT*.
13 In fact, Ted Nagle's father Ed, a trader based at Fort Resolution, was among the first to stake claims (in 1898) at what eventually would become the Pine Point Mine.

14 Ryan Silke, "Yellowknife's First... Prospector," *EdgeYK*, 1 October 2015; McMeekan, *Jock McMeekan's Yellowknife Blade*, 13.
15 Geological Survey of Canada, *Summary Report on the Operations of the Geological Survey for the Year 1899*, 104.
16 Bell's report of the 1899 to 1900 expedition is contained in Geological Survey of Canada, *Annual Report vol. 13, 1900*, 95–103. Camsell was born in Fort Liard to a Hudson's Bay Company factor and a Métis mother.
17 Camsell, "The Unexplored Areas of Continental Canada," 249–57; Bell, "Great Slave Lake," 556–80; Zaslow, *The Opening of the Canadian North*, 285–6.
18 Piper, *The Industrial Transformation of Subarctic Canada*, chap. 1; Zaslow, *The Northward Expansion of Canada*, chap. 4.
19 Cronin, "Northern Visions," 303–30; Zaslow argues, "Aviation may also be credited with the introduction of the mining industry with its attendant effects into the Territories." See *The Northward Expansion of Canada*, 210.
20 Bell, *Far Places*, 26.
21 Fumoleau, *As Long as This Land Shall Last*; Abel, *Drum Songs*, chap. 8.
22 These are described in Yellowknives Dene First Nation, Trailmark Systems, and DownNorth Consulting, *Yellowknives Dene First Nation Knowledge and History of the Giant Mine*, 7–22; as well as in Helm, *The People of Denendeh*, chap. 9.
23 Fumoleau, *As Long as This Land Shall Last*, 127.
24 Evans, King, Freeman, and Degray, *Summary of Research on the Establishment, Administration and Oversight of the Giant Mine*, 9–11; Abel, *Drum Songs*, 194.
25 Piper, *When Disease Came to this Country*, 190.
26 Quoted in Piper, *When Disease Came to this Country*, 223.
27 Yellowknives Dene First Nation, Trailmark Systems, and DownNorth Consulting, *Yellowknives Dene First Nation Knowledge and History of the Giant Mine*, 22–5.
28 Government of Canada, *Regulations for the Disposal of Quartz Mining Claims on Dominion Lands in Manitoba, the North-West Territories, and the Yukon Territory*; Hoogeveen, "Sovereign Intentions," 81–102; Hoogeveen, "Sub-Surface Property, Free-Entry Mineral Staking and Settler Colonialism in Canada," 121–38.
29 Bankes and Sharvit, "Aboriginal Title and Free Entry Mining Regimes in Northern Canada."
30 Gordon, "Narratives Unearthed," 59–86; Zaslow, *The Opening of the Canadian North*, 211–12.
31 See Baker interview in Jackson, ed., *Yellowknife, NWT: An Illustrated History*, 14–16. The all-caps claim names are Baker's.
32 See Walt Humphries interview in Cyril John Baker ("Yellowknife Johnney") Fonds, N-1999-015 file 1-3, Northwest Territories Archives (hereafter NWTA), and an article by Baker published in the *CIM Reporter* in 1985 and collected in Cyril John Baker ("Yellowknife Johnney") Fonds, N-1999-015, file 1-5, NWTA. Of the popular accounts of the Yellowknife gold boom, only Webster's *The Prospector's Pick* tends to downplay the role of Baker, who receives only passing mention. Prospector turned

newspaperman Jock McMeekan also tended to credit "the contribution of many persons" to the discovery and development of Giant. McMeekan, *Jock McMeekan's Yellowknife Blade*, 41.

33 Jackson, ed., *Yellowknife, NWT*, 15.

34 Liza Piper, *The Industrial Transformation of Subarctic Canada*, 40. This pattern of uncredited Indigenous assistance and knowledge is common in settler accounts.

35 Several versions of this story are recounted in Yellowknives Dene First Nation Elders Advisory Council, *Weledeh Yellowknives Dene*; Eddie Sikyea interview, 9 May 2011.

36 C.J. Baker to S. Taylor, 8 October 1936. Cyril John Baker ("Yellowknife Johnney") Fonds, N-1999-015, file 1–4, NWTA.

37 See Jolliffe interview in Jackson, ed., *Yellowknife, NWT*, 17–20. Advice to prospectors and details of local geology were printed regularly in the *Northern Miner*. A detailed compilation of information on geology, mining, and travel in the region was later published in Lord, *Mineral Industry of the Northwest Territories*.

38 Silke, *The Operational History of Mines in the Northwest Territories*, 248–9.

39 "Yellowknife Facts, Figures Reveal New Camp in Making," *Northern Miner*, 5 January 1939, 17.

40 "Mining Regulations in the NWT Encourage Prospector," *Northern Miner*, 27 October 1938, 120.

41 Evans, King, Freeman, and Degray, *Summary of Research on the Establishment, Administration and Oversight of the Giant Mine*, 10.

42 Fumoleau, *As Long as This Land Shall Last*, 399.

43 Abel, *Drum Songs*, 213.

44 Yellowknives Dene First Nation, Trailmark Systems, and DownNorth Consulting, *Yellowknives Dene First Nation Knowledge and History of the Giant Mine*, 26. Baker himself noted the presence of the village and the disturbance of the "Indian graveyard" at Burwash; see Walt Humphries interview, Cyril John Baker ("Yellowknife Johnney") Fonds, N-1999-015, file 1-3, NWTA.

45 Yellowknives Dene First Nation, Trailmark Systems, and DownNorth Consulting, *Yellowknives Dene First Nation Knowledge and History of the Giant Mine*, 31.

46 Fred Sangris interview, 4 May 2011. This image is also invoked by Mary Rose Sundberg in Benoit's documentary film *Guardians of Eternity*. On use of the Con Mine area, see John Drygeese interview, 9 May 2011.

47 Helen Tobie (Dettah) interview, in Foster and Heming, eds, *Yellowknife Tales*, 7.

48 Yellowknives Dene First Nation Elders Advisory Council, *Weledeh Yellowknives Dene*, 14.

49 Yellowknives Dene First Nation, Trailmark Systems, and DownNorth Consulting, *Yellowknives Dene First Nation Knowledge and History of the Giant Mine*, 31.

50 See maps and discussion in Degray, "Indigenous Risk Perceptions and Land Use in Yellowknife, NT"; and Evans, King, Freeman, and Degray, *Yellowknives Dene First Nation Knowledge and History of the Giant Mine*.

51 Evans, King, Freeman, and Degray, *Yellowknives Dene First Nation Knowledge of the Giant Mine*, 50.
52 Piper, *The Industrial Transformation of Subarctic Canada*, 98.
53 McMeekan, *Jock McMeekan's Yellowknife Blade*, 28.
54 "Camsell Impressed by Yellowknife," *Northern Miner*, 22 September 1938, 9. Nor was this practice confined to the 1930s. Yellowknife historian Geddes Webster claims that "[i]n 1945 a large area east of Yellowknife was deliberately burned-off by prospectors, so then after a good rainstorm, the bare rocks were easily examined." Webster, *The Prospector's Pick*, 33.
55 Interview with Isadore Tsetta, 12 May 2011. Log books and inventories from the Burwash operation include references to payments to local Dene for meat and wood. See Cyril John Baker ("Yellowknife Johnney") Fonds, N-1999-015, file 1-4, NWTA.
56 A series of these detailed cordwood contracts and receipts are found in N-1980-002, Box 5, files 7–9, NWTA.
57 Yellowknives Dene First Nation, *The Giant Gold Mine: Our Story*, 18; Yellowknives Dene First Nation Elders Advisory Council, *Weledeh Yellowknives Dene: A History*, 54.
58 Silke, *The Operational History of Mines in the Northwest Territories, Canada*, 112–14.
59 "First Year's Gold Output at Yellowknife Important," *Northern Miner*, 26 October 1939, 25.
60 "Canada's Last Frontier Yields to Invading Army," *Northern Miner*, 12 May 1938, 1.
61 A. Kelso Roberts, "8,000 Miles by Air, Including Yellowknife Tour, in 6½ Days," *Northern Miner*, 10 August 1939, 17.
62 "Yellowknife Facts, Figures Reveal New Camp in Making," *Northern Miner*, 5 January 1939, 17. The origins and early experiences of Yellowknife settlers are colourfully documented in Jackson, ed., *Yellowknife, NWT*; and Foster and Heming, eds., *Yellowknife Tales*.
63 "Survey Settlement at Yellowknife," *Northern Miner*, 14 July 1938, 35.
64 Charles Perkins, oral interview, in Foster and Heming, eds., *Yellowknife Tales*, 14.
65 Zaslow, *The Northward Expansion of Canada*, 217.
66 Piper, *The Industrial Transformation of Subarctic Canada*, 118–19.
67 Grant, *Sovereignty or Security*, chap. 2. In the pages of the *Yellowknife Blade*, Jock McMeekan frequently denounced the administration of Yellowknife settlement by unelected bureaucrats.
68 Zaslow, *The Northward Expansion of Canada*, 216.
69 Lord, *Mineral Resources of the Northwest Territories*, 23.
70 Zaslow, *The Northward Expansion of Canada*, 217.
71 Weledeh oral history, 15, 20.
72 Charles Perkins, oral interview in Foster and Heming, eds., *Yellowknife Tales*, 19. Perkins's observation is echoed in Zaslow, *The Northward Expansion of Canada*, 217.

73 John Drygeese interview, 9 May 2011.
74 "Gold Officially Classed 'Essential Industry,'" *Northern Miner*, 18 July 1940, 1.
75 Piper, *The Industrial Transformation of Subarctic Canada*, 252
76 Writing on the mining history of the American West, Kent Curtis has similarly argued that the common "just-so" story, whereby "metals rested in places in the landscape and miners went and got them," ignores the crucial contextual factors that give rise to mining development. As Curtis suggests, for much of mining history, getting the ores was the setting within which other developments – technological, social, economic, and cultural – took place. See Curtis, *Gambling on Ore*, 203.
77 Sundberg related this story in the documentary film *Guardians of Eternity* (Benoit, 2015).
78 Michel Paper interview, 13 May 2011.

Chapter Two

1 "Yellowknife's Fine Fortune," *Northern Miner*, 9 March 1944. Clipping of article found in RG 85, vol. 253, file 999-2, Library and Archives Canada (hereafter LAC).
2 E.V. Neeland, Consulting Engineer, and A.K. Muir, General Manager, Giant Yellowknife Gold Mines, Memorandum Re Mining Potentialities and Hydro Electric Power Development in the Yellowknife District, n.d. RG 85, vol. 253, file 999-2, LAC. K.J. Christie, Chief Mining Inspector, "Mining Activity During 1948 Season in the Yellowknife District, Northwest Territories," n.d. RG 85, vol. 1509, file 999-9-2, LAC.
3 Cpl W.L. Casselman, RCMP Fort Smith Detachment report, 1 June 1942. RG 85, vol. 253, file 999-2, LAC. Early developments at Giant Mine were described in an article with "Giant Yellowknife Installs Mill," *Northern Miner*, 4 September 1941. Clipping found in RG 85, vol. 253, file 999-2, LAC.
4 "Yellowknife's Fine Fortune," 9 March 1944. RG 85, vol. 253, file 999-2, LAC.
5 John M. Grant, "Giant Yellowknife Is Planning Big Development in Postwar," *Saturday Nigh*t, 25 November 1944. Clipping found in RG 85, vol. 253, file 999-2, LAC.
6 "Giant Financing Makes Record," *Northern Miner*, 31 January 1946. Clipping found in RG 85, vol. 253, file 999-2, LAC. The *Northern Miner* published a letter skeptical of the Giant development on 11 October 1945. Clipping found in RG 85, vol. 253, file 999-2, LAC.
7 Early construction of the power plant is described in "Giant Y'knife has Markings of Big, Profitable Mine," *Northern Miner*, 25 July 1946, 1, 4.
8 "200 Tons for Giant on First Boat," *Northern Miner*, 15 March 1945. Clipping found in RG 85, vol. 253, file 999-2, LAC. Records of the woodcutting program are not complete, though snippets of amounts cut and hauled are found in the monthly reports for January to March 1946, N-2001-014, Box 1, File 3, NWTA.
9 Neeland and Muir, Memorandum Re Mining Potentialities and Hydro Electric Power Development in the Yellowknife District, n.d. RG 85, vol. 253, file 999-2, LAC.

10 Details on the Snare River completion and the pouring of the first gold brick were found in Christie, "Mining Activity During 1948 Season in the Yellowknife District, Northwest Territories," n.d. RG 85, vol. 1509, file 990-9-2, LAC. Employment figures came from Giant Mine's monthly reports from 1946, found in N-2001-014, box 1, file 3; and monthly reports from 1948, found in N-2001-014, box 1, file 5, NWTA.

11 Hugh Keenleyside, "Mineral Output in N.W.T. Moving Up and Other Developments Important," *Northern Miner*, 25 November 1948, 122, 123. The figures for the first year of production, running from May 1948 to May 1949, were found in Silke, *The Operational History of Mines in the Northwest Territories*, 269.

12 Mackay Meikle, District Administrator of the Mackenzie Region, to Roy A. Gibson, Deputy Commissioner of the Northwest Territories, 3 July 1944. RG 85, vol. 253, file 999-2, LAC.

13 A good deal of this waste was returned underground to backfill mined-out stopes. Other material was deposited in tailings areas, where process water treated to remove arsenic was also disposed. See technical descriptions in a 1976 report by J. Grainge, regional engineer, G-2009-020 box 13, file 5, NWTA; a more recent mineralogical and technical description of the Giant milling process is found in Jamieson, 'The Legacy of Arsenic Contamination from Mining and Processing Refractory Gold Ore at Giant Mine," 533–51.

14 Department of Mines and Resources, Bureau of Mines, Report of the Ore Dressing and Metallurgical Laboratories, Investigation No. 2078, 17 July 1946. RG 85, vol. 253, file 999-2, LAC.

15 Parsons to Gibson, 27 August 1946. RG 85, vol. 253, file 999-2, LAC.

16 Gibson to Fred Fraser, 30 August 1946. RG 85, vol. 253, file 999-2, LAC.

17 For details on these smelter disputes, see LeCain, "The Limits of 'Eco-Efficiency,'" 336–51; Wirth, *Smelter Smoke in North America*; Munton and Temby, "Smelter Fumes, Local Interests, and Political Contestation in Sudbury," 24–36; Kuhlberg and Miller, "Protection to the Sulphur-Smoke Tort-Feasors," 225–57.

18 The Anaconda stack, by comparison, was 585 feet, and even the much smaller McLeod-Cockshutt Mine near Geraldton built a somewhat larger 230-foot stack. For the Anaconda stack, see LeCain, *Mass Destruction*. For the McLeod Mine, see Thunder Bay Public Library, Gateway to Northwestern Ontario History, "McLeod Mine," accessed 24 February 2021, https://images.ourontario.ca/gateway/55815/data?n=3.

19 This estimate is based on Kingsley Kay's report that in December 1949 Con had emitted two to three tons (four to six thousand pounds) of arsenic air pollution per day between July 1948 and the installation of pollution control equipment in August 1949, while Giant emitted eight tons (sixteen thousand pounds) of arsenic dust between January 1949 and the installation of a Cottrell electrostatic precipitator in October 1951. See Kingsley Kay, Chief, Industrial Health Laboratory, to Dr K.C. Charron, Chief, Industrial Health Division, Department of National Health and Welfare, "Arsenic at Yellowknife," 6 December 1949. RG 29, vol. 2342, file 455-10-13, LAC.

20 Evans, King, Freeman, and Degray, *Summary of Research on the Establishment, Administration and Oversight of the Giant Mine.*

21 For general historical material and medical research on arsenic, see Meharg, *Venomous Earth*; and Hughes et al., "Arsenic Exposure and Toxicology," 305–32. The Canadian arsenic standard was noted in Kay to Charron, "Arsenic at Yellowknife," 6 December 1949. RG 29, vol. 2342, file 455-10-13, LAC. See also Mitchell, "Health Risks Associated with Chronic Exposures to Arsenic in the Environment," 435–49; and Sambu and Wilson, "Arsenic in Food and Water," 217–26. For an overview of the arsenic standard in Canadian drinking water, see Federal-Provincial-Territorial Committee on Drinking Water, *Guidelines for Canadian Drinking Water Quality.*

22 Kingsley Kay, R.J. Traill, Chief of Metallurgy, Department of Mines, and K.J. Christie, Chief Mining Inspector, "Report of Committee on Evaluation of Arsenic Problem at Yellowknife, Northwest Territories," n.d. RG 29, vol. 2342, file 455-10-13, LAC.

23 K.J. Christie, "The Arsenic Problem at Yellowknife, N.W.T.," 26 May 1951. RG 29, vol. 2342, file 455-10-13, LAC.

24 Barbara Bromley, interview in Foster and Heming, *Yellowknife Tales*, 97–8; Helen Kilkenny, interview in Jackson, ed., *Yellowknife, NWT*, 114–15.

25 Kay to Charron, "Arsenic at Yellowknife," 6 December 1949. RG 29, vol. 2342, file 455-10-13, LAC. In addition to the reports of wildlife mortality, this report contains details on the Con settlement with the Bevans. This report is based on the first of many inspection trips and surveys that public health expert Kingsley Kay conducted in the area.

26 S. Homulos to K.J. Christie, 26 May 1949. RG 85, vol. 1509, file 990-9-2, LAC.

27 Jewitt to Roy Gibson, 7 June 1949. RG 29, vol. 2342, file 455-10-13.

28 An overview of the problems with pollution from the impinger sludge is contained in K. Raht to Jewitt, 28 June 1951. RG 85, vol. 40, file 139-7, LAC. See also Kay to Charron, Chief of the Industrial Health Division, National Health and Welfare, 23 December 1949. RG 29, vol. 2342, file 455-10-13. The figure for the arsenic content in the sludge came from Kay to Charron, "Arsenic at Yellowknife," 6 December 1949. RG 29, vol. 2342, file 455-10-13, LAC.

29 Kay to Charron, "Arsenic at Yellowknife," 6 December 1949. RG 29, vol. 2342, file 455-10-13, LAC.

30 Kay's bio was taken from his obituary by Alfred E. Clark, "Dr. Kingsley Kay, 68, Widely Known Expert on Insecticide Toxicity," *New York Times*, 28 February 1981, 19.

31 Kay to Charron, "Arsenic at Yellowknife," 6 December 1949. RG 29, vol. 2342, file 455-10-13, LAC. Kay had travelled to Yellowknife with the K.J. Christie, chief inspector of mines, and R.J. Traill, chief of metallurgy in the Bureau of Mines. The arrival of the delegation received brief mention in the *News of the North* on 2 December 1949, in an article titled "Discharge of Arsenic Being Probed," found on the back page (8) of the edition.

32 G.D.W. Cameron to Gibson, 14 December 1949. RG 29, vol. 2342, file 455-10-13, LAC.

33 Memorandum for File, Telephone Conversation with Mr K.J. Christie, 21 December 1949. RG 29, vol. 2342, file 455-10-13, LAC.

34 Minutes of Special Meeting of the Northwest Territories Council, 22 December 1949. RG 29, vol. 2342, file 455-10-13, LAC.

35 F.S. Parney, Assistance Director of Health Services to G.D.W. Cameron, Deputy Minister of National Health, 27 December 1949. RG 29, vol. 2342, file 455-10-13, LAC. See also Kay to Charron, 23 December 1949. RG 29, vol. 2342, file 455-10-13, LAC.

36 Keenleyside to Cameron, 13 January 1950. RG 29, vol. 2342, file 455-10-13, LAC.

37 See Grant, *Sovereignty or Security*, 188–210.

38 Minutes of a Special Meeting of the Northwest Territories Council, 19 January 1950. RG 29, vol. 2342, file 455-10-13, LAC.

39 The meeting is described in a letter from Gibson to J.G. McNiven, Manager, Negus Mines, 23 January 1950. RG 29, vol. 2342, file 455-10-13, LAC.

40 Charron to Cameron, 24 January 1950. RG 29, vol. 2342, file 455-10-13, LAC. Our emphasis.

41 Stanton to Gibson, 30 January 1950. RG 29, vol. 2342, file 455-10-13, LAC.

42 Jewitt to Gibson, 7 June 1949. RG 29, vol. 2342, file 455-10-13, LAC.

43 Notes on meeting held in the office of Mr R.A. Gibson, 9 February 1950. RG 29, vol. 2342, file 455-10-13, LAC. Stanton to Charron 21 January 1950. RG 29, vol. 2342, file 455-10-13, LAC. Stanton posted small ads in the *News of the North* (in English only) warning people not to drink water melted from snow or found in puddles or pools. The ads appeared in the 21 April and 28 April 1950 edition of the paper, and they emphasized that the situation was particularly dangerous due to the spring runoff. A similar ad appeared in the *Yellowknife Blade* on 29 April 1950.

44 Minutes of a Special Meeting of the Northwest Territories Council, 19 January 1950. RG 29, vol. 2342, file 455-10-13, LAC.

45 A good biography was contained in his obituary. See "Dr. O.L. Stanton Dies," *News of the North*, 9 January 1970, 3.

46 Cameron to Keenleyside, 10 January 1950. RG 29, vol. 2342, file 455-10-13, LAC.

47 Kay to Cameron, 6 January 1950. RG 29, vol. 2342, file 455-10-13, LAC.

48 According to Kay, Kam Lake was showing arsenic levels of 1.5 parts per million, Rat Lake 5 parts per million, and Pud Lake 35 parts per million. See Kingsley Kay, "Digest Report on Yellowknife Visit, June 29th to July 5th, 1950." RG 29, vol. 2342, file 455-10-13, LAC.

49 Stanton to Gibson, 14 June 1950. RG 29, vol. 2342, file 455-10-13, LAC.

50 Laurie Cinnamon, Interview, in Jackson, ed., *Yellowknife, NWT*, 85. We do not believe these are the same horses as the Bourke horses because there is a picture on the NWTA site showing Laurie Cinnamon as a teenage girl, with the same last name, suggesting her father's last name would have been Cinnamon (married names are given for some of the other girls).

51 For the delays in the delivery of the Cottrell unit, see Minutes of Meeting held to Discuss the Death of Indian Boy, Latham Island, 1 June 1951. RG 29, vol. 2977, file 851-5-2, pt. 1, LAC.

52 The temperature and precipitation data were found at the Government of Canada's historical weather data website, https://climate.weather.gc.ca/historical_data/search_historic_data_e.html. The date for freeze-up on Yellowknife Bay was found in the Giant Mine monthly report for October 1950, N-2001-014, Box 1, File 7, NWTA.

53 The report on heavy arsenic concentrations was cited in Minutes of Meeting held to Discuss the Death of Indian Boy, Latham Island, 1 June 1951. RG 29, vol. 2977, file 851-5-2, pt. 1, LAC.

54 Grant, *Sovereignty or Security*, 195–9.

55 The death was reported in a telegram from mining inspector Steve Homulos to G.E.B. Sinclair, 17 May 1951. RG 29, vol. 2342, file 455-10-13, LAC. References to other Yellowknives being poisoned are found in correspondence from Dr Matas to Dr Falconer, 16 May 1951. RG 29, vol. 2977, file 851-5-2, pt. 1, LAC. Reference to a "few" Yellowknives being treated for arsenic poisoning is made in a report from Kay to Charron, 25 May 1952. RG 29, vol. 2342, file 455-10-13, LAC. The latter report is second hand, however, and only refers to those people in hospital. Collected correspondence indicates that G.E.B. Sinclair, director of the Northern Administration and Lands Branch in the Department of Resources and Development, had become the department's point person on the arsenic issue after Gibson's death.

56 Sinclair wrote to Charron twice about the issue, on 23 May 1951 and 28 May 1951. RG 29, vol. 2342, file 455-10-13, LAC.

57 Stanton to H.A. Young, Commissioner of the Northwest Territories, 18 May 1951. RG 29, vol. 2342, file 455-10-13, LAC.

58 Both of the April 1951 ads were on page five of the newspaper. The July 1951 ad was placed on page six.

59 The water deliveries are mentioned in the letter from Stanton to Young, 18 May 1951. RG 29, vol. 2342, file 455-10-13, LAC.

60 See Minutes of Meeting held to Discuss the Death of Indian Boy, Latham Island, 1 June 1951. RG 29, vol. 2977, file 851-5-2, pt. 1, LAC. The roaster became operational on 29 October 1952. A.C. Callow, Giant Yellowknife Gold Mines' secretary, informed Sinclair of the Cottrell commencing operations in a letter dated 30 October 1951. RG 85, vol. 40, file 139-7, LAC.

61 Muir informed Sinclair of the settlement in an undated letter. RG 85, vol. 40, file 139-7, LAC. The compensation that the Abel's received would amount to $7,973 in 2023 dollars, while the Bevans would have received $212,615 in 2023 dollars.

62 Yellowknives Dene First Nation, *The Giant Gold Mine: Our Story*, 17. The quote also appears (unattributed) in Yellowknives Dene First Nation Elders Advisory Council, *Weledeh Yellowknives Dene: A History*, 52.

63 Interviewee quoted in Yellowknives Dene First Nation, Trailmark Systems, and DownNorth Consulting, *Yellowknives Dene First Nation Knowledge and History of the Giant Mine*, 55.
64 Yellowknives Dene First Nation, *The Giant Gold Mine: Our Story*, 17.
65 Interviewee quoted in Yellowknives Dene First Nation, Trailmark Systems, and DownNorth Consulting, *Yellowknives Dene First Nation Knowledge and History of the Giant Mine*, 56.
66 Tester, "Mad Dogs and (Mostly) Englishmen," 129–47.
67 Evans, King, Freeman, and Degray, *Summary of Research on the Establishment, Administration and Oversight of the Giant Mine*, 22.
68 See Voyles, *Wastelanding*.
69 Yellowknives Dene First Nation, *The Giant Gold Mine: Our Story*, 20.
70 The arsenic emission totals were found in a memo from J.P. Windish, Industrial Hygienist, Occupational Health Division, to A.T. Jordan, Chief Mining Engineers, Department of Northern Affairs and National Resources, 24 November 1960. RG 29, vol. 2977, file 851-5-2, pt. 1, LAC. A survey report published in 1969 placed the emissions at Con Mine at a much higher rate of 434 pounds per day, but the rates cited for Giant for the years 1955 to 1957 were lower (see table 3.1). See de Villiers and Baker, *An Investigation into the Health Status of Inhabitants of Yellowknife, Northwest Territories*, 5. De Villiers and Baker acknowledged that their numbers were estimates of arsenic emissions. Windish's memo does not indicate a method used to determine stack emissions. Ore production numbers were derived from Giant Yellowknife Gold Mine's annual reports for 1955 to 1957, N-1991-082, Giant Mine Fonds, NWTA.
71 Kay to C.K. LeCapelain, Chief, Lands Division, Department of Resources and Development, 29 September 1953. RG 85, vol. 40, file 139-7, pt. 1, LAC. Kay's plans for the survey included testing of snow, water, air, vegetation, and people for arsenic. See Kay to G.E.B. Sinclair, 25 October 1951. RG 85, vol. 40, file 139-7, pt. 1, LAC.
72 Stanton to F.J. Cunningham, Deputy Commissioner of the Northwest Territories, 5 June 1954. RG 85, vol. 40, file 139-7, pt. 1, LAC.
73 On this issue, see Nash, "Purity and Danger," 651–68; Vogel, "From 'the Dose Makes the Poison' to 'the Timing Makes the Poison,'" 667–73.
74 At the meeting to discuss the death of Frank Abel, the Northwest Territories Council had mentioned the 0.05 parts per million arsenic standard as the measure that should be used. 1 June 1951. RG 29, vol. 2977, file 851-5-2, pt. 1, LAC.
75 Dr O. Schaefer, Northern Medical Research Unity to the A/Regional Director, Northern Region, Department of National Health and Welfare, 4 November 1971. RG 29, vol. 2977, file 851-5-2, pt. 1, LAC.
76 P.E. Moore, Director, Indian Health Services, To L.I. Pugsley, Laboratory Services, 16 November 1952. RG 85, vol. 40, file 139-7, pt. 1, LAC.
77 This information was contained in a report, with authorship not stated, titled "Report of Phase II: Clinical and Laboratory Examination of Persons Previously

Screened for Arsenic Exposure," n.d. (but the trial clearly took place in June 1975). RG 29, accession 1996-97-706, box 6, file 8726-1-1, vol. 3, LAC.

78 K. Raht wrote a lengthy overview of the arsenic disposal issue in a letter to Jewitt, 28 June 1951. RG 85, vol. 40, file 139-7, pt. 1, LAC. Kay's approval of the Crank Lake disposal site was affirmed in notes on a meeting held with Raht, Homulos, and C.E. White on 30 June 1950. RG 29, vol. 2342, file 455-10-13, LAC.

79 C.E. White to H.C. Giegerich, 2 August 1951. N-1980-002, Box 6, File 33, NWTA.

80 Meeting Held to Discuss the Arsenic Problem at Yellowknife as the Result of the Proposal of Negus Mines Limited to Commence Roasting Operations, 1 August 1951. RG 29, vol. 2342, file 455-10-13, LAC.

81 Silke, *The Operational History of Mines in the Northwest Territories*, 112.

82 Miramar Northern Mining, *Con Mine Final Closure and Reclamation Plan*; Northwest Territories Health and Social Services, "Arsenic in Lakes around Yellowknife," Advisory, 5 July 2019, accessed 5 July 2019, https://www.hss.gov.nt.ca/en/newsroom/arsenic-lake-water-around-yellowknife; Madi Parett et al., "Impacts on Aquatic Biota from Salinization and Metalloid Contamination by Gold Mine Tailings in Sub-Arctic Lakes," 116815.

83 Kay, Digest Report on Yellowknife Visit, June 29 to July 5th, 1950. RG 29, vol. 2342, file 455-10-13, LAC.

84 Muir to G.E.B. Sinclair, 24 February 1951. RG 29, vol. 2342, file 455-10-13, LAC.

85 Gibson to Muir, 21 July 1950. RG 29, vol. 2342, file 455-10-13, LAC.

86 Muir to G.E.B. Sinclair, 24 February 1951. RG 29, vol. 2342, file 455-10-13, LAC.

87 Dufresne to Sinclair, 30 June 1951. RG 29, vol. 2342, file 455-10-13, LAC.

88 "Arsenic Disposal: Methods Adopted by Companies facing Similar Problems," n.d. RG 29, vol. 2342, file 455-10-13, LAC.

89 Gilchrist to Muir, 22 November 1950. Letter obtained by Kevin O'Reilly through an information request during the Mackenzie Valley Review Board environmental assessment of the Giant Mine Remediation Project.

90 Meeting Held to Discuss the Arsenic Problem at Yellowknife as the Result of the Proposal of Negus Mines Limited to Commence Roasting Operations, 1 August 1951. RG 29, vol. 2342, file 455-10-13, LAC.

91 O.L. Stanton to G.E.B. Sinclair, 27 February 1951. Letter obtained by Kevin O'Reilly through an Information Request during the Mackenzie Valley Review Board environmental assessment of the Giant Mine Remediation Project.

92 We are referring particularly to RG 29, vol. 2977, file 851-5-2, pt. 1, LAC, which jumps abruptly from documents dated in the early 1950s to 1964.

93 Robert H. Winters, "Mines Minister Issues Progress Report on NWT Activities, 1951," *News of the North*, 7 December 1951, 5.

Chapter Three

1 Employment numbers at Giant were recorded in monthly reports contained in the Giant Yellowknife Gold Mines Fonds, N-2001-014, NWTA. Production numbers were derived from Bullen and Robb, "Social-Economic Impacts of Gold Mining in the Yellowknife Mining District," 2. For population numbers, see Sabin, "Contested Colonialism," 116.

2 See Bourne, *Yellowknife, NWT*. For an overview of political developments in Yellowknife, see Sabin, "Contested Colonialism"; and Grant, *Sovereignty or Security*, 195–200. See also Hamilton, *Arctic Revolution*.

3 As noted in the previous chapters, there are contradictory numbers on arsenic emissions in 1959. The figures used here are from de Villiers and Baker, *An Investigation into the Health Status of Inhabitants of Yellowknife, Northwest Territories*, 5. A lower number of 266 pounds per day for 1959 was cited in a memo from J.P. Windish, Industrial Hygienist, Occupational Health Division, to A.T. Jordan, Chief Mining Engineers, Department of Northern Affairs and National Resources, 24 November 1960. RG 29, vol. 2977, file 851-5-2, pt. 1, LAC.

4 A Summary of Grainge's Report, "Water Pollution, Yellowknife Bay, NWT," December 1963. G-2009-020, box 13, file 5, NWTA. See also US Department of Health, Education and Welfare, Public Health Service, *Public Health Service Drinking Water Standards*. Grainge's reflections on the 1963 study (which he remembered as taking place in 1962) are contained in a memoir about his work in the Northwest Territories: Grainge, *The Changing North*.

5 United Steelworkers of America, A Brief to the CPHA Task Force on Arsenic, 14 March 1977. RG 29, vol. 2978, file 851-5-2, pt. 5, LAC

6 M17 to Dr Procter, 10 December 1965, and M17 to Dr Procter, 20 December 1965. RG 29, vol. 2977, file 851-5-2, pt. 1, LAC.

7 Butler to A.B. Yates, 1 November 1967. RG 29, vol. 2977, file 851-5-2, pt. 1, LAC. The data sheets, titled "Arsenic Survey: Water Samples Taken at Yellowknife," are in the same file. They also show very high readings from tap water at Giant Mine, which had a separate intake in Yellowknife Bay.

8 Mention of the anemia is made in memos from Dr Butler, Chief Medical Officer and Regional Director, Department of National Health and Welfare, to Dr Frost, Director General, Medical Services, Ottawa, 24 August 1967 and 17 August 1967. RG 29, vol. 2977, file 851-5-2, pt. 1, LAC.

9 Butler to Procter, 30 October 1967, and Procter to Butler, 29 September 1967. RG 29, vol. 2977, file 851-5-2, pt. 1, LAC.

10 Butler to A.B. Yates, 1 November 1967; Proctor to Butler, 27 November 1967; Butler to Procter, 6 December 1967. RG 29, vol. 2977, file 851-5-2, pt. 1, LAC.

11 Butler to Wiebe, 23 September 1970. RG 29, vol. 2977, file 851-5-2, pt. 1, LAC.

12 Hodgson to Chrétien, 25 September 1970. RG 29, vol. 2977, file 851-5-2, pt. 1, LAC.

13 Chrétien to Munro, 1 October 1970. RG 29, vol. 2977, file 851-5-2, pt. 1, LAC.

14 Munro to Chrétien, 15 October 1970. RG 29, vol. 2977, file 851-5-2, pt. 1, LAC.

15 Briefing notes for Chrétien, 9 October 1970. RG 29, vol. 2977, file 851-5-2, pt. 1, LAC.
16 Butler to A.J. Richardson, Secretary, Consumers' Association of Canada, Yellowknife Branch, 16 November 1970. RG 29, vol. 2977, file 851-5-2, pt. 1, LAC. Richardson's letter is dated from 16 October 1970, and no doubt Butler held off answering as he awaited the development of a communications strategy from his superiors.
17 The information about the cost-shared nature of the program came from Grainge, *The Changing North*, 167.
18 De Villiers and Windish, "Lung Cancer in a Fluorspar Mining Community," 94–109.
19 De Villiers and Baker, *An Investigation into the Health Status of Inhabitants of Yellowknife, Northwest Territories*, 46–7.
20 De Villiers and Baker, *An Investigation into the Health Status of Inhabitants of Yellowknife, Northwest Territories*. The fallout data came from page 4, while the water contamination analysis was found on page 7.
21 See, for example, B. Olszamowski, Secretary-Treasurer, City of Yellowknife, to Butler, 9 June 1970. RG 29, vol. 2977, file 851-5-2, pt. 1, LAC; C.A. Lewis, District Manager, Environmental Protection Branch, Environment Canada, to M. Morrison, Chairman, Northwest Territories Water Board, 8 November 1974. RG 29, vol. 2977, file 851-5-2, pt. 2, LAC; A. Brian Deer, Director of Information Services, National Indian Brotherhood, to Marc Lalonde, Minister of National Health and Welfare, n.d. (received by Lalonde's office 10 January 1975). RG 29, vol. 2977, file 851-5-2, pt. 2, LAC. Wiebe referred to pressure to obtain copies of the report from the CBC, the commissioner of the Northwest Territories, and the city of Yellowknife in a memo to E.A. Watkinson, Director General of Health Services, 1 December 1969. RG 29, vol. 2977, file 851-5-2, pt. 1, LAC. The Northwest Territories Council was still desperately seeking a copy of the report on January 1975, with Councillor Searle pleading with the Commissioner of the Northwest Territories to table a copy of the report at a meeting held 13 January 1975. See an excerpt of the council meeting, "Question W1-54," 13 January 1975. G-2009-020, Box 13, file 5, NWTA.
22 Butler to the Director General of Medical Services, 3 September 1970, and Butler to the Director General of Medical Services, 30 November 1970. RG 29, vol. 2977, file 851-5-2, pt. 1, LAC.
23 De Villiers's comments on staffing problems are contained in a memo to E.A. Watkinson, Director General, Health Services Branch, 26 August 1969, and the issue with the statistician was outlined in a memo from Wiebe to Butler, 7 January 1970. Both memos are found in RG 29, vol. 2977, file 851-5-2, pt. 1, LAC. The issue of de Villiers's tardiness with communication and frequent travel crops out throughout the archival documents; for instance, a set of handwritten notes on a memo between Butler and Wiebe, dated 3 September 1970, lamented de Villiers's failure to reply to return correspondence, proposed to follow up with him the following Monday, but then lamented that he was in Geneva. RG 29, vol. 2977, file 851-5-2, pt. 1, LAC.

24 Brett to the Assistant Deputy Minister of Medical Services, 10 August 1972. RG 29, vol. 2977, file 851-5-2, pt. 1, LAC.
25 Wiebe to Butler, 14 May 1971. RG 29, vol. 2977, file 851-5-2, pt. 1, LAC.
26 Schaefer to Regional Director, Northern Region. 4 November 1971. RG 29, vol. 2977, file 851-5-2, pt. 1, LAC.
27 D.B. Dewar, Assistant Deputy Minister, Medical Services Branch, to Paul Woodstock, Principal Executive Officer to A/DM Health, 10 January 1974. RG 29, vol. 2977, file 851-5-2, pt. 2, LAC.
28 Details on the committee are found in a memo from Maurice LeClair, M.D., to Ian Howard, Executive Assistant to the Minister, 26 November 1970. RG 29, vol. 2977, file 851-5-2, pt. 1, LAC. The first set of recommendations from the committee are contained in a memo from Wiebe to Butler, 3 December 1970. RG 29, vol. 2977, file 851-5-2, pt. 1, LAC.
29 W.H. Frost, Arsenic – Yellowknife, 28 October 1970. RG 29, vol. 2977, file 851-5-2, pt. 1, LAC.
30 Wiebe to Butler, 30 October 1970. RG 29, vol. 2977, file 851-5-2, pt. 1, LAC.
31 O'Toole, Clark, Malaby, and Trauger, "Environmental Trace Element Survey at a Heavy Metals Refining Site," 172–85.
32 James J. O'Toole to the Board of Health, City of Yellowknife, 31 May 1972. RG 29, accession 1996-97-706, box 6, file 8726-1-1 vol. 1, LAC.
33 C.A. Pearson (on behalf of Health and Welfare Minister John Munro) to Helga Reismann, 1 May 1972. RG 29, accession 1996-97-706, box 6, file 8726-1-1 vol. 1, LAC.
34 James J. O'Toole to C.A. Pearson, 3 January 1973. RG 29, accession 1996-97-706, box 6, file 8726-1-1 vol. 1, LAC.
35 Wallace and Hardin, *Chemical and Biological Characteristics of Seepages from Tailings Areas at Giant Yellowknife Mines*, 5.
36 Ibid., 15.
37 Ibid.
38 Lanny Cook, "Pollution Secrecy Angers City Council," *News of the North*, 24 April 1974, 1–2.
39 Edward Ristan, Environmental Health Officer, to Dr A.O. Ugyar, Director, Mackenzie Zone, Department of National Health and Welfare, 23 October 1974. RG 29, vol. 2977, file 851-5-2, pt. 2, LAC. It was a common misperception that the Yellowknives Dene were Dogrib, but they are in fact a distinct cultural group with their own language.
40 Ron Verzuh, "Giant Mine Fined $2,000 for Arsenic Pollution in Back Bay Last April," *News of the North*, 26 February 1976, 1–2.
41 "Another Arsenic Spill at Giant," *News of the North*, 29 January 1975, 21.
42 De Smecht, Laguitton, and Bérubé, *Control of Arsenic Level in Gold Mine Waste Waters*.
43 Northwest Territories Water Board, Giant Yellowknife Mines, Public Hearing Under the Northern Inland Waters Act, April 22, 1975, Yellowknife, NWT

(obtained from the Mackenzie Valley Land and Water Board [hereafter MVLWB] Paper Public Registry, Yellowknife). See also "Giant to Spend $1.5 Million More for Pollution Control," *News of the North*, 30 April 1975, 12.

44 H. Bengts to M.L. Brown, Mining Engineer, 9 May 1973. RG 29, vol. 2978, file 851-5-2, pt. 5, LAC.

45 R.S. Brown, Giant Yellowknife Mines to A.K.C. [only the initials of the recipient were included on the letter], 1 August 1974. RG 29, vol. 2978, file 851-5-2, pt. 5, LAC.

46 Ron Wallace, Department of the Environment, to D. Fowler, Inland Waters Directorate, 5 December 1974. RG 29, vol. 2978, file 851-5-2, pt. 5, LAC.

47 Northwest Territories Water Board, Giant Yellowknife Mines, Ltd, Public Hearing Under the Northern Inland Waters Act, 22 April 1975, Yellowknife, NWT, MVLWB.

48 Jack Grainge, draft report on arsenic in the Yellowknife area, 14 June 1976. G-2009-020 box 13, file 5, NWTA.

49 Preliminary Report of a Special Committee Formed to Study the Levels of Arsenic in the Waters of Yellowknife (Appendix to Report, Present Views on NWT Government as to Future of Programs Presently Under NWT Region of Medical Services), 3 December 1975. RG 29, vol. 2978, file 851-5-2, pt. 5, LAC.

50 Arsenic Concentrations in Waters near Yellowknife, NWT, 1974. RG 29, vol. 2977, file 851-5-2, pt. 2, LAC.

51 Grainge, draft report, 14 June 1976. G-2009 box 13, file 5, NWTA.

52 See, for example, Lee and Fraumeni Jr., "Arsenic and Respiratory Cancer in Man," 1,045–52; Marvin Gerald Ott, Holder, and Gordon, "Respiratory Cancer and Occupational Exposure to Arsenicals," 250–55.

53 De Villiers and Baker, *An Investigation into the Health Status of Inhabitants of Yellowknife, NWT*, 10. Among the collection of papers in the archival files were Jackson and Grainge, "Arsenic and Cancer," 396–401 (n.b., the second author is not the same Jack Grainge who was an engineer in Yellowknife). In the US, the National Institute of Occupational Safety and Health (NIOSH) accepted arsenic as a suspected carcinogen in 1974. See "OSHA Is About to Move on a New Arsenic Standard," *Occupational Hazards* (September 1976): 83–4. Both articles were found in RG 29, accession 1996-97-706, box 6, file 8726-1-1, vol. 3, LAC.

54 Mary Chartrand for H. Veldhuizen, Head, Air Pollution Control Section, Environmental Protection Service, Northwest Region, to C.A. Lewis, District Manager, Environmental Protection Service, Yellowknife, 6 February 1975. RG 29, accession 1996-97-706, box 6, file 8726-1-1, vol. 2, LAC. The memo was also addressed to the district manager for the Environmental Protection Service in Yellowknife and copied to Richard Eaton in Health and Welfare.

55 Abel, *Drum Songs*; Gottesman, "Native Hunting and the Migratory Birds Convention Act," 67–89; Sandlos, *Hunters at the Margin*.

56 Johnson, "The Case of the Million-Dollar Duck," 56–86; Sissons, *Judge of the North*.

57 Sabin, "Settler Colonialism and the Administrative State," 149–65.

58 Page, *Northern Development*; Sabin, "Voices from the Hydrocarbon Frontier," 17–48.

59 For an overview of the "renaissance of Dene society," see the final chapter of Abel, *Drum Songs*; and Coulthard, *Red Skin, White Masks*, chap. 2. The National Indian Brotherhood was not incorporated until 1970.

60 Michel Sikyea to Jean Chrétien, 25 September 1973. Giant Mine Remediation Public Registry, accessed 21 October 2022, https://reviewboard.ca/upload/project_document/EA0809-001_Letter_-_YKDFN_to_DIAND_Minister_J__Chretien_-_Sept_1973.pdf. The letter was copied to Stuart Hodgson, commissioner of the Northwest Territories; Fred Henne, mayor of Yellowknife; and Colin Wynn, Yellowknife city alderman.

61 Northwest Territories Water Board, Public Hearing, Giant Yellowknife Mines, Ltd, 10 October 1974, MVLWB, 17.

62 Ibid. Sutton's comments are recorded on pages 12 to 16 of the transcript, while Chief Joseph Charlo's are recorded on pages 16 to 18.

63 See pages 20 to 21 of the public hearing transcript for 1974, MVLWB.

64 The USWA position in 1975 is summarized in United Steelworkers of America, "A Brief to the Canadian Public Health Association Task Force on Arsenic," 14 March 1977, 7–8. RG 29, vol. 2978, file 851-5-2, pt. 5, LAC. Giant Mine's workers had been represented by the USWA since a merger with the previous union, the notoriously radical International Union of Mine, Mill and Smelter Workers, in 1967. The merger was the result of a sustained raiding campaign by the USWA. See Powell, "Questioning Mine Mill in Yellowknife," 187–206.

Chapter Four

1 See, for instance, statements by Wally Firth, member of Parliament for the Northwest Territories, recorded in Hansard on 5 June 1975 and filed in RG29, vol. 2977, file 851-5-2, pt. 3, LAC.

2 O'Connor, *The First Green Wave*; Jennifer Read, "'Let Us Heed the Voice of Youth,'" 227–50; Clapperton, "The Ebb and Flow of Local Environmentalist Activism," 261–88; Leeming, *In Defence of Home Places*.

3 Anastasia M. Shkilnyk, *A Poison Stronger than Love*; Tobasonakwut, "The Marmion Lake Generating Station," 171–9.

4 Sabin, "Voices from the Hydrocarbon Frontier," 17–48; Sandlos and Keeling, "Pollution, Local Activism, and the Politics of Development in the Canadian North," 25–32.

5 Tataryn, *Dying for a Living*. For more on the aluminum controversy, see Jorgenson and Sandlos, "Dust Versus Dust," 1–26. For more on the occupational health issues at Elliot Lake, see MacDowell, "The Elliot Lake Uranium Miners' Battle to Gain Occupational Health and Safety Improvements," 91–118.

6 All quoted and paraphrased material was taken from a transcript of the *As It Happens* episode printed in the *Yellowknifer*, 11 January 1975, 2, 6–8.

7 Sikyea and Betsina's comments are reprinted on page 6 of the *Yellowknifer* reprint.
8 The press release of the Indian Brotherhood was quoted extensively in the news article "Brotherhood Outraged by Revelations," *News of the North*, 15 January 1975, 20.
9 Ibid, 20.
10 "What Was Hidden from the Public and Why?" *Yellowknifer*, 11 January 1975, 4.
11 Ibid., 4.
12 Ibid., 4.
13 United Steelworkers of America, "A Brief to the Canadian Public Health Association Task Force on Arsenic," 14 March 1977, 16–21. RG 29, vol. 2978, file 851-5-2, pt. 5, LAC.
14 "Ecology North Asks About Other Unpublished Reports," *Yellowknifer*, 16 January 1975, 23.
15 Carolyn and Brian Holstein to Frank Philbrook, MP, 8 January 1975. RG 29, vol. 2977, file 851-5-2, pt. 2, LAC.
16 Josie Toews to Marc Lalonde, 27 January 1975. RG 29, vol. 2977, file 851-5-2, pt. 2, LAC.
17 Wiese to Trudeau, n.d., and Wiese to Lalonde, n.d. RG 29, vol. 2977, file 851-5-2, pt. 2, LAC. The underlined emphasis is from Wiese's letter to Trudeau.
18 This was indeed done, as recorded in a memo from J.H. Wiebe to Butler, 28 May 1971. RG 29, vol. 2977, file 851-5-2, pt. 1, LAC.
19 Butler to Assistant Deputy Minister, Medical Services Branch, 19 May 1971. RG 29, vol. 2977, file 851-5-2, pt. 1, LAC.
20 D.B. Dewar, Assistant Deputy Minister, Medical Services Branch to Paul Woodstock, Principal Executive Officer to Assistant Deputy Minister of Health, 10 January 1975. RG 29, vol. 2977, file 851-5-2, pt. 2, LAC. The memo noted that Chrétien's concerns had been prompted by a note of caution from the commissioner of the Northwest Territories, and then "the RD [regional director] was instructed not to make public comments."
21 Lewis to M. Morrison, Chair, Northwest Territories Water Board, 8 November 1974. RG 29, vol. 2977, file 851-5-2, pt. 2, LAC. Lewis did obtain a copy of the report.
22 "Preliminary Report of a Special Committee Formed to Study the Levels of Arsenic in the Waters of Yellowknife," 16 January 1975. RG 29, vol. 2978, file 851-5-2, pt. 5, LAC.
23 Ibid.
24 "Brief Notes on Meeting Held to Discuss Yellowknife Environmental Survey," 21 January 1975. G-2009-020, box 13, file 5, NWTA.
25 "Arsenic Hair Tests Are a Flop," *Native Press*, 26 February 1975. Clipping found in G-2009-020, box 13, file 5, NWTA. An internal Health and Welfare report counted fifty-five Indigenous participants and noted disappointment in this number, in spite of recruitment being in the Dene language and "visits to each home by an Indian girl" to recruit participants. See "Report on Arsenic Program," memo,

Department of National Health and Welfare, 14 April 1975. RG 29, vol. 2977, file 851-5-2, pt. 3, LAC.

26 "Southerner Deplores Arsenic Tests," and "Editorial," *Yellowknifer*, 13 March 1975, 6, 9.

27 Department of National Health and Welfare Canada, "Yellowknife Arsenic Study Results Published," news release, 27 May 1975. RG 29, vol. 2977, file 851-5-2, pt. 3, LAC.

28 "General position of the Standing Committee on Arsenic Pollution in the Yellowknife Area on National Health and Welfare Press Release on Hair Sampling Program Results," undated memo, G-2009-020, box 13 file 5, NWTA.

29 "Analysis of Hair Arsenic Results, Yellowknife, 1975," memo, Dr R.D.P. Eaton, G-2008-028, box 9, file 17, NWTA; W. Cheveldayoff, "Miners, Not Other Yellowknife Residents, Face Arsenic Danger, Health Report Shows," *Globe and Mail*, 28 May 1975. Clipping found in RG 29, vol. 2977, file 851-5-2, pt. 3, LAC.

30 Telex to Hon. Marc Lalonde, Minister of National Health and Welfare, from United Steelworkers of America – Northwest Territories, 2 June 1975. RG 29, vol. 2977, file 851-5-2, pt. 3, LAC.

31 "Arsenic Threat to Miners," *Yellowknifer*, 29 May 1975, 28–9.

32 Marsh F. Hawes to Marc Lalonde, 2 June 1975; Lalonde to Hawes, 20 June 1975; D.B. Dewar, Medical Services Branch, to Marsh F. Hawes, 17 June 1975. RG 29, vol. 2977, file 851-5-2, pt. 3, LAC.

33 This critique culminated in the passing of the Dene Declaration in 1975 by the Indian Brotherhood of the Northwest Territories and the Métis Association of the Northwest Territories, which asserted Dene nationhood and self-determination, and advocated for self-government. Watkins, ed., *Dene Nation*; Peter J. Usher, "Northern Development, Impact Assessment and Social Change," 111; Coulthard, *Red Skin, White Masks*, 57–8.

34 National Indian Brotherhood, "Arsenic in Yellowknife: Federal Study Misses Poisoned Children, Ignores Cancer Hazard," news release, 2 June 1975. RG 29, vol. 2977, file 851-5-2, pt. 3, LAC. The critique of Schaeffer's sampling method was also discussed in Tataryn, *Dying for a Living*, 116.

35 National Indian Brotherhood, "Arsenic in Yellowknife."

36 Peter Gorrie, "Arsenic Tests Inadequate, Say Steelworkers, Indian Brotherhood," *News of the North*, 4 June 1975, 1; Peter Gorrie, "Arsenic Worries Continue," *News of the North*, 11 June 1975, 6; "Findings on Arsenic Challenged by Indians," *Globe and Mail*, 3 June 1975, 2.

37 Northwest Territories Water Board, Public Hearing, Giant Yellowknife Mines, Ltd, 22 April 1975, 46. A transcript of hearing was accessed in the public registry of the MVLWB.

38 Ibid., 21.

39 Ibid., 15–16.

40 Ibid. Wynne's comments are on page 28, Jacobsen's on pages 28 to 29, Burnford's on page 47, Bintner's on page 45, Hason's on pages 49–50, and Anderson's on page 50.
41 Ibid., 31.
42 "Giant to Spend $1,500,000 on Arsenic Control," *Yellowknifer*, 21 April 1976, 1, 11.
43 "Arsenic Exposure in Workplace Areas of Yellowknife Gold Mines and Mills, Northwest Territories," Occupational Health Unit, Medical Services Branch, July 1975. RG 29, vol. 2978, file 851-5-2, pt. 6A, LAC.
44 Memorandum, F.H. Hicks, Medical Services Branch, 7 April 1975. RG 29, vol. 2977, file 851-5-2, pt. 3, LAC.
45 "Arsenic Exposure in Workplace Areas of Yellowknife Gold Mines and Mills, Northwest Territories," Occupational Health Unit, Medical Services Branch, July 1976. RG 29, vol. 2978, file 851-5-2, pt. 6A, LAC.
46 D.A. Gemmill, "Summary Report, Yellowknife Environmental Survey," July 1976. RG 29, vol. 2977, file 851-5-2, pt. 4, LAC. Much of the data from these studies was eventually published as D.A. Gemmill, ed., *Technical Data Summary*.
47 Report by J. Grainge, regional engineer, to Standing Committee on Arsenic, 14 June 1976. G-2009-020, Box 13, file 5, NWTA.
48 Ibid.
49 Minutes of Standing Committee on Arsenic, 30 September 1976. G-2009-020, box 13, file 6, NWTA. This file also contains the draft public statement on arsenic that cast doubt on the links between arsenic and cancer. It included weirdly simplistic messages containing possibly inaccurate statements like "everybody eats a little arsenic."
50 Jon Ferry, "Arsenic in Yellowknife Poisons Experts' Teamwork," *Edmonton Journal*, 12 October 1976, 40. Both Gemmill and Grainge may have attempted to suppress or criticize internally the other's report; Grainge acknowledges as much in his memoir, *The Changing North*, 169.
51 Catherine Lawson, "Study a Worse Problem than Arsenic," *News of the North*, 20 October 1976, 10.
52 Jervis, *Statement RE: Yellowknife Arsenic Pollution Problem*.
53 National Indian Brotherhood, the United Steelworkers of America, and the University of Toronto, *Document Released by the National Indian Brotherhood, the United Steelworkers of America, and the University of Toronto*.
54 See Tataryn, *Dying for a Living*, 124–5. Tataryn claimed that the cancer rates in Yellowknife were higher than the national average, and that they had climbed over the years that arsenic had been emitted in Yellowknife. He did note that the Statistics Canada demographers had cautioned that the small sample size of the Yellowknife population compromised the statistical significance of the cancer data.
55 Quoted in *Document Released by the National Indian Brotherhood, the United Steelworkers of America, and the University of Toronto*, 3. Notably, at the same time that controversy raged over the YES studies, the USWA was being displaced

as the union representing workers at Giant. After a dispute over the management of union dues, Giant employees voted for a new union in 1976, the Canadian Aluminum Smelter and Allied Workers (CASAW), which framed its takeover in nationalistic terms as a locally controlled, Canadian union replacing the distant US-based Steelworkers. By the end of 1976, CASAW began to negotiate a new contract with Giant. Nevertheless, the USWA continued to advocate on the arsenic issue in Yellowknife, as discussed below.

56 "Yellowknife Tests Show Arsenic Level 'Horrendously High,'" *Toronto Star*, 17 January 1977, A1 (Erasmus comments on page A2). The same story was reprinted in the *Ottawa Journal* and other newspapers. See also Victor Malarek, "Yellowknife Arsenic Level 'Horrendously High,'" *Globe and Mail*, 17 January 1977, A1–2.

57 The television program was summarized and quoted in Roman Semjanovs, "Arsenic Back to Haunt Us," *Yellowknifer*, 20 January 1977, 3, 7.

58 Jon Ferry, "Private Study Says Yellowknife Arsenic Level Dangerously High," *Edmonton Journal*, 17 January 1977, 1. Ferry's study also included a reference by Tataryn to the past deaths of Dene children from eating arsenic-laden snow.

59 "Yellowknife Mine Sure of Safeguards," *Albertan*, 18 January 1977, 2.

60 Department of National Health and Welfare Canada, "Task Force to Study Arsenic," news release, 18 January 1977. RG 29 vol. 2977, file 851-5-2, pt. 4, LAC.

61 "Lalonde Denies Cover-Up on Yellowknife Arsenic," *Calgary Herald*, 19 January 1977, 2. Lalonde took on the NIB in the media and in letters to Tataryn and others, which are collected in RG 29 vol. 2977, file 851-5-2, pts. 4 and 5, LAC.

62 Caron to Bruce Rawson, DM, 21 January 1977 RG 29, vol. 2977, file 851-5-2, pt. 4, LAC.

63 Gerald H. Dafoe, Executive Director, CPHA, to Noel Starblanket, President, NIB, 17 February 1977. RG 29 vol. 2978, file 851-5-2, pt. 5, LAC; Canadian Public Health Association, "CPHA Task Force on Arsenic Convenes," news release, 18 February 1977. RG 29, vol. 2978, file 851-5-2, pt. 5, LAC. Erasmus, president of the Indian Brotherhood of the Northwest Territories, also requested a seat and was denied: Erasmus to Marc Lalonde, 26 January 1977. RG 29, vol. 2978, file 851-5-2, pt. 4, LAC.

64 "Ottawa Hides the Poison," *Globe and Mail*, 19 January 1977, A6.

65 Richard Gwyn, "How a Bureaucracy Played Down Poison," *Toronto Star*, 22 January 1977, C1.

66 Jon Ferry, "New Arsenic Study More Hype than Fact," *Edmonton Journal*, 24 January 1977, 15.

67 Letter, Marc Lalonde to *Toronto Star*, 3 February 1977, RG 29 vol. 2978, file 851-5-2, pt. 6A, LAC.

68 "A Brief to the CPHA Task Force on Arsenic," United Steelworkers of America, 14 March 1977. RG 29, vol. 2978, file 851-5-2, pt. 5. LAC.

69 Ibid. The somewhat sketchy hearing transcripts in the same file echo these claims. A delegation from the CASAW local also testified, urging stronger pollution controls and protections for workers.

70 The substance of the NIB brief was published later by Starblanket and journalist Lloyd Tataryn as "Notes from the Territories," 12–15.

71 Sheila Brady, "Do Anything to Clean Up Arsenic, Indians Ask Government," *Ottawa Journal*, 29 March 1977. Clipping found in RG 29, vol. 2978, file 851-5-2, pt. 6A, LAC.

72 "Arsenic Task Force Hearing, Yellowknife, NWT," 14 March 1977. Transcript found in RG 29, vol. 2978, file 851-5-2, pt. 5, LAC.

73 Ibid.; "Family Fled Arsenic Level, Miner Is Ill," *Globe and Mail*, 16 March 1977, 9.

74 "Miners Use Polluted Water Probe Told," *Montreal Gazette*, 15 March 1977, 15; Jon Ferry, "Arsenic Hearing Traces Fears of Miners," *Edmonton Journal*, 16 March 1977, 29.

75 R.D.P. Eaton to Regional Director, NWT Region, 16 March 1977. RG 29, vol. 2978, file 851-5-2, pt. 5, LAC.

76 O. Schaefer, MD, to Dr M.B. Wheatley, acting co-ordinator, environmental contaminant program, Department of National Health and Welfare Canada, 4 April 1977. RG 29 vol. 2978, file 851-5-2, pt. 6A, LAC.

77 Grainge, *The Changing North*, 170–1.

78 Bruce Rawson, Deputy Minister of National Health and Welfare, Memo to the Minister, RG 29, vol. 2978, file 851-5-2, pt. 6A, LAC. There is no date on this memo but handwritten notes suggest it was drafted in July 1977.

79 H.P. Blejer, "Evaluation of Canadian Public Health Association Task Force on Arsenic Interim Report of May 1977." RG 29, vol. 2978, file 851-5-2, pt. 6B, LAC.

80 Victor Malarek, "US Expert Denounced 'Sloppy' Federal Study of Yellowknife Arsenic Contamination," *Globe and Mail*, 15 September 1977, 4. In addition to his media comments, Falkowski highlighted Blejer's "ignored" conclusions: *Presentation to The National Indian Brotherhood 8th Annual General Assembly*, 4.

81 Canadian Public Health Association, *Task Force on Arsenic.*

82 Ibid., 55–6.

83 Rosemary Cairns, "Most of YK Safe from Arsenic," *News of the North*, 4 January 1978, 1–2.

84 "Giant Striving to Control Emissions," *Yellowknifer*, 5 January 1978, 19.

85 Ronald J. Hawkes, President, NWT Chamber of Mines, to Hon. Monique Begin, Minister of National Health and Welfare, 15 February 1978. RG 29, vol. 2978, file 851-5-2, pt. 7. The recommendation for an environmental review board also immediately raised a question of its constitutionality, as it would mandate a Government of the Northwest Territories agency to review the decisions of federal ministers.

86 Cairns, "Most of YK Safe from Arsenic."

87 The USWA's point-by-point response is documented in Marsh Hawes, chairman, Steelworkers Arsenic Committee, to Monique Begin, Minister of National Health and Welfare, 18 January 1978. RG 29, vol. 2978, file 851-5-2, vol. 7; Peter Gorrie, "Report Downplays Arsenic Scare Story in Yellowknife," *Edmonton Journal*, 4 January 1978, 22.

88 Robert Blake, "Most Safe from Evils of Arsenic Latest Report Reveals," *Yellowknifer*, 5 January 1978, 5; Robert Blake, "Task Force Findings Just the Beginning," *Yellowknifer*, 2 February 1978, 19; Hubert Johnson, "Views Mixed Over Yellowknife Arsenic Report Findings," *Edmonton Journal*, 17 November 1978, 104. The NIB also released a short critical summary of the risks of environmental arsenic exposures: *Is the Arsenic in Yellowknife's Streets Good for You?*

89 The setup of the renewed committee is documented in RG 29, vol. 2978, file 851-5-2, pt. 6A and pt. 7, LAC; Terms of Reference are noted in G-1993-006, box 52, file 10 017 119, vol. 1, NWTA. As with the pre-1977 Standing Committee, Indigenous organizations never sent representatives.

90 Some of the hair and urine sample results for both workers and Dene children are reviewed in G-2008-028, box 9, file 13. In an interesting example of "refusal," there are some indications that Dene families were uneasy about being included in another round of hair studies – see R.D.P. Eaton to B. Wheatley, Memorandum RE: Arsenic in Yellowknife, Hair Levels in Indian Children, 20 March 1978. RG 29, vol. 2978, file 851-5-2, pt. 7, LAC.

91 Correspondence between R.D.P. Eaton and Marsh Hawes, United Steelworkers of America, 3 May 1978. G-2008-028, box 9, file 16, NWTA.

92 Canadian Public Health Association, news release, 15 November 1978. G-1993-006, box 5, file 10 017 119, NWTA.

93 O. Schaefer, MD, to Dr M.B. Wheatley, Co-ordinator, Environmental Contaminant Program, Department of National Health and Welfare Canada, 1 May 1978. G2008-028, box 9, file 16, NWTA.

94 R.B. Sutherland, MD, to Dr J.A. Hildes, Medical Health Unit, Faculty of Medicine, University of Manitoba, 20 April 1978. G-2008-028, box 9, file 16, NWTA.

95 Minutes, Standing Committee on Arsenic Meeting in Yellowknife, 31 January 1978. RG 29, vol. 2978, file 851-5-2, pt. 7, LAC. Moore's thoughts on the arsenic standard were communicated by letter to D. Egli, a member of the Standing Committee on Arsenic and also the NWT Chamber of Mines, 19 January 1978. G-1993-006, Box 52, file 10 017 119, NWTA.

96 R.D.P. Eaton to Regional Director, Medical Services Branch, Memorandum RE: United Steelworkers Comments on T.F. Report, 24 January 1978. RG 29, vol. 2978, file 851-5-2, pt. 7, LAC. NIOSH is a nongovernmental agency associated with the US Centres for Disease Control, focused on workplace safety. Thus, its studies and recommendations were not necessarily adopted by government agencies.

97 Occupational Exposure to Inorganic Arsenic, Final Standard, Occupational Safety and Health Administration, US Department of Labor, 5 May 1978. A copy was filed in G-1993-006, Box 52, File 10 017 113, Vol. 1, NWTA.

98 Correspondence with Mackenzie and others revealed this dilemma: if there was "no safe level" for arsenic, then establishing any permissible standard above zero could be seen as arbitrary. But studies of long-term, low-level occupational exposure were inconclusive, and in any case, it was impossible to detect arsenic below

two micrograms per cubic metre of air. So, adopting a standard that was "reasonable" and "attainable," given technological limitations, appeared to be the best strategy. See letters in G-2008-028, box 9, file 17, NWTA.

99 These problems continued into the early 1980s – see memos and correspondence in G-2008-028, box 9, file 17, NWTA.

100 Memorandum, Bruce Rawson, Deputy Minister, to Minister of National Health and Welfare, 19 January 1978. RG 29, vol. 2978, file 851-5-2, pt. 7, LAC. People in "Rainbow Valley" (Ndilǫ) occasionally used water from Back Bay, in spite of posted warnings against drinking or swimming. See CBC Mackenzie Network Summary, 12 May 1978. G-1993-006, box 52, file 10 017 119, vol. 2, NWTA.

101 Regional Director, NWT Region, to Associate Director General, Medical Services Branch, 11 October 1984. G-2008-028 box 9 file 17, NWTA.

102 Preliminary Report of a Special Committee Formed to Study the Levels of Arsenic in the Waters of Yellowknife, 13 January 1975. RG 29, vol. 2978, file 851-5-2, pt. 5, LAC.

103 W.D. Frost, MD, "Arsenic – Yellowknife," 25 January 1977. RG 29, vol. 2978, file 851-5-2, pt. 5, LAC.

104 Canadian Public Health Association, *Task Force on Arsenic*, 59–62.

105 Report by J. Grainge, regional engineer, to Standing Committee on Arsenic (Table 5), 4 June 1976. G-2009-020, Box 13, file 5, NWTA.

106 "Arsenic Waste Causes Concern," *Calgary Herald*, 9 February 1977, 17; see also *Victoria Daily Colonist*, 9 February 1977, 1.

107 Jon Ferry, "Arsenic in Permafrost May Pose Major Pollution Problem," *Edmonton Journal*, 8 February 1977, 26; Jon Ferry, "Natural Flooding May Allow Arsenic to Seep Out," *Calgary Herald*, 10 February 1977, 26.

108 Rosemary Cairns, "Giant Says There Is Not Now nor Ever Will Be an Arsenic Problem," *News of the North*, 16 February 1977, 6.

109 "Briefing Notes on the February 8 Episode of Arsenic in Yellowknife." RG 29, vol. 2978, file 851-5-2, pt. 5, LAC.

110 Canadian Public Health Association, *Task Force on Arsenic*, 63–4.

111 Victor Malarek, "Yellowknife's Arsenic Enough to Poison the World, Inquiry Told," *Globe and Mail*, 29 March 1977, 10.

112 Marsh Hawes, chairman, Steelworkers Arsenic Committee, to Monique Begin, Minister of National Health and Welfare, 18 January 1978. RG 29, vol. 2978, file 851-5-2, pt. 7, LAC.

113 Tataryn, "Arsenic and Red Tape," 30.

114 Falkowski, *Presentation to the National Indian Brotherhood 8th Annual General Assembly*, 1.

Chapter Five

1 Canadian Public Health Association, *Task Force on Arsenic*, 113.

2 Gold Roasting Industry Task Force on Arsenic Emissions, Notes on Third Meeting, 16 May 1978. G-1993-006, box 52, file 10 017 113, NWTA. Billing was introduced in chapter 3 and was the chief environmental protection officer for the Northwest Territories government.

3 Moore, Wheeler, and Sutherland, *The Effect of Metal Mines on Aquatic Ecosystems in the Northwest Territories*. The information on non-compliance issues with Baker Creek effluent was found in J. Redburn and A. MacDonald, Inspectors Under the Northern Inlands Water Act, "Report on the Compliance of Giant Yellowknife Mines, Ltd with Water Licence N1L3-0043, 27 November 1985. 1985 Water Board Hearings, MVLWB.

4 See Regional Public Affairs, News Summary No. 57–78, CBC Mackenzie Summary, 12 May 1978. G-1993-006, box 52, file 10 017 119, vol. 2, NWTA. Moore's comments were contained in: Notes by W.A. Moore on Report entitled, "The Effects of Metal Mines on Aquatic Ecosystems in the NWT – Giant Yellowknife Mines," 15 May 1978. G-1993-006, box 52, file 10 017 119, vol. 2, NWTA.

5 Moore reported this figure in the transcript, Northwest Territories Water Board Public Hearing, Application for Water License Renewal by Giant Yellowknife Mines, Ltd, 27 January 1981. Water Board Hearings, 1981, MVLWB.

6 The data regarding contaminant reductions in the effluent were contained in Environment Canada, Submission to the Water Board on an Application by Giant Yellowknife Mines, Ltd, for Water License Renewal, 27 November 1985. File titled: 1985 Water Board Hearings, Northwest Territories Water Board, MVLWB. The same file also contained a typed manuscript of a paper on water treatment at Giant Mine that two of the company's employees had presented at the Canadian Institute of Mining and Metallurgy Conference, Smithers, BC, October 1983.

7 Giant Yellowknife Mines, Annual Report, 1982. Copy found in a Giant Mine clippings file maintained by the NWTA.

8 For the company's claims about reduced seepage, see Giant Yellowknife Mines, Ltd, A Submission to the Northwest Territories Water Board, 5 January 1987, contained in the file titled: Royal Oak Mines, Abandonment and Restoration, 1980s, MVLWB.

9 Northwest Territories Water Board Public Hearing on an Application by Giant Yellowknife Mines, Ltd Yellowknife Operations to Renew Water Licence N1L3-0043. Contained in a file titled: 1985 Water Board Hearings, MVLWB.

10 The data on spills was obtained from J. Redburn and A. MacDonald, Inspectors Under the Northern Inlands Water Act, "Report on the Compliance of Giant Yellowknife Mines, Ltd with Water Licence N1L3-0043, 27 November 1985. 1985 Water Board Hearings, MVLWB, and Government of the Northwest Territories, Department of Renewable Resources, Pollution Control Division, Reported Spills – Summary. G 1993-006, box 46, file 165 022, NWTA. Although the impacts of these

spills are not recorded in the available documents, the amounts of wastewater spills ranged from 2,000 to 74,000 litres, the tailings spills ranged from 22,700 to 90,000 litres, and the two arsenic spills involved 100 and 200 kilograms of material.

11 The request for an amendment to the existing water licence (to allow deposition in Baker Creek) came in a letter from Ken Blower, General Manager, Giant Mine, to Glenn Warner, Chair, Northwest Territories Water Board, 21 June 1985; Warner communicated his approval to Blower on 18 July 1985. Both documents were located in the file: Abandonment and Restoration 1980s and Background Documents, MVLWB.

12 Northwest Territories Water Board Public Hearing on an Application by Giant Yellowknife Mines, Ltd. Yellowknife Operations to Renew Water Licence N1L3-0043. Contained in a file titled: 1985 Water Board Hearings, MVLWB.

13 Donnelly to W.A. Moore, 18 June 1979. N-2005-022, box/file 36-2, NWTA.

14 Occupational Health Unit, Medical Services Branch, Department of National Health and Welfare, "Arsenic Exposure in Workplace Areas at Giant Yellowknife Mines, Yellowknife NWT," n.d. G-1993-006, box 29, file 13 408 024, NWTA. The company sent a formal memo to employees on 27 October 1981 emphasizing the use of protective gear in areas with arsenic dust, perhaps unintentionally underlining the fact that exposure levels in some work areas were still not safe. G. Aaltonen, "Safe Working Procedures in Arsenic Exposure Areas," 27 October 1981. N-2005–022, box/file 36-4, NWTA.

15 The primary purpose of the task force was described in the minutes of its first meeting, 5–6 July 1977, Ottawa. G-1993-006, box 52, file 10 017 113, vol. 1, NWTA.

16 Price to Earl Gagan, Environment Canada, 10 August 1977. G-1993-006, box 52, file 10 017 113, vol. 1, NWTA. Gagan was the chair of the Gold Processing Industry Task Force on Arsenic Emissions. Environment Canada's proposed stack limit was contained in Minutes of the Gold Processing Industry Task Force on Arsenic Emissions, 5–6 July 1977, Ottawa. G-1993-006, box 52, file 10 017 113, vol. 1, NWTA.

17 W.A. Moore to L.S. Price, Manager, Environmental Controls, Giant Yellowknife Mines, Ltd, 17 August 1977. G-1993-006, box 52, file 10 017 113, vol. 1, NWTA.

18 Gold Roasting Industry Task Force on Arsenic Emissions, Notes on Third Meeting, 16 May 1978. G-1993-006, box 52, file 10 017 113, vol. 1, NWTA.

19 The figure of 29 pounds/day was drawn from the previously cited Memo from Regional Director, Medical Services Branch, NWT Region to the Associate Director, Medical Services Branch, 11 October 1984. G-2008-028, box 9, file 17, NWTA. The lower figure of 20 pounds/day and the below limit readings in the 1970s were taken from K.W. Hall, Stack Testing Report – 1979, 22 January 1980. G-1993–006 box 29, file 13 408 024, NWTA. For evidence of ongoing reductions, see R.J. Kent, Environmental Protection Service, A Report on Arsenic Emissions During August 1981 at Giant Yellowknife Mines, January 1982, G-1993-006, box 29, file 13 408 024, NWTA.

20 Lorne James, Pollution Control Engineer, Government of the Northwest Territories to Robert Janes, Science Institute of the Northwest Territories, 23 June 1986. G-1993-006, box 19, file 13 408 024, NWTA.

21 Air Quality Monitoring in the Northwest Territories, 1989 Data. Document found in Kevin O'Reilly's personal collection. Over the course of three decades of activism on the Giant Mine issue, O'Reilly collected a trove of reports, newspaper articles, and archival documents. He graciously shared this material with us.

22 For a full discussion of threshold limit values, see Boudia, "Managing Scientific and Political Uncertainty," 95–112; Vogel, "From 'The Dose Makes the Poison' to 'The Timing Makes the Poison,'" 667–73; Western, "Arsenic Lost Years," 1–36; Ziem and Castleman, "Threshold Limit Values," 910–18. For a more general discussion, see Langston, *Toxic Bodies*; Liboiron, *Pollution Is Colonialism*; Nash, *Inescapable Ecologies*. For a study of corporate resistance to pollution controls, see Markowitz and Rosner, *Deceit and Denial*.

23 Occupational Exposure to Inorganic Arsenic, Final Standard, Occupational Safety and Health Administration, US Department of Labor, 5 May 1978. A copy was filed in G-1993-006, box 52, file 10 017 113, vol. 1, NWTA.

24 Ibid. See also "Commentary by the Science Advisory Board of the Northwest Territories on the Final Report of the CPHA Task Force on Arsenic," Working Paper No. 1, 27 January 1978. G-1993-006 box 52, file 10 017 119, vol. 1, NWTA.

25 Gemmill forwarded most of these papers between late 1977 and throughout much of 1978. Unlike today's electronic repositories, these papers were difficult to access and share. Yet, on one occasion Gemmill managed to forward eleven papers. See Gemmill to Billing, 2 November 1977. G-1993-006, box 52, file 10 017 119, vol. 1, NWTA. There were many other papers scattered through this first volume of the arsenic files and also volume 2 of the same file.

26 David Halliburton, Mining, Mineral and Metallurgical Division, Abatement and Compliance Branch, Air Pollution Control Directorate, Department of National Health and Welfare Atmospheric Emissions and Control Technology – Gold Roasting Operations, April 1978. G-1993-006, box 52, file 10 017 113, vol. 1, NWTA.

27 M. Friesen, Chief Engineer, Giant Yellowknife Mines, Collection and Storage of Arsenic-Bearing Dust, and Giant Yellowknife Mines. Company report (November 1971; revised and updated August 1984). Copy located in the personal files of Kevin O'Reilly.

28 Giant Yellowknife Mines, Ltd Restoration and Abandonment Plans, 16 October 1985. Copy found in the folder, Royal Oak Mines Abandonment and Restoration Plans and Background Documents, 1980s, MVLWB. For the WAROX controversy, see List of Environmental Concerns and Recommendations: Regional Environmental Review Committee, NAP, INAC, Yellowknife, NWT, Re: Giant Yellowknife Mines, Ltd Proposed WAROX Transfer Facility at Enterprise, NWT, October 1988. G-1993-006, box 46, file 165 022, NWTA. Concerns about the WAROX plan in Enterprise are referenced in a letter from K. Morton, Project

Supervisor, Giant Yellowknife Mines, Ltd to Winnie Cadieux, Chair, Enterprise Settlement Council, 2 November 1988; and concerns at Hay River are outlined in a news article, "Council Objects to Site Request for Arsenic Transfer," *The Hub*, 24 August 1988. Both documents were found in G-1993-006, box 46, file 165 022, NWTA. The idea for the transfer plant at Enterprise dated back to 1978 and was tied directly to Giant Yellowknife Mines' relationship to Koppers. See John Hite, President, Koppers, to David Emery, President, Giant Yellowknife Mines, Ltd, 1 August 1971. G-1993-006, box 52, file 10 017 119, vol. 2, NWTA. The unsuitability of Giant Mine's arsenic in the Koppers plan is mentioned in Royal Oak Mines, Ltd, "An Assessment of Scientific Data Relating to the Permanent Storage of Arsenic Trioxide in the Underground Mine Workings at the Giant Mine." Terms of reference for an environmental study for the Northwest Territories Water Board, 1993. Personal files of Kevin O'Reilly.

29 This assessment is based on a survey of the notes for the Joint (management and union) Health and Safety Committee at Giant Mine through the 1980s, and also the minutes of the Joint Health and Safety Committee from 1987 to 1989. N-2005-022, Box/File 1-1, 1-3 and 1-4, NWTA. To be fair to the union, some of the relative decline in attention paid to arsenic may be because the committee members from the union had a lot of pollution issues to address, including asbestos in old buildings, PCB exposure, and the handling of cyanide. Exposure to silica dust remained a concern, even if levels stayed below thresholds for much of the decade.

30 Selleck and Thompson, *Dying for Gold*, 8. Profit numbers for Giant Mine were found in the "Year to Date" column in the December 1978 and 1979 Summary of Operations for the mine, N-2001-014, Giant Yellowknife Mines, Ltd Fonds, box 6, files 3 and 4, NWTA. Details on CASAW's wage demands and the company's perceptions of picket line violence were taken from a memo sent from W.A. Moore to Giant President D.J. Emery, 6 October 1980. N-2001-014, Giant Yellowknife Mines, Ltd Fonds, box 7, file 1, NWTA. Gold price data was taken from Macrotrends, "Gold Prices – 100 Year Historical Chart." Accessed 15 May 2023. https://www.macrotrends.net/1333/historical-gold-prices-100-year-chart.

31 N-2001-014, Giant Yellowknife Mines, Ltd Fonds, box 7, files 2 and 6, NWTA.

32 See Selleck and Thompson, *Dying for Gold*, 8–11.

33 Selleck, "The Giant Mine Tragedy," 32–6. The industry's struggles in this period, which led to a wave of mine closures and bankruptcies, are recounted in McAllister and Alexander, *A Stake in the Future*.

34 Selleck and Thompson, *Dying for Gold*, 12–23; Selleck, "The Giant Mine Tragedy," 32–6; Danielson, "The Northern Miner's 1991 'Mining Man of the Year': Margaret (Peggy) Witte." Year-to-date operational profits were taken from income statements found in N-2001-014, Giant Yellowknife Mines, Ltd Fonds, Box 9, File 1 and 2, NWTA.

35 Selleck and Thompson, *Dying for Gold*, 23–38.

36 In addition to Selleck and Thompson, see Staples and Owens, *The Third Suspect*; Hunter and O'Malley, *Giant Mine*; Zelniker, *Giant: Murder Underground*.

37 Singh, Zinni, and Jain, "The Effects of the Use of Striker Replacement Workers in Canada," 61–85.

38 The early stages of the strike are described evocatively in Selleck and Thompson, *Dying for Gold*, 35–74; and also Zelniker, *Giant: Murder Underground*, episode 2, "The Lockout," https://www.cbc.ca/listen/cbc-podcasts/1066-giant, which contains extensive audio recordings from events described in this paragraph.

39 David Staples and Greg Owens, "Murder in the Mine: The Nine Doomed Miners Were Making a Routine Descent into the Gold-Rich, Strike-Torn Giant Mine when an Echoing Blast Signaled Trouble Below," *Edmonton Journal*, 26 September 1992, G1.

40 The quote from Hoddinott and other details come from Zelniker, *Giant: Murder Underground*, episode 3, "The Explosion"; episode 4, "The Investigation"; episode 5, "The Interrogation"; episode 6, "Judgment."

41 Canadian Press, "Labor Board Rules Against Mine Owners; Bad-Faith Charge Upheld," *Edmonton Journal*, 12 November 1993, A1. See also *Royal Oak Mines Inc. v. Canada (Labour Relations Board)*, 1996 CanLII 220 (SCC), [1996] 1 SCR 369, accessed 28 May 2023, https://www.canlii.org/en/ca/scc/doc/1996/1996canlii220/1996canlii220.html.

42 Minutes of the Joint Health and Safety Committee from 1987 to 1989. N-2005-022, Box/File 1-8 to 1-14, NWTA.

43 May, "Brian Mulroney and the Environment," 381–92. On anti-logging blockades, see Hodgins, Lischke, and McNab, eds., *Blockades and Resistance*; and Stefanick, "Baby Stumpy and the War in the Woods," 41–68. The Green Plan has been criticized for focusing more on disseminating information than promoting meaningful policy changes. See Hoberg and Harrison, "It's Not Easy Being Green," 119–37.

44 The initial request for the amendment to the water licence was made in a letter from Connell to Nickerson, 15 June 1993, and the company's analysis of the reasons for the ammonia spike were included in the text of a presentation to the water board's Technical Advisory committee, given on June 14, detailing the background to the issue. Both documents located in N1L3-0043, 1991–93, MVLWB.

45 Nickerson approved the new fifteen-parts-per-million limit in a memo to Connell, 19 June 1993. Connell's second request for the lifting of all ammonia limits was sent 23 July 1993. Nickerson's response is dated 30 July 1993. All documents located in N1L3-0043, 1991–93, MVLWB.

46 Canadian Press, "Gold-Mine Owners Seek Laxer Environmental Laws," *Edmonton Journal*, 32 July 1993, F2. The cartoon was from the 8 July 1994 edition of the *Yellowknifer*. Clipping from Kevin O'Reilly's personal files. The editorial was titled "Environmental Threat Must Be Assessed," *Yellowknifer*, 3 November 1993. Clipping from O'Reilly's personal files.

47 See Peter Atamanenko to Northwest Territories Water Board, 26 October 1993; and Clark Marcino, Public Hearing Submission to the Northwest Territories Water Board on the Application by Royal Oak Mines to Delete Ammonia

Emission Standards from, Licence N1L3-0043, 26 October 1993. All documents located in N1L3-0043, 1991–93, MVLWB. Subsequent documents indicate that Atamanenko was secretary of Northwest Territories EnviroWatch.

48 Beaulieu to Nickerson, 26 October 1993. N1L3-0043, 1991–93, MVLWB.

49 For an account of the hearings, see Nancy Rempel, "Fifty Attend Giant Water Licence Review," *Northern Star*, 3 November 1993. Clipping from personal files of Kevin O'Reilly. For more detailed information on the positions of key players, see the written submission of Royal Oak Mines and the Department of Indian and Northern Affairs, both dated 26 October 1993, and the joint submission of Environment Canada and the Department of Fisheries and Oceans, 15 October 1993. N1L3-0043, 1991–93, MVLWB.

50 Northwest Territories Water Board Reasons for Decision, Licence Number N1L3-0043, n.d. N1L3-0043, 1999–October 2000, MVLWB. Environment Canada's assessment of the ammonia situation in 1998 is contained in its Submission to the Northwest Territories Water Board on an Application for Water License Renewal, N1L3-0043, Royal Oak Mines, Inc., 16 January 1998. N1L3-0043, 1997–98, MVLWB.

51 Munton and Temby, "Smelter Fumes, Local Interests, and Political Contestation in Sudbury," 24–36; Kuhlberg and Miller, "'Protection to the Sulphur-Smoke Tort-Feasors,'" 225–57; Wirth, *Smelter Smoke in North America*; Macdonald, *The Politics of Pollution*.

52 O'Reilly was quoted in Judy Langford, "Giant Gases Cause Tree Damage: Study," *Northern Star*, 7 July 1992, 1. The impact of sulphur dioxide, especially its impacts on local vegetation, was mentioned in the early 1970s in O'Toole, Clark, Malaby, and Trauger, "Environmental Trace Element Survey at a Heavy Metals Refining Site," 172–85.

53 Arlene Bell, Letter to the Editor, "Giant's Insidious Emissions," *Yellowknifer*, 2 August 1995, 8.

54 Hocking, Kuchar, Plambeck, and Smith, "The Impact of Gold Smelter Emissions on Vegetation and Soils of a Sub-Arctic Forest-Tundra Transition Ecosystem," 133–7.

55 Chris O'Brien and Kevin O'Reilly to Titus Allooloo, Minister of Renewable Resources, Northwest Territories, 22 April 1991. Personal files of Kevin O'Reilly. The report cited in the letter was D. Maynard and S. Malhotra, "The Impact of SO_2 on the Soils and Vegetation Near Giant Mine," *Forestry Canada*, 1990. Allooloo's reply to O'Brien and O'Reilly was dated 4 June 1991, and also located in O'Reilly's personal files.

56 Meeting Minutes, Giant Mines: SO_2 Emissions, 23 October 1990. Personal files of Kevin O'Reilly.

57 The information on air quality monitoring came from the document, *Northwest Territories Renewable Resources Department, Yellowknife Air Quality Monitoring, 1991 and 1992 Data*. The air quality report, which was responding to O'Reilly and O'Brien's request for an investigation, was produced by the Environmental

Protection Division, Department of Renewable Resources, Government of the Northwest Territories, "An Investigation of Atmospheric Emissions from the Royal Oak Giant Mine," June 1993. All documents located in O'Reilly's personal files.

58 Judy Langford, "Giant Gases Cause Tree Damage: Study," *Northern Star*, 7 July 1993, 1.

59 Editorial, "Report Fails to Clear the Air," *Yellowknifer*, 9 July 1993, 7.

60 Editorial, "Where's Mr. Wizard When You Need Him?" *Yellowknifer*, 14 July 1993, 7.

61 Don McNealy, Norm Plante, and Dale Johnston, "Arsenic a Danger at Giant Mine," *Northern Star*, 25 August 1993. Clipping from the personal files of Kevin O'Reilly.

62 Editorial, "Cleaning Up the Neighborhood," *Northern Star*, 7 July 1993, 6.

63 Nuttall's comments are quoted in Doug Schmidt, "No 'Imminent Health Hazard' from Giant Emissions: Report," *Yellowknifer*, 23 July 1993, 3, 28. Nuttall may have derived the line about "no imminent health hazard" from an advisory document that J.R. Hickman, director general of the environmental health directorate, sent to Dr Ian Gilchrist, medical director, Northwest Territories Health, on 6 July 1993. The document deals with sulphur dioxide and arsenic, and it notes that, despite the lack of an immediate threat, arsenic is a "known human carcinogen," and should be "reduced to the lowest possible level." Document from the personal files of Kevin O'Reilly.

64 Royal Oak Mines, "Atmospheric Emissions at the Giant Mine," press release, 9 July 1993. Personal files of Kevin O'Reilly.

65 Kevin O'Reilly, guest column, "Zero Discharge the Only Solution," *Yellowknifer*, 26 July 1995, 9.

66 Draft Motion on Giant Mine Air Emissions, n.d. Royal Oak's response to the passage of this motion is recorded in a letter from Sadek El-Alfy, Vice President of Operations, Royal Oak Mines, 4 October 1995. Both documents from the personal files of Kevin O'Reilly.

67 A transcript of Judy Langford's report on CBC radio, 24 May 1995, was found in the personal files of Kevin O'Reilly.

68 Michel Paper, Evidence, Parliamentary Hearings on Canadian Environmental Protection Act, 11 May 1995, accessed 3 March 2021, http://www.parl.gc.ca/content/hoc/archives/committee/351/sust/evidence/122_95-05-11/sust122_blk-e.html#0.1.SUST122.000001.AA1040.A.

69 Testimony of Michel Paper, Isadore Tsetta, and Fred Sangris, Yellowknife Hearings, Standing Committee on Environment and Sustainable Development, House of Commons, Canada, 11 May 1995, accessed 14 June 2023, https://www.ourcommons.ca/content/archives/committee/351/sust/evidence/122_95-05-11/sust122_blk-e.html.

70 Bill Erasmus, Jonas Sangris, and Darrell Beaulieu to Mary O'Neill, Special Assistant, Office of the Minister of the Environment, 17 May 1995. Personal files of Kevin O'Reilly.

71 Stephen Kakfwi, Minister of Renewable Resources, "Reducing Local Sulphur Dioxide Air Pollution." Transcript of an address in the Legislative Assembly found in O'Reilly's personal files. A copy of the draft "Gold Roaster Discharge Regulations" under CEPA were also found in O'Reilly's personal files. A search of the online *Northwest Territories Gazette* for the years 1996 to 1999 revealed no listing for any regulations related to Giant Mine's roaster emissions. O'Reilly recalls that "nothing further happened" regarding the roaster discharge regulations. See Kevin O'Reilly, "Liability, Legacy, and Perpetual Care," 348.

72 Steven Mitchell, Letter to the Editor, "Royal Oak Is Irresponsible," *Yellowknifer*, 31 July 1996. Clipping from the personal files of Kevin O'Reilly.

73 *Yellowknife Area Air Quality Monitoring, 1997 Data*. This report was found in the personal files of Kevin O'Reilly, and (despite the title) also includes readings from 1998 and multi-year averages.

74 Mary O'Neill, Special Assistant to Copps, to Bill Erasmus, Dene National Chief, 11 September 1995. The information on the designation of arsenic as toxic came from a backgrounder, "Priority Substances Assessment Program," 10 February 1994. Both documents were found in the personal files of Kevin O'Reilly.

75 The cost–benefit analysis is contained in a report authored by Environment Canada, Health Canada, and the Government of the Northwest Territories Health and Social Services, "Controlling Arsenic Releases to the Environment in the Northwest Territories: Discussion of Management Options," April 1997. Unpublished report for consultation, found in the personal files of Kevin O'Reilly. The quote on Royal Oak is from page 54 of the report and the financial projections are from page 47.

76 Resource Futures International, report prepared for Environment Canada, *Socio-Economic Analysis of Three Management Options to Reduce Atmospheric Emissions of Arsenic from Gold Roasting*, 9 September 1996, 27. Personal files of Kevin O'Reilly.

77 The federal government did lower the drinking water guidelines from 0.05 milligrams per litre to 0.01 milligrams per litre, but not until 2006. See Health Canada, *Guidelines for Canadian Drinking Water Quality*.

78 Resource Futures International, *Socio-Economic Analysis of Three Management Options to Reduce Atmospheric Emissions of Arsenic from Gold Roasting*, 53; and Environment Canada, Health Canada, and Government of the Northwest Territories Health and Social Services, *Controlling Arsenic Releases to the Environment in the Northwest Territories: Discussion of Management Options*, April 1993, 18. Both reports found in the personal files of Kevin O'Reilly.

79 Resource Futures International, Report Prepared for Environment Canada, *Socio-Economic Analysis of Three Management Options to Reduce Atmospheric Emissions of Arsenic from Gold Roasting*, 58–9.

80 Testimony of Fred Sangris, Yellowknife Hearings, Standing Committee on Environment and Sustainable Development, House of Commons, Canada, 11 May 1995, accessed 14 June 2023, https://www.ourcommons.ca/content/archives/committee/351/sust/evidence/122_95-05-11/sust122_blk-e.html.

81 Resource Futures International, *Socio-Economic Analysis of Three Management Options to Reduce Atmospheric Emissions of Arsenic from Gold Roasting*, 59. Data on Indigenous employment at Giant Mine is hard to come by because the company did not keep track of this in its annual reports. One news report from 1969 stated that just 3.5 per cent of the workforce at that time was Indigenous. See "Giant Mine: The Story of What Makes the North," *News of the North*, 24 April 1969. Article found in a clipping file created by the NWTA

Chapter Six

1 The employment figure was cited in Bob Weber, "Lights Out at Mine Means Giant Changes for Yellowknife," *Lethbridge Herald*, 2 November 1999, A7.

2 Employment figures were taken from Royal Oak Mines, Inc., April 1997 Highlights. N-2001-014, box 11, file 2, NWTA. For the issues surrounding the diamond mines, see Bielawski, *Rogue Diamonds*; DiFrancesco, "A Diamond in the Rough," 114–34; Hall, "Diamond Mining in Canada's Northwest Territories," 376–93.

3 Reference to the depths of the chambers was found in Golder Associates, *Final Abandonment and Restoration Plan, Miramar Giant Mine*, 26 September 2001, vol. 2, p. A-6-5. A copy of the report was found at the MVLWB.

4 Doug Ashbury, "Rocky Road Ahead: Civic Leaders Fear More Layoffs in Mining Sector," *Yellowknifer*, 21 November 1997, A3.

5 Royal Oak's financial challenges are described in a background document, likely produced by the Government of the Northwest Territories, authored by Balesh Konda, Royal Oak Mines, Inc., 10 November 1997. G-2012-026, File 1-8, NWTA. See also Allan Robison, "Losses Mount at Royal Oak," *Globe and Mail*, 1 April 1998, B1, B12.

6 Analysis of the Economic Impact of the Closure of Giant Mine, 4 October 1999. G-2013-029, file 1-2, NWTA.

7 Canadian Autoworkers Local 2304, Socioeconomic Impact Study of Giant Mine Closure. 20 September 1999. G-2013-029, file 1-2, NWTA.

8 NWT Executive Council, Assistance for Con and Royal Oak/Giant Mines, 25 February 1995. G-2013-029, file 1-8, NWTA. See also Information Brief, States of Giant and Con Mines, Yellowknife, n.d. G-2013-029, file 1-2, NWTA.

9 Government of the Northwest Territories, Communications Plan: Exploration and Development Assistance to Royal Oak (Giant) Mine, n.d. G-2013-029, file 1-2, NWTA.

10 Ibid.

11 Connell's comments are found in Northwest Territories Water Board Public Hearing on an Application by Royal Oak Mines, Inc., for the Renewal of Water

License N1L3-0043, 14 January 1993. The comment on cold air being pumped into the mine is recorded on page 20 and there are further comments on page 72. A standalone copy of the transcript was found in the paper public registry of the MVLWB. The conditions for the water licence are found in Pt. B, Northwest Territories Water License, N1L2-0043, 1 May 1994. Miramar Giant Mine, 1999–October 2000, MVLWB.

12 Neil Jamieson, Director, Public Works and Engineering, City of Yellowknife, to Jim McCaul, Head, Regulatory Approvals Section, Northwest Territories Water Board, 20 June 1997. Miramar Giant Mine, 1997–98, MVLWB.

13 Wray to Tim Acton, Vice President of Operations, Royal Oak Mines, 16 June 1997. Northwest Territories Water License, N1L2-0043. Miramar Giant Mine, 1997–98, MVLWB.

14 Ed Szol, Executive Vice President and Chief Operations Officer, to Gordon Wray, Chair, Northwest Territories Water Board, 18 August 1997. Northwest Territories Water License, N1L2-0043. Miramar Giant Mine, 1997–98, MVLWB.

15 Dillon Consulting, *Giant Mine Arsenic Trioxide Management.*

16 Northwest Territories Water Board Public Hearing on an Application by Royal Oak Mines, Inc. Giant Mine, Water Licence N1L2-0043, 28–29 January 1998. MVLWB, p. 25.

17 Ibid., 26–9.

18 Ibid., 129–31, quote on page 131.

19 Ibid., 136.

20 Ibid., 137.

21 Ibid., 117.

22 Peter Atamanenko, General Secretary, NWT EnviroWatch, to Vicki Loser, Northwest Territories Water Board, 21 May 1997. Northwest Territories Water License, N1L2-0043. Miramar Giant Mine, 1997–98, MVLWB.

23 Dave Talbot, Submission to the Northwest Territories Water Board, January 1998. Northwest Territories Water License, N1L2-0043. Miramar Giant Mine, 1997–98, MVLWB.

24 Gordon Wray, Chair, Northwest Territories Water Board to Margaret Witte, President and CEO, Royal Oak Mines, 13 February 1998. Northwest Territories Water License, N1L2-0043. Miramar Giant Mine 1997–98, MVLWB.

25 Royal Oak Mines, Inc., "Arsenic Trioxide Management, Giant Mine, Yellowknife, NWT," 31 March 1998. Unpublished report prepared for the Northwest Territories Water Board, re: licence N1L2-0043. Royal Oak Documents Binder, MVLWB.

26 Anne-Marie Jennings, "Giant Gets a Break," *Yellowknifer*, 1 April 1998. Clipping found in the personal files of Kevin O'Reilly.

27 Northwest Territories Water Board Reasons for Decisions, License Number N1L2-0043, 23 November 1999. Northwest Territories Water License, N1L2-0043. Miramar Giant Mine, 1999–2000, MVLWB.

28 M.J. Brodie, Brodie Consulting, to Neill Thompson, 5 March 1999. Northwest Territories Water License, N1L2-0043. Miramar Giant Mine, 1999–2000,

MVLWB. The reference to wooden bulkheads was found in Northwest Territories Water Board Public Hearing on an Application by Royal Oak Mines, Inc. Giant Mine, Water Licence N1L2-0043, 28-29 January 1998. MVLWB, p. 22.

29 Dene Nation, "Dene Nation Concern over Royal Oak Mines, Inc.," press release, 16 February 1999. Found in the personal files of Kevin O'Reilly.

30 James Stevenson, "Eulogy Read for Royal Oak," *Victoria Times Colonist*, 16 April 1999, D1. See also Keith Damsell, "Royal Oak Placed in Receivership, Board Resigns," *Financial Post*, 17 April 1999. Clipping found in the personal files of Kevin O'Reilly.

31 Dane Gibson, "Cashless Mine Owes Big," *Yellowknifer*, 7 May 1999, A9.

32 Allan Robinson and Paul Waldie, "Royal Oak Simply 'Unlucky,' Witte Contends," *Globe and Mail*, 20 April 1999, B3; Allan Robinson, Mining Reporter, "Royal Oak Board Quits, Firm in Receivership: Witte and Directors Resign as Debt Cripples Company; Miner Unable to Find Rescue Plan," *Globe and Mail*, 17 April 1999, B1.

33 Allan Robinson, "Taxpayers May Face Giant Cleanup Bill," *Globe and Mail*, 20 April 1999, B3.

34 The surface cleanup figure is from Det'on Cho Environmental Alliance, "Environmental Site Assessment and Cost Estimate of Giant Mine." Unpublished report for the Government of the Northwest Territories and DIAND, November 1999. Copy located at the MVLWB. The figure was reported in the media several times. See, for example, "Giant Mine Surface Cleanup Tab $16 Million," *Edmonton Journal*, 9 December 1999, A9. For Colomac, see Ian McKinnon, "Royal Oak May Leave Taxpayers on Hook: Cleanup at NWT Mines Likely to Top $256 Million," *National Post*, 9 March 1999, C1; Richard Gleeson, "Cleanup Dollars in Short Supply: $3 Million to Cover This Year's Work at Both Giant and Colomac Mines," *News North*, 26 June 2000, A5. Royal Oak also owed $575,000 in property taxes to the City of Yellowknife. See John Monroe, Manager, Tax Policy, Fiscal Policy Division, Department of Finance, Government of the Northwest Territories, Update on Miramar Con and Giant Mines Discussions, 6 March 1998. G-2013-029, File 1-2, NWTA. For Hope Brook, see "Province Seeks Clean-Up Costs," *Telegram* (St John's), 29 July 1999, Metro/Provincial News, 4; and Editorial, "How Does the Province Clean Up Old Mines," *Telegram* (St John's), 14 May 1999, 10.

35 Quoted in Ian McKinnon, "Royal Oak May Leave Taxpayers on Hook: Cleanup at NWT Mines Likely to Top $256 Million," *National Post*, 9 March 1999, C1.

36 Quoted in ibid.

37 An attitude captured in Matthew McClearn, "Mining: Sh*t Happens but You Move On," *Canadian Business Magazine*, 27 May 2009, 68–74.

38 Canadian Press Wire, "MLA Urges Cleanup of Arsenic at Infamous Gold Mine," 4 June 1999. E-mailed version of the story found in the personal files of Kevin O'Reilly.

39 Dane Gibson, "DIAND Under Giant Pressure," *Yellowknifer*, 4 June 1999, A5.

40 Northwest Territories Federation of Labour, press release, 28 April 1999. Personal files of Kevin O'Reilly.

41 Editorial, "Dealer's Choice," *Yellowknifer*, 11 June 1999, A7.

42 Richard Gibson, "Willing to Bend: DIAND 'Flexible' on Giant Arsenic Liability," *Yellowknifer*, 4 June 1999, A5.

43 "Union Under Gun to Produce Plan to Buy Struggling Mine," *Edmonton Journal*, 8 September 1999, H3.

44 Keith Damsell, "Union Abandons Its Drive to Save Notorious Mine," *National Post*, 21 September 1999, C1.

45 Department of Resources, Wildlife, and Economic Development submission to the Financial Management Board, n.d. G-2012–026, file 1-6, NWTA.

46 The reference to the ten-dollar purchase price was found in Jorge Barrera, "A Small Step Forward: Cuts to Giant Pensions Less than Expected," *Yellowknifer*, 16 June 2000, A13. More details on the sale were found in a press release from Miramar, "Miramar Acquires Giant Mine Assets, Boosts Production and Lowers Costs," 14 December 1999. Personal files of Kevin O'Reilly. See also Government of the Northwest Territories' Role in Giant Mine Surface Reclamation, 18 November 1999. G-2012-026, file 1-6, Government of the Northwest Territories.

47 Department of Resources, Wildlife, and Economic Development, Government of the Northwest Territories, "Operation and Sale of Giant Mine," 12 August 1999. G-2012-026, file 1-7, NWTA.

48 Quoted in Bob Weber, "Yellowknife Bids Farewell to Giant: With Historic Gold-Mining Industry Losing Its Lustre, NWT City Works to Find New Identity," *Globe and Mail*, 1 November 1999, A5.

49 Transcript of CBC Radio segment, "Lupin Mine May Hire Laid-Off Giant Mine Employees," 15 November 1999. G-2012-026, file 1-6, NWTA.

50 Bob Weber, "Yellowknife Bids Farewell to Giant," A5.

51 These quotes were found in a transcript of the CBC Radio segment, "Last Day of Work for Giant Employees," 12 November 1999. G-2012-026, file 1-6, NWTA.

52 Jorge Barrera, "A Small Step Forward: Cuts to Giant Pensions Less than Expected," *Yellowknifer*, 16 June 2000, A13.

53 Giant Mine's environmental liabilities just prior to Royal Oak's demise are detailed in the appendix to a report by the Department of Resources, Wildlife, and Economic Development, Government of the Northwest Territories, "Abandonment and Cleanup of Giant Mine," 28 September 1999. G-2012-026, file 1-6, NWTA.

54 Transcript of the CBC Radio segment, "Shut Down of Giant's Roaster Results in Cleaner Air for Yellowknife," 4 May 2000. Personal files of Kevin O'Reilly. The improvement to asthma symptoms was reported in a focus group study: Lutra Associates, Ltd, "Awareness Testing: Findings from the Focus Groups on Giant Mine and the Arsenic Trioxide." Unpublished report prepared for DIAND, January 2002. Northwest Territories Water License, N1L2-0043. Miramar Giant Mine, February 2002–September 2002, MVLWB.

55 See Department of Resources, Wildlife, and Economic Development submission to the Financial Management Board, Cleanup of Giant Mine Surface Environmental Liabilities, 7 March 2000. G-2012–026, file 1-6, NWTA. Reference to the legal opinion on DIAND's responsibilities was found in a briefing produced by the Department of Resources, Wildlife, and Economic Development, Government of the Northwest Territories. Operation and Sale of Giant Mine, 12 August 2000. G-2012-026, file 1-7, NWTA. The background on the transfer of the Giant Mine lease to the Government of the Northwest Territories, the possible liability associated with it, and the reasons why the Government of the Northwest Territories would only be responsible for surface issues, is found in a position paper by the staff of the Department of Municipal and Community Affairs, "Government of the Northwest Territories Role in Giant Mine Surface Reclamation," forwarded under cover letter from Gay Kennedy on 18 November 1999, G-2012-026, file 1-6, NWTA.

56 Miramar Mining Corporation, "Miramar Intends to Return to Giant Mine at Year-End," news release, 22 June 2001. Personal files of Kevin O'Reilly. More details were found in a transcript of a CBC Radio report, "Miramar Will Keep Giant Mine Operating," 3 August 2001. Personal files of Kevin O'Reilly.

57 Det'on Cho Environmental Alliance, "Environmental Site Assessment and Cost Estimate of Giant Mine." Unpublished report for the Government of the Northwest Territories and DIAND, November 1999. Copy located at the MVLWB. The reporting on Det'on Cho's lobbying for a role in the cleanup, along with Sangris's and Beaulieu's comments, came in a report by Ian McKinnon, "Giant a 'Ticking Time Bomb,'" *National Post*, 22 May 1999, D3.

58 SRK Consulting and SENES Consultants, "Giant Mine Remediation Plan."

59 Givens, "From Here to Eternity," 159–79; Tannenbaum, *Communication Across 300 Generations*; Weitzberg, *Building on Existing Institutions to Perpetuate Knowledge of Waste Repositories*.

60 Department of Indian and Northern Affairs, "Information: Giant Mine Arsenic Trioxide Technical Workshop," n.d. Personal files of Kevin O'Reilly. See also Dane Gibson, "Arsenic Options on the Table: Arsenic Experts Focus on Giant," *Yellowknifer*, 25 June 1999, A6.

61 Terriplan Consultants, "Giant Mine Underground Arsenic Trioxide Management Alternatives Workshop," 19.

62 SRK Consulting, "Giant Mine Arsenic Trioxide Management Alternatives."

63 Terriplan Consultants, *Giant Mine Underground Arsenic Trioxide Management Alternatives*, 26.

64 "Arsenic Management Options: Giant Mine," presentation by Yellowknife MLAs, 26 May 2003. Personal files of Kevin O'Reilly.

65 Terriplan Consultants, *Giant Mine Underground Arsenic Trioxide Management Alternatives*, 22.

66 Ibid., p. E-11. The final question about the pumps was recorded in Lutra Associates, *Awareness Testing: Findings from the Focus Groups on Giant Mine and*

the Arsenic Trioxide, Final Report. Prepared for the Communications Directorate, Department of Indian Affairs and Northern Development, January 2002, 14. Personal files of Kevin O'Reilly.

67 Giant Mine Remediation Project, Smokehouse Café, Ndilǫ, 22 January 2003, 4. Personal files of Kevin O'Reilly.

68 Ibid., 6.

69 Ibid., 2.

70 Ibid., 8.

71 Ibid.

72 "Cooperation Agreement Respecting the Giant Mine Remediation Project," 15 March 2005, accessed 26 August 2023, https://www.gov.nt.ca/ecc/sites/ecc/files/resources/cooperation_agreement_2005.pdf. For background to the formal adoption of the freeze option in 2004, see SRK Consulting and SENES Consultants, "Giant Mine Remediation Plan," 23.

73 SRK Consulting and SENES Consultants, "Giant Mine Remediation Plan."

74 For a summary of the city's position, see O'Reilly, "Liability, Legacy, and Perpetual Care," 356.

75 SRK Consulting and SENES Consultants, "Giant Mine Remediation Plan," 2–5. See also Sandlos and Keeling, "Aboriginal Communities, Traditional Knowledge, and the Environmental Legacies of Extractive Development in Canada," 278–87.

76 O'Reilly, "Liability, Legacy, and Perpetual Care," 355–6.

77 Gordon Van Tighem, Mayor of Yellowknife, to the Mackenzie Valley Environmental Impact Review Board, 7 April 2008. Mackenzie Valley Environmental Impact Review Board online registry for Giant Mine Remediation Project, EA-0809-001, accessed 2 September 2023, https://reviewboard.ca/upload/project_document/EA0809-001_Letter_of_Referral_from_the_City_of_Yellowknife.pdf.

78 Chiefs, Yellowknives Dene First Nation, to Gordon Van Tighem, Mayor of Yellowknife, 17 March 2008. Mackenzie Valley Environmental Impact Review Board online registry for Giant Mine Remediation Project, EA 0809-001, accessed 2 September 2023, https://reviewboard.ca/upload/project_document/EA0809-001_Letter_of_Referral_from_the_City_of_Yellowknife.pdf.

79 Kevin O'Reilly, Notes for Special City Council Meeting, 18 March 2008. Mackenzie Valley Environmental Impact Review Board online registry for Giant Mine Remediation Project, EA 0809-001, accessed 2 September 2023, https://reviewboard.ca/upload/project_document/EA0809-001_Letter_of_Referral_from_the_City_of_Yellowknife.pdf.

80 Sabin, "Alternatives North," 125–40.

81 Raffensberger, *Principles of Perpetual Care*; Joan Kuyek, *The Theory and Practice of Perpetual Care of Contaminated Sites.*

82 Alternatives North and Yellowknives Dene First Nation, *From Despair to Wisdom*.

83 Taylor and Kenyon, *Giant Mine Perpetual Care Funding Options*. For a general overview of the issues surrounding community trust, health, and the Giant Mine remediation, see Banfield and Jardine, "Consultation and Remediation in the North," 21,231.

84 Yellowknives Dene First Nation, *The Giant Gold Mine: Our Story*.

85 Department of Indian Affairs, Canada and Government of the Northwest Territories, *Giant Mine Remediation Project: Developer's Assessment Report*, EA 0809-001, October 2010, pp. 14–18, accessed 8 September 2023, https://reviewboard.ca/upload/project_document/EA0809-001_Giant_DAR.pdf; O'Reilly, "Liability, Legacy, and Perpetual Care," 356.

86 DIAND and Government of the Northwest Territories, *Giant Mine Remediation Project: Developer's Assessment Report*, chap. 6, p. 35. Of course, 237,000 tons of arsenic slowly melting and then leaching into groundwater and then leaking into the surrounding environment could seriously worsen the "more immediate" health and environmental impacts associated with a future crisis.

87 Ibid., chap. 2, p. 6.

88 Ibid., chap. 2, pp. 13–21, 28–9.

89 O'Reilly, "Liability, Legacy, and Perpetual Care," 359. The ballooning price tag only came to light through an access to information request from O'Reilly.

90 Mackenzie Valley Environmental Impact Review Board, Giant Mine Remediation Project, Environmental Assessment Hearing, EA-0809-001, 10 September 2012, p. 108, accessed 14 September 2023, https://reviewboard.ca/upload/project_document/EA0809-001_Giant_Mine_hearing_transcripts_-_September_10__2012.pdf.

91 Mackenzie Valley Environmental Impact Review Board, Giant Mine Remediation Project, Environmental Assessment Hearing, EA-0809-001, 11 September 2012, p. 254, accessed 14 September 2023, https://reviewboard.ca/upload/project_document/EA0809-001_Giant_Mine_heaing_transcripts_-_September_11__2012.pdf.

92 The testimony of Elders was spread throughout the five days of the hearings, but the comments of most were concentrated on the third day. See Mackenzie Valley Environmental Impact Review Board, Giant Mine Remediation Project, Environmental Assessment Hearing, EA-0809-001, 12 September 2012, 177–215, accessed 14 September 2023, https://reviewboard.ca/upload/project_document/EA0809-001_Giant_Mine_hearing_transcript_-_September_12__2012.

93 The preceding sentences are a summary of major themes in the public testimony. Transcripts for the hearings held 13 September 2012 can be found at Mackenzie Valley Environmental Impact Review Board online registry for Giant Mine Remediation Project, EA 0809-001, https://reviewboard.ca/upload/project_document/EA0809-001_Giant_Mine_public_hearing_transcript_-_Sept_13__2012.pdf (accessed 14 September 2023); and for 14 September 2012, https://reviewboard.ca/upload/project_document/EA0809-001_Giant_Mine_

public_hearing_transcript_-_September_14__2012.pdf (accessed 14 September 2023).

94 Environmental Assessment Hearing, EA-0809-001, 12 September 2012, 344–52.

95 Environmental Assessment Hearing, EA-0809-001, 12 September 2012, 108.

96 Environmental Assessment Hearing, EA-0809-001, 10 September 2012. The discussion of the perpetual care and community oversight plans is on page 43, while the chair's request for AANDC to answer questions came in an exchange on pages 53–4.

97 Environmental Assessment Hearing, EA-0809-001, 11 September 2012, 170.

98 The one non-Indigenous member of the board, John Curran, recused himself from the final decision on the remediation project after he accused Alternatives North of being a "clandestine" organization. "Board Member Removes Himself from Giant Mine Cleanup Review," CBC News, 16 October 2012, accessed 20 September 2023, https://www.cbc.ca/news/canada/north/board-member-removes-himself-from-giant-mine-cleanup-review-1.1184554.

99 Joanna Ankersmit, Director, Contaminated Sites Program, Aboriginal Affairs and Northern Development, and Ray Case, Assistant Deputy Minister, Corporate and Strategic Planning, Environment and Natural Resources, Government of the Northwest Territories, to Richard Edjericon, Chair, MVLWB, 12 October 2012. Mackenzie Valley Environmental Impact Review Board online registry for Giant Mine Remediation Project, EA 0809-001, accessed 13 September 2023, https://reviewboard.ca/upload/project_document/EA0809-001_Closing_comments-_Developer.pdf.

100 Mackenzie Valley Review Board, Report of Environmental Assessment and Reasons for Decision, 20 June 2013. Mackenzie Valley Environmental Impact Review Board online registry for Giant Mine Remediation Project, EA 0809-001, p. i, accessed 22 September 2023, https://reviewboard.ca/upload/project_document/EA0809-001_Giant_Report_of_Environmental_Assessment_June_20_2013.pdf.

101 Ibid., iii.

102 Ibid., 189–96.

103 Bernard Valcourt, Minister of AANDC, to JoAnne Deneron, Chairperson, Mackenzie Valley Environmental Impact Review Board, 11 August 2014. Mackenzie Valley Environmental Impact Review Board online registry for Giant Mine Remediation Project, EA 0809-001, accessed 22 September 2023, https://reviewboard.ca/upload/project_document/EA0809-001_Final_decision_letter_from_AANDC_Minister_to_MVRB_Chairperson.pdf.

104 Beckett, "Beyond Remediation," 1,389–412.

105 Gottlieb, "Beyond NEPA and Earth Day," 1–14.

Conclusion

1 Paper is quoted in Alternatives North, *From Despair to Wisdom*, 4.

2 Sidney Cohen, "Cost of Cleaning Up Yellowknife's Giant Mine Now Pegged at $4.38B, Up from $1B," CBC News, 10 November 2022, accessed 27 September 2023, https://www.cbc.ca/news/canada/north/giant-mine-remediation-cost-4-billion-1.6647952.

3 H.E. Jamieson, "The Legacy of Arsenic Contamination from Mining and Processing Refractory Gold Ore at Giant Mine," 545.

4 Chételat et al., "Remobilization of Legacy Arsenic from Sediment in a Large Subarctic Waterbody Impacted by Gold Mining"; Palmer et al., *The Concentration of Arsenic in Lake Waters of the Yellowknife Area*. NWT Open File 2015-06, 2015, 29.

5 Thienpont et al., "Multi-Trophic Level Response to Extreme Metal Contamination from Gold Mining in a Subarctic Lake."

6 Degray, "Indigenous Risk Perceptions and Land-Use in Yellowknife, NT"; Yellowknives Dene First Nation, Trailmark Systems, and DownNorth Consulting, *Yellowknives Dene First Nation Knowledge and History of the Giant Mine*."

7 Canada North Environmental Services, *Giant Mine Human Health and Ecological Risk Assessment*.

8 For the criticism from Yellowknives Dene First Nation Chief Edward Sangris, and Chan's response, see CBC News, "Giant Mine Contamination Not a Big Health Concern, Study Finds, but Not Everyone's Satisfied," 27 February 2023, https://www.cbc.ca/news/canada/north/giant-mine-contamination-toenail-arsenic-exposure-1.6760191.

9 Terriplan Consultants, "Giant Mine Underground Arsenic Trioxide Management Alternatives Workshop," 22.

10 Mackenzie Valley Environmental Impact Review Board, Giant Mine Remediation Project, Environmental Assessment Hearing, EA-0809-001, 11 September 2012, 248, accessed 8 January 2025, https://reviewboard.ca/upload/project_document/EA0809-001_Giant_Mine_heaing_transcripts_-_September_11__2012.pdf.

11 Nash, *Inescapable Ecologies*. A similar claim to the existence of a cancer cluster occurred in the Sahtu Dene community of Délı̨nę, where Sahtúot'į̨nę had worked to load uranium ore in burlap sacks from the Port Radium mine from the 1930s to the 1960s. A federal government study of the issue, the Canada-Délı̨nę Uranium Table, concluded that there would be no means to reconstruct a historical epidemiological study of the links between exposure to uranium and cancer. Nonetheless, the community of Délı̨nę still believes that historical exposure to uranium made their community a "village of widows." For more discussion, see Délınę Uranium Team, *If Only We Had Known*; Délı̨nę Uranium Committee, *They Never Told Us These Things*.

12 Beckett, "Beyond Remediation," 1392. In past work, we have used a similar metaphor to refer to Giant as one of several "zombie" mines across Northern Canada: a closed and abandoned site that nevertheless continues to exert a negative social

and environmental legacy for local communities. Keeling and Sandlos, "Ghost Towns and Zombie Mines," 377–420.

13 McNeill, *The Great Acceleration*.

14 Renewed efforts are being made by provincial and federal governments to create comprehensive inventories of orphaned and abandoned mine sites, which some estimates place at over 10,000. See Natural Resources Canada, Lands and Minerals Sector, "National Inventory of Orphaned and Abandoned Mines," Natural Resources Canada, Federal Geospatial Platform, 2024, https://osdp-psdo.canada.ca/dp/en/search/metadata/NRCAN-FGP-1-330ec960-cc52-47d9-840b-d93470347ab4. See also Castrilli, *Report on the Legislative, Regulatory, and Policy Framework*.

15 Commissioner of Environment and Sustainable Development, *Contaminated Sites in the North*, 22.

16 See Macpherson, "Cyprus Anvil Mine," 111–49; Dena Cho Environmental and Remediation, *Review of the Faro Remediation Project* YESAB *Proposal*.

17 Russell, "The Spectacular Fall of Victoria Gold, Once the Darling of Yukon Mining."

18 Standing Committee on Economic Development and Environment, *Report on the Prevention and Management of Contaminated Sites*. For another overview, see Dance et al., "Mine Remediation Policy and Practice in Northern Canada," 196–230. For a broad analysis of the lax remediation regime in the Alberta oil sands, see Carter, *Fossilized*.

19 Emma Grant, "Alberta Won't Force Oil Sands Companies to Pay More for Cleanup Costs," *Globe and Mail*, 3 October 2024, B1, B6.

20 During the environmental assessment process, the federal government vigorously resisted the creation of an independent oversight board. For the Giant Mine Oversight Board's research on solutions to the problem of underground arsenic, see Giant Mine Oversight Board, Research Program Report, November 2023, https://gmob.ca/wp-content/uploads/2023/11/2023-11-GMOB-Research-Program-Public-Meeting-Report-F.pdf.

21 The agreement to work toward an apology and compensation is called the Collaborative Process Protocol Agreement, the agreement to work collaboratively on the environmental and social legacies of mining is simply called the Memorandum of Cooperation, and the economic agreement is called the Community Benefits Agreement. See Crown-Indigenous Relations and Northern Affairs Canada, "Government of Canada Signs Apology and Compensation Agreements for Giant Mine with the Yellowknives Dene First Nation," press release, 13 August 2021, accessed 3 October 2024, https://www.canada.ca/en/crown-indigenous-relations-northern-affairs/news/2021/08/government-of-canada-signs-apology-and-compensation-agreements-for-giant-mine-with-the-yellowknives-dene-first-nation.html.

Bibliography

Personal Papers

The authors derived a great deal of primary research material from the personal files of Kevin O'Reilly, who has been collecting material on Giant Mine for over forty years. The file folders included reports, newspaper articles, letters, e-mail correspondences, transcripts of radio programs, transcripts of public meetings/consultations, and scientific research papers. The authors wish to extend a special thanks to Kevin for letting us have access to this material.

Archives

NORTHWEST TERRITORIES ARCHIVES, PRINCE OF WALES NORTHERN HERITAGE CENTRE

G-1993-006, Department of Renewable Resources Fonds, Government of the Northwest Territories (GNWT)

G-2008-028, Department of Health and Social Services Fonds, Environmental Contaminants – Arsenic Protection Program, GNWT

G-2009-020, Department of Health and Social Services Fonds, GNWT

G-2012-026, Department of Municipal and Community Affairs, GNWT

G-2013-029, Department of Finance, GNWT

N-1999-015 Cyril John Baker ("Yellowknife Johnney") Fonds

N-1980-002, Consolidated Mining and Smelting Company of Canada Fonds

N-1991-082, Giant Mine Fonds

N-2001-014, Giant Mine Fonds

N-2005-022, The Canadian Association of Smelter and Allied Workers (CASAW)/ Canadian Auto Workers (CAW), Local 2304 Fonds

N-2018-010 Native Communications Society Fonds

LIBRARY AND ARCHIVES CANADA

RG 29, Department of National Health and Welfare, Government of Canada

RG 85, Northern Affairs Program (records of various federal government departments that held the northern affairs portfolio)

MACKENZIE VALLEY LAND AND WATER BOARD
(FORMERLY NORTHWEST TERRITORIES WATER BOARD)
PUBLIC REGISTRY

Golder Associates, "Final Abandonment and Restoration Plan, Miramar Giant Mine," 26 September 2001.

Multiple Files under Reference Code: N1L3-0043, Giant Mine Water License Applications, 1985–2003

Royal Oak Mines, Abandonment and Restoration and Background Documents, 1980s (file)

Transcripts of Public Hearings and Background Documents for Giant Mine Water License Applications

MACKENZIE VALLEY REVIEW BOARD: ONLINE REGISTRY

Giant Mine Remediation Project, EA0809-001, https://reviewboard.ca/registry/ea0809-001

Oral History Interviews in Dettah and Ndilǫ, Northwest Territories, April–May 2011

John Drygeese
Michel Paper
Eddie Sikyea
Fred Sangris
Isadore Tsetta

Media

The Albertan

Benoit, France, dir. *Guardians of Eternity*. ShebaFilms, 2015. https://vimeo.com/150291898.

Calgary Herald

Canadian Broadcasting Corporation (CBC), news website

Canadian Business

Canadian Press

CIM (Canadian Institute of Mining, Metallurgy and Petroleum) Reporter

EdgeYK Magazine

Edmonton Journal

Financial Post

National Post

Ottawa Journal
Giant: Murder Underground, CBC podcast series
Globe and Mail
Ideas, CBC radio program
Lethbridge Herald
Montreal Gazette
New York Times
News of the North (*News/North*)
Northern Miner
Northern News
Northern Star
Saturday Night
Toronto Star
Victoria Times Colonist
Yellowknife Blade
Yellowknifer

Reports and Government Documents

Alternatives North and Yellowknives Dene First Nation. *From Despair to Wisdom: Perpetual Care and the Future of the Giant Mine, A Report on a Community Workshop*. Yellowknife, NWT, 26–27 September 2011. https://alternativesnorth.ca/wp-content/uploads/2016/02/2011-09-26-giant-perpetual-care-workshop-report.pdf.

Bourne, L.S. *Yellowknife, NWT: A Study of its Urban and Regional Economy*. Northern Co-ordination and Research Centre, Department of Northern Affairs and National Resources, September 1963. https://publications.gc.ca/collections/collection_2017/aanc-inac/R42-3-1963-8-eng.pdf.

Canada North Environmental Services. *Giant Mine Human Health and Ecological Risk Assessment: Final Report*. Prepared for Public Services and Procurement Canada, Western Region. Markham, ON: Canada North Environmental Services, 2018. https://mvlwb.com/registry.

Canadian Public Health Association (CPHA). *Task Force on Arsenic: Final Report, Yellowknife Northwest Territories*. Ottawa: CPHA, 1977.

Castrilli, Joseph. *Report on the Legislative, Regulatory, and Policy Framework Respecting Collaboration, Liability, and Funding Measures in Relation to Orphaned/Abandoned, Contaminated, and Operating Mines in Canada*. Ottawa: National Orphaned/Abandoned Mines Initiative, 2007.

Commissioner of Environment and Sustainable Development. *Contaminated Sites in the North*. Ottawa: Auditor General of Canada, 2024.

Délı̨nę Uranium Committee. *They Never Told Us These Things: A Record and Analysis of the Deadly and Continuing Impacts of Radium and Uranium Mining on the Sahtu Dene of Great Bear Lake*. Délı̨nę, NWT: Délı̨nę First Nation, 1998.

Délı̨nę Uranium Team. *If Only We Had Known: The History of Port Radium as Told by the Sahtúot'ı̨nę*. Délı̨nę, NWT: Délı̨nę Uranium Team, 2005.

Dena Cho Environmental and Remediation. *Review of the Faro Remediation Project YESAB Proposal*. Report filed with Yukon Environmental and Socioeconomic Assessment Board Public Registry, August 2020, Document Number: 2019-0149-0555. https://yesabregistry.ca/projects/39ca43c0-bd52-4dcd-90c7-37d55a305ebd.

Department of Indian Affairs, Canada and Government of the Northwest Territories. *Giant Mine Remediation Project: Developer's Assessment Report*. EA 0809-001, October 2010. https://reviewboard.ca/upload/project_document/EA0809-001_Giant_DAR.pdf.

De Smecht, Louis M., Daniel Laguitton, and Yves Bérubé. *Control of Arsenic Level in Gold Mine Waste Waters*. Ottawa/Quebec City: Northern Affairs Canada and Centre de recherches sur l'eau, Laval University, 1975.

de Villiers, A.J., and P.M. Baker. *An Investigation into the Health Status of Inhabitants of Yellowknife, Northwest Territories*. Ottawa: Occupational Health Division, Department of National Health and Welfare, 1969.

Dillon Consulting. *Giant Mine Arsenic Trioxide Management, Technical Meeting Proceedings*, 28, 29, and 30 October 1997. Appendix PI in *Giant Mine Remediation Plan Public Consultation and Communications*, Department of Indian Affairs and Northern Development, 2005. https://mvlwb.com/registry.

– *Giant Mine Arsenic Trioxide Technical Workshop: Final Summary Report*. Department of Indian Affairs and Northern Development, 1999. https://mvlwb.com/registry.

Evans, Peter, David King, Randy Freeman, and Amanda Degray. *Summary of Research on the Establishment, Administration and Oversight of the Giant Mine and Its Impacts on the Yellowknives Dene First Nation*. Trailmark Systems and DownNorth Consulting, 2020. https://giantminemonster.ca/wp-content/uploads/2020/11/Giant-mine-report-20201124-min.pdf.

Falkowski, Paul. "Presentation to the National Indian Brotherhood 8th Annual General Assembly." Winnipeg, MB, 14 September 1977, University of Alberta Libraries.

Federal-Provincial-Territorial Committee on Drinking Water. *Guidelines for Canadian Drinking Water Quality: Guideline Technical Document – Arsenic*. Ottawa: Health Canada, 2006. https://healthycanadians.gc.ca/publications/healthy-living-vie-saine/water-arsenic-eau/alt/water-arsenic-eau-eng.pdf.

Gagan, Earl W. *Arsenic Emissions and Control Technology: Gold Roasting Operations*. Mining, Mineral and Metallurgical Division, Abatement and Compliance Branch, Air Pollution Control Directorate, Report EPS 3-AP-79-5. https://publications.gc.ca/collections/collection_2023/eccc/en42/En42-1-3-79-5-eng.pdf.

Gemmill, D.A., ed. *Technical Data Summary: Arsenic in the Yellowknife Environment*, rev. ed. Yellowknife: Ad Hoc Standing Committee on Arsenic, 1977.

Geological Survey of Canada. *Annual Report, vol. 13, 1900*. Ottawa: King's Printer, 1903.

– *Summary Report on the Operations of the Geological Survey for the Year 1899*. Ottawa: King's Printer, 1900.

Giant Mine Oversight Board. *Research Program Report*. Yellowknife: Giant Mine Oversight Board, 2023. https://gmob.ca/wp-content/uploads/2023/11/2023-11-GMOB-Research-Program-Public-Meeting-Report-F.pdf.

Government of Canada. *Regulations for the Disposal of Quartz Mining Claims on Dominion Lands in Manitoba, the North-West Territories, and the Yukon Territory*. Ottawa: Department of the Interior, 1899.

Hoffman, G. Christian. *Report of the Section on Chemistry and Mineralogy*. Geological Survey of Canada Annual Report, vol. 11, 1898. Ottawa: Queen's Printer, 1900.

Jervis, Robert E., Department of Chemical Engineering and Applied Chemistry, and Institute for Environmental Studies. "Statement RE: Yellowknife Arsenic Pollution Problem." Unpublished document. Edmonton: Boreal Institute for Northern Studies Library, University of Alberta, 1977.

Kitto, F.H. *The North West Territories*. Ottawa: King's Printer, 1930.

Kuyek, Joan. *The Theory and Practice of Perpetual Care of Contaminated Sites*. Yellowknife: Alternatives North, 2011. https://reviewboard.ca/upload/project_document/EA0809-001_Perpetual_Care_of_Contaminated_Sites_Theory_and_Practice_1311181243.pdf.

Lord, C.S. *Mineral Industry of the Northwest Territories*. Ottawa: Department of Mines and Resources, 1941.

Moore, James, Susan Wheeler, and David Sutherland. "The Effects of Metal Mines on Aquatic Ecosystems in the Northwest Territories – 2: Giant Yellowknife Mines Limited." Unpublished report. Environmental Protection Service, Fisheries and Environment Canada, EPS 5-NW-78-9, June 1978. https://publications.gc.ca/collections/collection_2022/eccc/En42-1-5-78-9-eng.pdf.

National Indian Brotherhood. *Is the Arsenic in Yellowknife's Streets Good for You?* Ottawa: National Indian Brotherhood, 1978.

National Indian Brotherhood, the United Steelworkers of America, and the University of Toronto. "Document Released by the National Indian Brotherhood, the United Steelworkers of America, and the University of Toronto." Boreal Institute for Northern Studies Library, University of Alberta, 15 January 1977.

Palmer, Mike, Jennifer Galloway, Heather Jamieson, R. Timothy Patterson, Hendrik Falck, and Steve Kokelj. *The Concentration of Arsenic in Lake Waters of the Yellowknife Area*. NWT Open File 2015-06, 2015.

Raffensberger, Carolyn. *Principles of Perpetual Care: The Giant Mine, Yellowknife, Northwest Territories*. Yellowknife: Alternatives North, 2011. https://reviewboard.ca/upload/project_document/EA0809-001_Principles_of_Perpetual_Care-_Report_from_Alt_North.pdf.

Sandlos, John. "Communicating with Future Generations." Summary of Working Group Discussions on Giant Mine, Yellowknife, NWT, 2015. http://www.toxiclegacies.com/wordpress/wp-content/uploads/CFG-working-group-SUMM-report-JKS.pdf.

– "Communicating with Future Generations at Giant Mine." A report on a workshop discussing strategies for Giant Mine, Yellowknife, Northwest Territories, 21–22 September 2017. http://www.toxiclegacies.com/wordpress/wp-content/uploads/CFG-workshop-report-1.pdf.

Sandlos, John, and Arn Keeling. *Giant Mine: Historical Summary*. Report drafted as background to the environmental assessment of the Giant Mine Remediation Project, 2012. http://reviewboard.ca/upload/project_document/EA0809-001_Giant_Mine__History_Summary.pdf.

Sandlos, John, Arn Keeling, and Kevin O'Reilly. "Communicating Danger: A Community Primer on Communicating the Arsenic Hazards at Yellowknife's Giant Mine to Future Generations." 2014. http://www.toxiclegacies.com/wordpress/wp-content/uploads/Comm_Future_Gen_YK_Report_Sep-2014-FINAL.pdf.

Silke, Ryan. "The Operational History of Mines in the Northwest Territories, Canada." Unpublished report, 2009. https://www.miningnorth.com/_rsc/site-content/library/NWT_Mines_History_RSilke2009.pdf.

SRK Consulting. "Giant Mine Arsenic Trioxide Management Alternatives: Final Report." Unpublished report prepared for the Department of Indian Affairs and Northern Development, December 2002. https://reviewboard.ca/upload/project_document/EA0809-001_Final_Report__Arsenic_Trioxide_Management_Alternatives_1328900495.pdf.

SRK Consulting and SENES Consultants. "Giant Mine Remediation Plan." Prepared for Giant Mine Remediation Project, Department of Indian Affairs, July 2007. https://reviewboard.ca/upload/project_document/EA0809-001_Giant_Mine_Remediation_Plan_1328900464.pdf.

Standing Committee on Economic Development and Environment. *Report on the Prevention and Management of Contaminated Sites*. Nineteenth Legislative Assembly of the Northwest Territories, 2023. https://www.ntlegislativeassembly.ca/sites/default/files/legacy/2023-02-07_-_scede_cr_39-192_contaminated_sites.pdf.

Tataryn, Lloyd. *Arsenic and Red Tape*. Ottawa: National Indian Brotherhood, 1978.

Taylor, Amy, and Duncan Kenyon. *Giant Mine Perpetual Care Funding Options*. Report prepared for Alternatives North and Yellowknives Dene First Nation. Yellowknife: Pembina Institute, 2012. https://www.ntassembly.ca/sites/assembly/files/12-06-14td50-173.pdf.

Terriplan Consultants, Giant Mine Underground Arsenic Trioxide Management Alternatives Workshop, 11–12 June 2001, Yellowknife, NWT. Workshop report, prepared for the Department of Indian and Northern Affairs, August 2001. https://reviewboard.ca/upload/project_document/EA0809-001_Giant_Mine_Arsenic_Management_Workshop_Summary_Report_July_2003.pdf.

Terriplan Consultants. *Giant Mine Underground Arsenic Trioxide Management Alternatives – Moving Forward: Selecting a Management Alternative*. Report prepared for Giant Mine Remediation Project, Indian Affairs and Northern

Development, NWT Regions, July 2003. https://reviewboard.ca/upload/project_document/EA0809-001_Giant_Mine_Arsenic_Management_Workshop_Summary_Report_July_2003.pdf.

US Department of Health, Education and Welfare, Public Health Service. *Public Health Service Drinking Water Standards*. Public Health Service Publication No. 956. Washington: Government Printing Office, 1962.

Usher, Peter. *Fur Trade Posts of the NWT, 1870–1970*. Ottawa: Department of Indian Affairs and Northern Development, 1971. http://parkscanadahistory.com/publications/north/nsrg-71-4.pdf.

Wallace, Ron, and M.J. Hardin. "Chemical and Biological Characteristics of Seepages from Tailings Areas at Giant Yellowknife Mines, Ltd., into Great Slave Lake, Northwest Territories, in 1974." Environmental Protection Service, Northwest Region, Report Number EPS-5-NW-74-1, November 1974.

Yellowknives Dene First Nation. *The Giant Gold Mine: Our Story – Impact of the Yellowknife Giant Gold Mine on the Yellowknives Dene: A Traditional Knowledge Report*. Dettah, NWT: Yellowknives Dene First Nation Council, 2005. https://mvlwb.com/registry.

Yellowknives Dene First Nation Elders Advisory Council. *Weledeh Yellowknives Dene: A History*. Dettah, NWT: Yellowknives Dene First Nation, 1997.

Yellowknives Dene First Nation, Trailmark Systems, and DownNorth Consulting. "Yellowknives Dene First Nation Knowledge and History of the Giant Mine: Concerns, Recommendations, and Closure." Unpublished report prepared for the Giant Mine Remediation Plan, March 2019.

Journal Articles and Books

Abel, Kerry M. *Drum Songs: Glimpses of Dene History*, 2nd ed. Montreal and Kingston: McGill-Queen's University Press, 2005.

Adcock, Tina. "Many Tiny Traces: Northern Exploration and Antimodernism Between the Wars." In *Ice Blink: Navigating Northern Environmental History*, edited by Stephen Bocking and Brad Martin, 131–77. Calgary: University of Calgary Press, 2017.

Aiken, Katherine G. "'The Environmental Consequences ... Were Calamitous': Smelter Smoke Controversies in Progressive Era America, 1899–1918." *Technology and Culture* 60, no. 1 (January 2019): 132–64.

Andrews, Thomas G. *Killing for Coal: America's Deadliest Labor War*. Cambridge, MA: Harvard University Press, 2008.

Athabasca Chipewyan First Nation, with Sabina Trimble and Peter Fortna. *Remembering Our Relations: Dënesų̨łiné Oral Histories of Wood Buffalo National Park*. Calgary, AB: University of Calgary Press, 2023.

Banfield, Laura, and Cynthia (Cindy) G. Jardine. "Consultation and Remediation in the North: Meeting International Commitments to Safeguard Health and Well-Being." *International Journal of Circumpolar Health* 72, no. 1 (2013): 21231.

Bankes, Nigel, and Cheryl Sharvit. "Aboriginal Title and Free Entry Mining Regimes in Northern Canada." Northern Minerals Working Paper, Ottawa, Canadian Arctic Resources Committee, 1998.

Barnes, Trevor. "Borderline Communities: Canadian Single Industry Towns, Staples, and Harold Innis." In *B/Ordering Space*, edited by Olivier Kramsch and Henk van Houtum, 109–22. New York: Routledge, 2005.

Beckett, Caitlynn. "Beyond Remediation: Containing, Confronting and Caring for the Giant Mine Monster." *Environment and Planning E: Nature and Space* 4, no. 4 (2021): 1389–412.

Bell, J. Mackintosh. *Far Places*. Toronto: MacMillan, 1931.

– "Great Slave Lake." *Geographical Journal* 19, no. 4 (1929): 556–80.

Berger, Stefan, and Peter Alexander. *Making Sense of Mining History: Themes and Agendas*. New York: Routledge, 2019.

Bielawski, Ellen. *Rogue Diamonds: The Rush for Northern Riches on Dene Land*. New York: Douglas and McIntyre, 2003.

Black, Megan. *The Global Interior Mineral Frontiers and American Power*. Cambridge, MA: Harvard University Press, 2018.

Blondin, George. *When the World Was New: Stories of the Sahtú Dene*. Yellowknife: Outcrop, 1990.

Bothwell, Robert. *Eldorado: Canada's National Uranium Company*. Toronto: University of Toronto Press, 1984.

Boudia, Soraya. "Managing Scientific and Political Uncertainty." In *Powerless Science? Science and Politics in a Toxic World*, edited by Soraya Boudia and Nathalie Jas, 95–112. New York: Berghahn Books, 2014.

Bridge, Gavin. "Contested Terrain: Mining and the Environment." *Annual Review of Environment and Resources* 29, no. 1 (2004): 205–59.

Bruno, Andy. *The Nature of Soviet Power: An Arctic Environmental History*. New York: Cambridge University Press, 2016.

Bullen, Warwick, and Malcom Robb. "Social-Economic Impacts of Gold Mining in the Yellowknife Mining District." Unpublished report, 2004. https://www.miningnorth.com/_rsc/site-content/library/economics/Robb-Bullen-Socio-Economic_Impacts_of_GoldMining_in_Yellowknife2004.pdf.

Camsell, Charles. "The Unexplored Areas of Continental Canada." *Geographical Journal* 48, no. 3 (1916): 249–57.

Carter, Angela V. *Fossilized: Environmental Policy in Canada's Petro-Provinces*. Vancouver: UBC Press, 2021.

Chételat, John, Michael J. Palmer, Katrina Paudyn, Heather Jamieson, Marc Amyot, Reed Harris, Raymond Hesslein, Nicolas Pelletier, and Ines Peraza. "Remobilization of Legacy Arsenic from Sediment in a Large Subarctic Waterbody Impacted by Gold Mining." *Journal of Hazardous Materials* 452 (2023): 131230. https://doi.org/10.1016/j.jhazmat.2023.131230.

Clapperton, Jonathan. "The Ebb and Flow of Local Environmentalist Activism: The Society for Pollution and Environmental Control (SPEC), British Columbia."

In *Environmental Activism on the Ground: Small Green and Indigenous Organizing*, edited by Jonathan Clapperton and Liza Piper, 261–88. Calgary: University of Calgary Press, 2019.

Clapperton, Jonathan, and Liza Piper, eds. *Environmental Activism on the Ground: Small Green and Indigenous Organizing*. Calgary: University of Calgary Press, 2019.

Clement, Wallace. *Hard-Rock Mining: Industrial Relations and Technological Changes at INCO*. Toronto: McClelland and Stewart, 1981.

Coulthard, Glen. *Red Skin, White Masks: Rejecting the Colonial Politics of Recognition*. Winnipeg: University of Manitoba Press, 1914.

Cronin, Marionne. "Northern Visions: Aerial Surveying and the Canadian Mining Industry, 1919–1928." *Technology and Culture* 48, no. 2 (2007): 303–30.

Curtis, Kent A. *Gambling on Ore: The Nature of Metal Mining in the United States, 1860–1910*. Boulder, CO: University Press of Colorado, 2013.

Dance, Anne, Miranda Monosky, Arn Keeling, and John Sandlos. "Mine Remediation Policy and Practice in Northern Canada." In *Extractive Industry and the Sustainability of Canada's Arctic Communities*, edited by Chris Southcott, Frances Abele, David Natcher, and Brenda Parlee, 196–230. Montreal and Kingston: McGill-Queen's University Press, 2022.

Danielson, Vivian. "The *Northern Miner*'s 1991 'Mining Man of the Year:' Margaret (Peggy) Witte," *Northern Miner*. https://republicofmining.com/2008/12/31/the-northern-miner%E2%80%99s-1991-%E2%80%9Cmining-man-of-the-year%E2%80%9D-margaret-peggy-witte-%E2%80%93-by-vivian-danielson.

Degray, Amanda. "Indigenous Risk Perceptions and Land-Use in Yellowknife, NT." Master's thesis, Memorial University of Newfoundland, 2020.

Demuth, Bathsheba. *Floating Coast: An Environmental History of the Bering Strait*. New York: W.W. Norton, 2019.

Derickson, Alan. "From Company Doctors to Union Hospitals: The First Democratic Health-Care Experiments of the United Mine Workers of America." *Labor History* 33, no. 3 (1992): 325–42.

De Villiers, A.J., and J.P. Windish. "Lung Cancer in a Fluorspar Mining Community: Radiation, Dust, and Mortality Experience." *British Journal of Industrial Medicine* 21 (1964): 94–109.

Dickerson, Mark. *Whose North? Political Change, Political Development, and Self-Government in the Northwest Territories*. Vancouver: University of British Columbia Press, 1992.

DiFrancesco, Richard J. "A Diamond in the Rough? An Examination of the Issues Surrounding the Development of the Northwest Territories." *Canadian Geographer/le Géographe Canadien* 44, no. 2 (2000): 114–34.

Elwell, Craig K. "Brief History of the Gold Standard in the United States." Congressional Research Service, 2011. https://sgp.fas.org/crs/misc/R41887.pdf.

Forestell, Nancy. "'And I Feel Like I'm Dying from Mining for Gold': Disability, Gender, and the Mining Community, 1920–1950." *Labor: Studies in Working-Class History of the Americas* 3, no. 3 (2006): 77–93.

Foster, Terry, and Ronne Heming, eds. *Yellowknife Tales: Sixty Years of Stories from Yellowknife*. Yellowknife: Outcrop, 2003.

Francaviglia, Richard V. *Hard Places: Reading the Landscape of America's Historic Mining Districts*. American Land and Life series. Iowa City: University of Iowa Press, 1991.

Fumoleau, René. *As Long as This Land Shall Last: A History of Treaty 8 and Treaty 11, 1870–1939*. Toronto: McClelland and Stewart, 1974.

Givens, David B. "From Here to Eternity: Communicating with the Distant Future." *ETC: A Review of General Semantics* 39 (1982): 159–79.

Gordon, Sarah. "Narratives Unearthed, or, How an Abandoned Mine Doesn't Really Abandon You." In *Mining and Communities in Northern Canada: History, Politics, Memory*, edited by Arn Keeling and John Sandlos, 59–86. Calgary: University of Calgary Press, 2015.

Gottesman, Dan. "Native Hunting and the Migratory Birds Convention Act: Historical, Political, and Ideological Perspectives." *Journal of Canadian Studies* 18, no. 3 (1983): 67–89.

Gottlieb, Robert. "Beyond NEPA and Earth Day: Reconstructing the Past and Envisioning a Future for Environmentalism." *Environmental History Review* 19, no. 4 (1995): 1–14.

– *Forcing the Spring: The Transformation of the American Environmental Movement*. Washington, DC: Island Press, 1993.

Grainge, Jack. *The Changing North: Recollections of an Early Environmentalist*. Edmonton: Canadian Circumpolar Institute, 1999.

Grant, Shelagh. *Sovereignty or Security? Government Policy in the Canadian North, 1936–1950*. Vancouver: UBC Press, 1988.

Green, Heather. "The Tr'ondëk Hwëch'in and the Great Upheaval: Mining, Colonialism, and Environmental Change in the Klondike, 1890–1940." PhD diss., University of Alberta, 2018.

Hall, Rebecca. "Diamond Mining in Canada's Northwest Territories: A Colonial Continuity." *Antipode* 45, no. 2 (2013): 376–93.

Hamilton, John David. *Arctic Revolution: Social Change in the Northwest Territories, 1935–1994*. Toronto: Dundurn Press, 1994.

Helm, June. *The People of Denendeh: Ethnohistory of the Indians of Canada's Northwest Territories*. Iowa City: University of Iowa Press, 2000.

Hesiod. *Hesiod's Works and Days*. Translated by David W. Tandy and Walter C. Neale. Berkeley: University of California Press, 1996.

Hoberg, George, and Kathryn Harrison. "It's Not Easy Being Green: The Politics of Canada's Green Plan." *Canadian Public Policy/Analyse de Politique* 20, no. 2 (1994): 119–37.

Hocking, Drake, Peter Kuchar, James A. Plambeck, and Roy A. Smith. "The Impact of Gold Smelter Emissions on Vegetation and Soils of a Sub-Arctic Forest-Tundra Transition Ecosystem." *Journal of the Air Pollution Control Association* 28, no. 2 (1978): 133–7.

Hodgins, Bruce W., David McNab, and Ute Lischke. *Blockades and Resistance: Studies in Actions of Peace and the Temagami Blockades of 1988–89*. Aboriginal Studies Series. Waterloo: Wilfrid Laurier University Press, 2003.

Hoogeveen, Dawn. "Sovereign Intentions: Gold Law and Mineral Staking in British Columbia." *BC Studies* 198 (2018): 81–102.

– "Sub-Surface Property, Free-Entry Mineral Staking and Settler Colonialism in Canada." *Antipide* 47, no. 1 (2015): 121–38.

Hughes, Michael F., Barbara D. Beck, Yu Chen, Ari S. Lewis, and David J. Thomas. "Arsenic Exposure and Toxicology: A Historical Perspective." *Toxicological Sciences* 123, no. 2 (2011): 305–32.

Hunter, John, and Martin O'Malley. *Giant Mine*. Television movie, directed by Penelope Buitenhuis. Toronto: CBC Television, 1996.

Isenberg, Andrew C. *Mining California: An Ecological History*. New York: Hill and Wang, 2005.

Jackson, Robert, and Jack Grainge. "Arsenic and Cancer." *Canadian Medical Association Journal* 113 (1975): 396–401.

Jackson, Susan, ed. *Yellowknife, NWT: An Illustrated History*. Yellowknife: Nor'West Publishing, 1990.

Jamieson, H.E. "The Legacy of Arsenic Contamination from Mining and Processing Refractory Gold Ore at Giant Mine, Yellowknife, Northwest Territories, Canada." *Reviews in Mineralogy and Geochemistry* 79, no. 1 (2014): 533–51. https://doi.org/10.2138/rmg.2014.79.12.

Johnson, Miranda. "The Case of the Million-Dollar Duck: A Hunter, His Treaty, and the Bending of the Settler Contract." *American Historical Review* 124, no. 1 (2019): 56–86.

Jorgenson, Mica. *The Weight of Gold: Mining and the Environment in Ontario, Canada, 1909–1929*. Reno: University of Nevada Press, 2023.

Jorgenson, Mica, and John Sandlos. "Dust Versus Dust: Aluminum Therapy and Silicosis in the Canadian and Global Mining Industries." *Canadian Historical Review* 102, no. 1 (2021): 1–26.

Josephson, Paul. "Industrial Deserts: Industry, Science and the Destruction of Nature in the Soviet Union." *Slavonic and East European Review* 85, no. 2 (2007): 294–321.

Josephson, Paul. "Technology and the Conquest of the Soviet Arctic." *Russian Review* 70, no. 3 (2011): 419–39.

Keeling, Arn. "'Born in an Atomic Test Tube': Landscapes of Cyclonic Development at Uranium City, Saskatchewan." *Canadian Geographer* 54, no. 2 (2010): 228–52.

Keeling Arn, and John Sandlos. "Environmental Justice Goes Underground? Historical Notes from Canada's Northern Mining Frontier." *Environmental Justice* 2, no. 3 (2009): 117–25. https://doi.org/10.1089/env.2009.0009.

– "Ghost Towns and Zombie Mines: Mine Abandonment, Reclamation, and Redevelopment in the Canadian North." In *Ice Blink: Navigating Northern*

Environmental History, edited by Stephen Bocking and Brad Martin, 377–420. Calgary: University of Calgary Press, 2017.

Keeling, Arn, and John Sandlos, eds. *Mining and Communities in Northern Canada: History, Politics, and Memory*. Calgary: University of Calgary Press, 2015.

Kirsch, Stuart. "Lost Worlds: Environmental Disaster, 'Culture Loss,' and the Law." *Current Anthropology* 42, no. 2 (2001): 167–98.

Kojola, Erik. "Divergent Memories and Visions of the Future in Conflicts over Mining Development." *Journal of Political Ecology* 27 (2020): 898–916.

Kuhlberg, Mark, and Scott Miller. "'Protection to the Sulphur-Smoke Tort-Feasors': The Tragedy of Pollution in Sudbury, Ontario, the World's Nickel Capital, 1884–1927." *Canadian Historical Review* 99, no. 2 (2018): 225–57.

Langston, Nancy. *Toxic Bodies: Hormone Disruptors and the Legacy of DES*. New Haven: Yale University Press, 2011.

LeCain, Timothy. "The Limits of 'Eco-Efficiency': Arsenic Pollution and the Cottrell Electrical Precipitator in the US Copper Smelting Industry." *Environmental History* 5, no. 3 (2000): 336–51.

– *Mass Destruction: The Men and Giant Mines That Wired America and Scarred the Planet*. New Brunswick, NJ: Rutgers University Press, 2009.

Leddy, Lianne. "Interviewing Nookomis and Other Reflections: The Promise of Community Collaboration." *Oral History Forum d'histoire Orale* 30 (2010): 1–18.

Leddy, Lianne C. *Serpent River Resurgence Confronting Uranium Mining at Elliot Lake*. Toronto: University of Toronto Press, 2022.

Lee, Anna M., and Joseph F. Fraumeni. "Arsenic and Respiratory Cancer in Man: An Occupational Study." *Journal of the National Cancer Institute* 42, no. 6 (1969): 1045–52.

Leech, Brian James. *The City That Ate Itself: Butte, Montana and Its Expanding Berkeley Pit*. University of Nevada Press, 2018.

Leeming, Mark R. *In Defence of Home Places: Environmental Activism in Nova Scotia*. Nature, History, Society. Vancouver: UBC Press, 2017.

Liboiron, Max. *Pollution Is Colonialism*. Durham, NC: Duke University Press, 2021.

Longley, Hereward. "Conflicting Interests: Development Politics and the Environmental Regulation of the Alberta Oil Sands Industry, 1970–1980." *Environment and History* 27, no. 1 (2019): 97–125.

Luby, Brittany. *Dammed: The Politics of Loss and Survival in Anishinaabe Territory*. Winnipeg: University of Manitoba Press, 2020.

Lynch, Martin. *Mining in World History*. Globalities. London: Reaktion Books, 2002.

Macdonald, Doug. *The Politics of Pollution: Why Canadians Are Failing Their Environment*. Toronto: McClelland and Stewart, 1991.

MacDowell, Laurel Sefton. "The Elliot Lake Uranium Miners' Battle to Gain Occupational Health and Safety Improvements, 1950–1980." *Labour/Le Travail* 69 (2012): 91–118.

MacPhee, Katrin. "Canadian Working-Class Environmentalism, 1965–1985." *Labour/Le Travail* 74 (2014): 123–49.

Macpherson, Janet. "Cyprus Anvil Mine." In *Northern Transitions: Northern Resource and Land Use Policy Study*, edited by Everett B. Peterson and Janet B. Writing, 111–49. Ottawa: Canadian Arctic Resources Committee, 1977.

Manuel, Jeffry T. *Taconite Dreams: The Struggle to Sustain Mining on Minnesota's Iron Range, 1915–2000*. Minneapolis: University of Minnesota Press, 2015.

Markowitz, Gerald, and David Rosner. *Deceit and Denial: The Deadly Politics of Industrial Pollution*. Berkeley: University of California Press, 2002.

May, Elizabeth. "Brian Mulroney and the Environment." In *Transforming the Nation: Canada and Brian Mulroney*, edited by Raymond Blake, 381–92. Montreal and Kingston: McGill-Queen's University Press, 2007.

McAllister Mary-Louise, and Cynthia Jacqueline Alexander. *A Stake in the Future: Redefining the Canadian Mineral Industry*. Vancouver: UBC Press, 1997.

McClearn, Matthew. "Mining: Sh*t Happens but You Move On," *Canadian Business* 27 (May 2009): 68–74.

McEvoy, Arthur F. "Working Environments: An Ecological Approach to Industrial Health and Safety." *Clio Medica* 41, no. 2 (1997): 59–89.

McMeekan, Jock. *Jock McMeekan's Yellowknife Blade*. Edited by Gladys McCurdy Gould. Duncan, BC: Lambrecht, 1984.

McNeill, John. *The Great Acceleration: An Environmental History of the Anthropocene since 1945*. Cambridge, MA: Belknap Press, 2016.

McNeill, John, and George Vrtis, eds. *Mining North America: An Environmental History since 1522*. Oakland: University of California Press, 2017.

Meharg, Andrew. *Venomous Earth: How Arsenic Caused the World's Worst Mass Poisoning*. New York: MacMillian, 2005.

Mellor, Robynne. "A Comparative Case Study of Uranium Mine and Mill Tailings Regulation in Canada and the United States." In *Mining North America: An Environmental History Since 1522*, edited by John McNeill and George Vrtis, 256–79. Oakland: University of California Press, 2017.

Mitchell, Valerie L. "Health Risks Associated with Chronic Exposures to Arsenic in the Environment." In *Arsenic: Environmental Geochemistry, Mineralogy, and Microbiology*, edited by Robert Bowell, Charles Alpers, Heather Jamieson, D. Kirk Nordstrom, and Juraj Majzlan, 435–49. Reviews in Mineralogy and Geochemistry, volume 79. Chantilly, VA: Mineralogical Society of America; Berlin: De Gruyter, 2014.

Montrie, Chad. *The Myth of Silent Spring: Rethinking the Origins of American Environmentalism*. Oakland: University of California Press, 2018.

– *A People's History of Environmentalism in the United States*. New York: Continuum Books, 2011.

Morse, Kathryn Taylor. *The Nature of Gold: An Environmental History of the Klondike Gold Rush*. Seattle: University of Washington Press, 2003.

Mouat, Jeremy. *Roaring Days: Rossland's Mines and the History of British Columbia*. Vancouver: University of British Columbia Press, 1995.

Mountford, Benjamin, and Stephen Tuffnell, eds. *A Global History of Gold Rushes*. Oakland: University of California Press, 2018.

Mudd, Gavin. "Global Trends in Gold Mining: Towards Quantifying Environmental and Resource Sustainability?" *Resources Policy* 32, nos. 1–2 (2007): 42–56.

Munton, Don, and Owen Temby. "Smelter Fumes, Local Interests, and Political Contestation in Sudbury, Ontario, During the 1910s." *Urban History Review* 44, nos. 1–2 (2015): 24–36.

Nagle, Ted, and Jordan Zinovich. *The Prospector: North of Sixty*. Edmonton: Lone Pine, 1989.

Nash, Linda. *Inescapable Ecologies: A History of Environment, Disease, and Knowledge*. Berkeley: University of California Press, 2006.

– "Purity and Danger: Historical Reflections on the Regulation of Environmental Pollutants." *Environmental History* 13, no. 4 (2008): 651–8.

Nelles, H.V. *The Politics of Development: Forests, Mines and Hydro-Electric Power in Ontario, 1849–1941*. Hamden, CT: Archon Books, 1974.

O'Connor, Ryan. *The First Green Wave: Pollution Probe and the Origins of Environmental Activism in Ontario*. Vancouver: University of British Columbia Press, 2015.

O'Reilly, Kevin. "Liability, Legacy, and Perpetual Care: Government Ownership and Management of the Giant Mine, 1999–2015." In *Mining and Communities in Northern Canada: History. Politics, Memory*, edited by Arn Keeling and John Sandlos, 341–76. Calgary: University of Calgary Press, 2015.

O'Toole, J.J., R.G. Clark, D.L. Malaby, and Trauger, D.L. "Environmental Trace Element Survey at a Heavy Metals Refining Site." In *Nuclear Methods in Environmental Research*, edited by James R. Vogt, Thomas F. Parkinson, and Robert L. Carter, 172–85. Columbia, MO: University of Missouri–Columbia, 1971.

Ott, Marvin Gerald, Benjamin B. Holder, and Harold L. Gordon. "Respiratory Cancer and Occupational Exposure to Arsenicals." *Archives of Environmental Health* 29, no. 5 (1974): 250–5.

Page, Robert. *Northern Development: The Canadian Dilemma*. Toronto: McClelland and Stewart, 1986.

Perrett, Madi, Branaavan Sivarajah, Cynthia L. Cheney, Jennifer B. Korosi, Linda Kimpe, Jules M. Blais, and John P. Smol. "Impacts on Aquatic Biota from Salinization and Metalloid Contamination by Gold Mine Tailings in Sub-Arctic Lakes." *Environmental Pollution* 278, no. 8 (2021): 116815.

Piper, Liza. *The Industrial Transformation of Subarctic Canada*. Vancouver: University of British Columbia Press, 2010.

– *When Disease Came to This Country: Epidemics and Colonialism in Northern North America*. Cambridge, MA: Cambridge University Press, 2023.

Piper, Liza, and John Sandlos. "A Broken Frontier: Ecological Imperialism in the Canadian North." *Environmental History* 12, no. 4 (2007): 759–95.

Pollon, Christopher. *Pitfall: The Race to Mine the World's Most Vulnerable Places*. Vancouver: Greystone Books, 2023.

Powell, Chris. "Questioning Mine Mill in Yellowknife: The Need for a Northern Labour History." *Northern Review* 28 (2008): 187–206.

Quivik, Fred. "The Historical Significance of Tailings and Slag: Industrial Waste as Cultural Resource." *Journal for the Society of Industrial Archaeology* 33, no. 2 (2007): 35–52.

Quivik, Fredric L. "Butte and Anaconda, Montana: Preserving and Interpreting a Vast Landscape of Extraction." *Change Over Time* 7, no. 1 (2017): 6–28.

Read, Jennifer. "'Let Us Heed the Voice of Youth': Laundry Detergents, Phosphates and the Emergence of the Environmental Movement in Ontario." *Journal of the Canadian Historical Association* 7 (1996): 227–50.

Rennie, Richard. *The Dirt: Industrial Carnage and Conflict at St. Lawrence, Newfoundland*. Toronto: Brunswick Books, 2008.

Rhatigan, James. "Mining Meaning: Telling Spatial Histories of the Britannia Mine." *Journal of Historical Geography* 67 (2020): 36–47.

Rosner, David, and Gerald Markowitz. *Deadly Dust: Silicosis and the Politics of Occupational Disease in Twentieth-Century America*. Princeton: Princeton University Press, 1991.

Russell, Rhiannon. "The Spectacular Fall of Victoria Gold, Once the Darling of Yukon Mining." *Walrus*, 2 October 2024.

Sabin, Jerald. "Alternatives North: A History." In *Care, Cooperation and Activism in Canada's Northern Social Economy*, edited by Frances Abele and Chris Southcott, 125–40. Edmonton: University of Alberta Press, 2016.

– "Contested Colonialism: The Rise of Settler Politics in Yukon and the Northwest Territories." PhD diss., University of Toronto, 2016.

– "Settler Colonialism and the Administrative State: The Transfer of the Government of the Northwest Territories to Yellowknife in 1967." *Canadian Public Administration* 67, no. 2 (2024): 149–65.

Sabin, Paul. "Voices from the Hydrocarbon Frontier: Canada's Mackenzie Valley Pipeline Inquiry (1974–1977)." *Environmental History Review* 19, no. 1 (1995): 17–48.

Sacco, Joe. *Paying the Land*. New York: Metropolitan Books, 2020.

Sambu, Sammy, and Richard Wilson. "Arsenic in Food and Water: A Brief History." *Toxicology and Industrial Health* 24, no. 4 (May 2008): 217–26.

Sandlos, John. *Hunters at the Margin: Native People and Wildlife Conservation in the Northwest Territories*. Vancouver: UBC Press, 2007.

Sandlos, John, and Arn Keeling. "Aboriginal Communities, Traditional Knowledge, and the Environmental Legacies of Extractive Development in Canada." *Extractive Industries and Society* 3, no. 2 (2016): 278–87.

– *Mining Country: A History of Canada's Mines and Miners*. Toronto: James Lorimer and Co., 2021.

– "Pollution, Local Activism, and the Politics of Development in the Canadian North." *RCC Perspectives* 4 (2016): 25–32.

Sandlos, John, Arn Keeling, Caitlynn Beckett, and Rosanna Nicol. "There Is a Monster Under the Ground: Commemorating the History of Arsenic Contamination at Giant Mine as a Warning to Future Generations." *Papers in Canadian History and Environment* 3 (2019): 1–55.

Scottie, Joan, Warren Bernauer, and Jack Hicks. *I Will Live for Both of Us: A History of Colonialism, Uranium Mining, and Inuit Resistance*. Winnipeg: University of Manitoba Press, 2022.

Selleck, Lee. "The Giant Mine Tragedy." *This Magazine* 36 (1992): 32–6.

Selleck, Lee, and Francis Thompson. *Dying for Gold: The True Story of the Giant Mine Murders*. Toronto: Harper Collins, 1997.

Sellers, Christopher C. *Hazards of the Job: From Industrial Disease to Environmental Health Science*. Chapel Hill: University of North Carolina Press, 1997.

Shkilnyk, Anastasia M. *A Poison Stronger than Love: The Destruction of an Ojibwa Community*. New Haven: Yale University Press, 1985.

Silke, Ryan. "The Operational History of Mines in the Northwest Territories, Canada." Unpublished report, 2009.

Singh, Parbudyal, Deborah Zinni, and Harish Jain. "The Effects of the Use of Striker Replacement Workers in Canada: An Analysis of Four Cases." *Labor Studies Journal* 30, no. 2 (2005): 61–85.

Sissons, Jack. *Judge of the North*. Toronto: McClelland and Stewart, 1968.

Skeard, Janelle. "Come Hell or High Water: Identity and Resilience in a Mining Town." *London Journal of Canadian Studies* 30 (2015): 90–109.

Smith, Duane A. *Mining America: The Industry and the Environment, 1800–1980*. Niwot, CO: University Press of Colorado, 1993.

Staples, David, and Greg Owens. *The Third Suspect: The Inside Story of the Hunt for the Yellowknife Mass Murderer*. Markham: Red Deer Press, 1995.

Stefanik, Lorna. "Baby Stumpy and the War in the Woods: Competing Frames of British Columbia Forests." *BC Studies* 130 (2001): 41–68.

Stewart, Sarah, and Raymond Yakeleya, eds. *We Remember the Coming of the White Man*. Calgary: Durvile and UpRoute Books, 2021.

Storm, Anna. *Post-Industrial Landscape Scars*. New York: Palgrave Macmillan, 2014.

Stuhl, Andrew. *Unfreezing the Arctic: Science, Colonialism and the Transformation of Inuit Lands*. Chicago: University of Chicago Press, 2016.

Tannenbaum, Percy. "Communication Across 300 Generations: Deterring Human Interference with Waste Deposit Sites." Columbus: Office of Nuclear Waste Isolation, 1984.

Tataryn, Lloyd. *Dying for a Living: The Politics of Industrial Death*. Toronto: Deneau and Greenberg, 1979.

– "Notes from the Territories: Arsenic Poisoning." *Alternatives Journal* 7, no. 2 (1978): 12–15.

Tester, Frank James. "Mad Dogs and (Mostly) Englishmen: Colonial Relations, Commodities, and the Fate of Inuit Sled Dogs." Études Inuit Studies 34, no. 2 (2010): 129–47.

Thienpont, Joshua R., Jennifer B. Korosi, Kathryn E. Hargan, Trisha Williams, David C. Eickmeyer, Linda E. Kimpe, Michael J. Palmer, John P. Smol, and Jules M. Blais. "Multi-Trophic Level Response to Extreme Metal Contamination from Gold Mining in a Subarctic Lake." *Proceedings of the Royal Society B: Biological Sciences* 283, no. 1836 (2016): 20161125. https://doi.org/10.1098/rspb.2016.1125.

Tobasonakwut, Peter Kinew. "The Marmion Lake Generating Station: Another Northern Scandal?" In *Environmentalism on the Ground: Small Green and Indigenous Organizing*, edited by Jonathan Clapperton and Liza Piper, 171–9. Calgary: University of Calgary Press, 2019.

Tuck, Eve. "Suspending Damage: A Letter to Communities." *Harvard Educational Review* 79, no. 3 (2009): 409–27.

Ureta, Sebastián, and Patricio Flores. *Worlds of Gray and Green: Mineral Extraction as Ecological Process*. Berkeley: University of California Press, 2022.

Usher, Peter J. "Northern Development, Impact Assessment and Social Change." In *Anthropology, Public Policy, and Native Peoples in Canada*, edited by Noel Dick and James Waldron, 98–130. Montreal and Kingston: McGill-Queen's University Press, 1993.

Van Horssen, Jessica. *A Town Called Asbestos: Environmental Contamination, Health, and Resilience in a Resource Community*. Vancouver: University of British Columbia Press, 2016.

Vogel, Sarah. "From 'The Dose Makes the Poison' to 'The Timing Makes the Poison': Conceptualizing Risk in the Synthetic Age." *Environmental History* 13, no. 4 (2008): 667–73.

Voyles, Traci Brynne. *Wastelanding: Legacies of Uranium Mining in Navajo Country*. Minneapolis: University of Minnesota Press, 2015.

Walker, Brett. *Toxic Archipelago: A History of Industrial Disease in Japan*. Seattle: University of Washington Press, 2010.

Watkins, Mel, ed., *Dene Nation: A Colony Within*. Toronto: University of Toronto Press, 1977.

Webster, Geddes, ed. *The Prospector's Pick: The People of the Yellowknife Gold Boom, 1936–1951*. Victoria: Trafford Publishing, 2007.

Weitzberg, Abraham. "Building on Existing Institutions to Perpetuate Knowledge of Waste Repositories." Technical report. Columbus: Office of Nuclear Waste Isolation, 1982.

Western, Sally Abbott. "Arsenic Lost Years: Pollution Control at Giant Mine from 1978 to 1999." *Northern Review* 51 (2021): 69–104.

Wirth, John D. *Smelter Smoke in North America: The Politics of Transborder Pollution*. Lawrence, KS: University Press of Kansas, 2000.

Zaslow, Morris. *The Northward Expansion of Canada, 1914–1967*. Toronto: McClelland and Stewart, 1988.

– *The Opening of the Canadian North, 1870–1917*. Toronto: McClelland and Stewart, 1971.

Zelniker, Rachel. *Giant: Murder Underground*. Eight-episode podcast series. Canadian Broadcasting Corporation, 21 September 2022. https://www.cbc.ca/listen/cbc-podcasts/1066-giant.

Ziem, Grace E., and Barry I. Castleman. "Threshold Limit Values: Historical Perspectives and Current Practice." *Journal of Occupational and Environmental Medicine* 31, no. 11 (November 1989): 910–18.

Index

McGill-Queen's Rural, Wildland, and Resource Studies Series

SERIES EDITORS: Jennifer Bonnell, James Murton, and R.W. Sandwell

1 How Agriculture Made Canada
Farming in the Nineteenth Century
Peter A. Russell

2 The Once and Future
Great Lakes Country
An Ecological History
John L. Riley

3 Consumers in the Bush
Shopping in Rural Upper Canada
Douglas McCalla

4 Subsistence under Capitalism
Nature and Economy in Historical and Contemporary Perspectives
Edited by James Murton, Dean Bavington, and Carly Dokis

5 Time and a Place
An Environmental History of Prince Edward Island
Edited by Edward MacDonald, Joshua MacFadyen, and Irené Novaczek

6 Powering Up Canada
A History of Power, Fuel, and Energy from 1600
Edited by R.W. Sandwell

7 Permanent Weekend
Nature, Leisure, and Rural Gentrification
John Michels

8 Nature, Place, and Story
Rethinking Historic Sites in Canada
Claire Elizabeth Campbell

9 The Subjugation of Canadian Wildlife
Failures of Principle and Policy
Max Foran

10 Flax Americana
A History of the Fibre and Oil That Covered a Continent
Joshua MacFadyen

11 At the Wilderness Edge
The Rise of the Antidevelopment Movement on Canada's West Coast
J.I. Little

12 The Greater Gulf
Essays on the Environmental History of the Gulf of St Lawrence
Edited by Claire E. Campbell, Edward MacDonald, and Brian Payne

13 The Miramichi Fire
A History
Alan MacEachern

14 Reading the Diaries of Henry Trent
The Everyday Life of a Canadian Englishman, 1842–1898
J.I. Little

15 Cultivating Community
Women and Agricultural Fairs in Ontario
Jodey Nurse

16 Being Neighbours
Cooperative Work and
Rural Culture, 1830–1960
Catharine Anne Wilson

17 The Lives of Lake Ontario
An Environmental History
Daniel Macfarlane

18 The Rough Poets
Reading Oil-Worker Poetry
Melanie Dennis Unrau

19 The Price of Gold
Mining, Pollution, and Resistance
in Yellowknife
John Sandlos and Arn Keeling